Teacher's Guide

PATHWAYS

Listening, Speaking, and Critical Thinking

4

Becky Tarver Chase
Ingrid Wisniewska

 NATIONAL GEOGRAPHIC LEARNING |  HEINLE CENGAGE Learning

Australia • Brazil • Japan • Korea • Mexico • Singapore • Spain • United Kingdom • United States

Pathways 4 Teacher's Guide
Listening, Speaking, and Critical Thinking

Publisher: Sherrise Roehr

Executive Editor: Laura Le Dréan

Acquisitions Editor: Tom Jefferies

Development Editor: Marissa Petrarca

Director of Global Marketing: Ian Martin

Marketing Manager: Caitlin Thomas

Marketing Manager: Emily Stewart

Director of Content and Media Production:
Michael Burggren

Sr. Content Project Manager: Daisy Sosa

Manufacturing Manager: Marcia Locke

Manufacturing Buyer: Marybeth Hennebury

Cover Design: Page 2 LLC

Cover Image: Terry W. Eggers/CORBIS

Interior Design: Page 2 LLC, Cenveo Publisher
Services/Nesbitt Graphics, Inc.

Composition: Cenveo Publisher Services/
Nesbitt Graphics, Inc.

ISBN-13: 978-1-111-34789-5

ISBN-10: 1-111-34789-1

National Geographic Learning
20 Channel Center St.
Boston, MA 02210
USA

Cengage Learning is a leading provider of customized learning solutions with office locations around the globe, including Singapore, the United Kingdom, Australia, Mexico, Brazil, and Japan. Locate your local office at: **international.cengage.com/region**

Cengage Learning products are represented in Canada by Nelson Education, Ltd.

Visit National Geographic Learning online at **ngl.cengage.com**
Visit our corporate website at **www.cengage.com**

Printed in the United States of America
4 5 6 7 8 9 10   20 19 18 17 16

Advantages of *Pathways Listening, Speaking, and Critical Thinking*

In *Pathways Listening, Speaking, and Critical Thinking*, real-world content from *National Geographic* publications provides a context for meaningful language acquisition. Students learn essential, high-frequency vocabulary, review important grammatical structures, and practice listening and speaking skills that will allow them to succeed in both academic and social settings.

Pathways Listening, Speaking, and Critical Thinking can be used in a wide variety of language-learning programs, from high schools and community colleges to private institutes and intensive English programs. The high-interest content motivates students and teachers alike.

The following features are included in *Pathways Listening, Speaking, and Critical Thinking*:

- Academic Pathways give students and teachers clear performance objectives for each unit.

- Opening pages introduce the unit theme and provide key vocabulary and concepts.

- Interesting content is used to present target vocabulary and to spark discussions.

- Extensive audio programs include lectures, interviews, conversations, and pronunciation models that expose students to many different kinds of speakers.

- Clear grammar charts present key grammar structures and explain language functions such as asking for clarification and sustaining a conversation.

- Presentation Skills boxes highlight skills for planning and delivering successful oral presentations.

- Student to Student boxes provide real-world expressions for making friends and working with classmates.

- An *Independent Student Handbook* and vocabulary index at the end of each level serve as tools to use in class or for self-study and review.

Teaching Language Skills and Academic Literacy

Students need more than language skills to succeed in an academic setting. In addition to teaching the English language, the *Pathways* series teaches academic literacy, which includes not only reading, writing, speaking, and listening skills, but also visual literacy, classroom participation and collaboration skills, critical thinking, and the ability to use technology for learning. Students today are expected to be motivated, inquisitive, original, and creative. In short, they're expected to possess quite an extensive skill set before they even begin their major course of study.

Using *National Geographic* Content in a Language Class

The use of high-interest content from *National Geographic* publications sets the *Pathways* series apart. Instead of working with topics that might seem irrelevant, students are engaged by fascinating stories about real people and places around the world and the issues that affect us all.

High-interest content is introduced throughout each unit—as context for target vocabulary, as content for lectures and conversation—and provides the information students need for lively discussions and interesting presentations.

The topics in the *Pathways Listening, Speaking, and Critical Thinking* series correspond to academic subject areas and appeal to a wide range of interests. For example:

Academic Subject Area	Unit Title	Unit Theme
Health Science	*Inside the Brain*	the physiology and psychology of the human brain
History / Archaeology	*Learning from the Past*	recent underwater discoveries and the lessons they impart about the value of history
Anthropology / Sociology	*Culture and Tradition*	traditions from cultures around the world, from cowboys to Caribbean music
Earth Science	*Fascinating Planet*	the geography and geology of national parks in China, Brazil, Madagascar, and New Zealand
Economics	*Money in Our Lives*	debt, understanding the global financial crisis, scientific studies on money and happiness

Increasing Visual Literacy

Photographs, maps, charts, and graphs can all convey enormous amounts of information. Lecturers and professors rarely give oral presentations without some kind of visual aid. Helping students to make sense of visuals is an important part of preparing them for academic success.

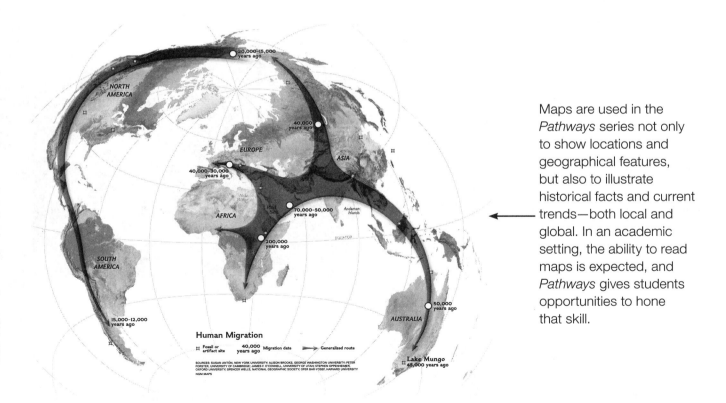

Maps are used in the *Pathways* series not only to show locations and geographical features, but also to illustrate historical facts and current trends—both local and global. In an academic setting, the ability to read maps is expected, and *Pathways* gives students opportunities to hone that skill.

v

Charts and graphs present numerical data in a visual way, and the *Pathways* series gives students practice in reading them. In addition to the standard pie charts and bar graphs, *Pathways* includes more unusual visuals from the pages of *National Geographic* publications.

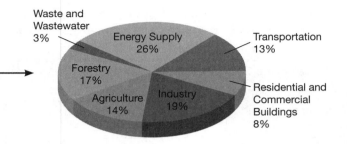

Graphic organizers have several functions in the *Pathways* series. They appeal to visual learners by showing relationships between ideas in a visual way. So, in addition to texts and listening passages, *Pathways* uses graphic organizers to present interesting content. Students are asked to use graphic organizers for a number of academic tasks such as generating topics or organizing notes for a presentation.

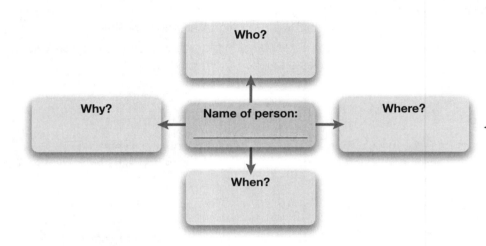

The photographs in the *Pathways* series go far beyond decorating the pages. Photographs introduce the unit theme and provide necessary background information for understanding listening passages and texts. Teachers will also want to exploit the photographs in *Pathways* to initiate discussions and reinforce the target language.

Building Critical Thinking Skills

Critical thinking skills are explicitly taught and practiced in *Pathways Listening, Speaking, and Critical Thinking*. One reason for this is that critical thinking—the ability to make judgments and decisions based on evidence and reason—is an essential skill for students in an academic setting, where they're expected to reflect on and analyze information rather than simply remember it. Students need to be prepared to think critically while listening, reading, writing, and participating in discussions. The skills of critical thinking do not develop on their own; they need to be taught, learned, and practiced.

The ability to think critically is also required in most careers, and critical thinking contributes to language acquisition by requiring deep processing of the language. In order to consider an idea in relation to other ideas and then articulate a response or an opinion about it, we must make complex associations in the brain. This in turn leads to better comprehension and retention of the target language.

Here are just a few examples of the academic tasks that require critical thinking skills:

- deciding which material from a lecture to take notes on
- determining a speaker's purpose when assessing the content of a talk
- forming an opinion on an issue based on facts and evidence
- relating new information to one's personal experiences
- giving specific examples to support one's main idea
- assessing the credibility of a source of information

The *Pathways* series gives explicit instruction on and practice of critical thinking skills. Each unit has a Critical Thinking Focus and several practice exercises. For example:

> **Critical Thinking Focus: Drawing Conclusions**
>
> When you draw a conclusion, you make a logical judgment about something based on the information you have. For example, *I might stop by your house. If there are no lights on, and when I knock on the door nobody answers, I'll probably conclude that nobody is home. I can't know this for certain since I can't go into the house and look around, but I do have enough information to reach a logical conclusion.*

  A | In a group, discuss the information from this unit about Angkor and the Khmer Empire and list some conclusions you can draw based on this information. Consider the topics below.

- The length of time that Angkor was the capital of the Khmer Empire
- The art and architecture that can be seen at Angkor
- The number of temples built at Angkor
- The size and sophistication of the water control systems in and around Angkor

> We can conclude that there were a lot of workers in Angkor. Somebody had to construct those huge man-made lakes.

- The fact that Angkor's wealth and power declined after losing river access to the sea
- The fact that Angkor Wat is on UNESCO's World Heritage site list

Teaching with *Pathways Listening, Speaking, and Critical Thinking*

Using the Opening Pages

Each unit of *Pathways Listening, Speaking, and Critical Thinking* begins with a unit opener and a two-page section called Exploring the Theme. These opening pages serve the important functions of raising student interest in the unit theme and introducing key vocabulary and concepts.

The Unit Opener

Every unit opener features a stunning photograph that draws students into the unit theme. You'll want to direct students' attention to the photograph and the unit title. Give students a chance to react to the photograph and give the class some of the background information that you'll find in the Teacher's Guide.

Every unit opener includes Think and Discuss questions that encourage students to interact with the photograph and to relate it to their own lives.

The unit opener also lists the Academic Pathways for each unit. These are clearly stated performance objectives that preview some of the main culminating activities in the unit. The Academic Pathways are also useful in assessing students' progress at the end of each unit.

Exploring the Theme

After you've worked with the unit opener, go on to the two-page Exploring the Theme section, which provides information in the form of maps, captioned photographs, and charts and graphs. This section gives students the background information and key terms they need before beginning the unit.

The Exploring the Theme questions check students' comprehension of the information and give them a chance to respond to it in a meaningful way.

Building Vocabulary

Each level of *Pathways Listening, Speaking, and Critical Thinking* contains approximately 200 target vocabulary words in addition to footnotes for less frequently used words. The target vocabulary words in the *Pathways* series are . . .

- **High-frequency:** Students are likely to use high-frequency words on a regular basis, which leads to greater acquisition and better fluency.

- **Level-appropriate:** The target vocabulary words in each level of the *Pathways* series are appropriate for the students studying in that level.

- **Useful for discussing the unit theme:** The vocabulary words in each unit are introduced in the vocabulary sections, used in the listening passages, and recycled in many of the activities.

- **Informed by the Academic Word List:** The *Pathways* series contains a high percentage of the words found on the Academic Word List.*

*The Academic Word List (AWL) is a list of the 570 highest-frequency academic word families that regularly appear in academic texts. The AWL was compiled by researcher Averil Coxhead based on her analysis of a 3.5-million-word corpus (Coxhead, 2000).

Developing Listening Skills

Each unit of *Pathways Listening, Speaking, and Critical Thinking* contains two listening sections. The listening passage in Lesson A takes place in a relatively formal context such as a lecture, a meeting, or a formal presentation. Lesson B presents an informal speaking situation such as a conversation between friends or a study group with classmates.

The language in the listening passages represents realistic situations, yet the language is controlled for level, and students may listen to each passage more than once. This guided listening gives students the chance to practice listening and note-taking skills and to develop the confidence and fluency they'll need before they are immersed in an academic setting.

Each listening section contains three parts:

- **Before Listening** activities provide background information and explicit instruction in listening skills.
- **While Listening** activities give students practice in listening for main ideas and smaller details and in making inferences.
- **After Listening** activities are designed to reinforce listening skills and to allow students to discuss and react to the listening passage.

Pronunciation

The pronunciation lessons are designed to increase students' listening comprehension as well as the comprehensibility of their own speech.

Note-Taking

Pathways Listening, Speaking, and Critical Thinking takes a scaffolding approach to building note-taking skills. Students begin by listening for specific information to fill in blanks. Later they complete partial notes and practice independent note-taking.

Listening Critically

Since critical thinking is an essential part of listening, skills such as identifying a speaker's purpose and summarizing the main points from a talk are part of the *Pathways* listening program.

Listening Homework

Extensive listening can play an important role in increasing listening comprehension. Students can expand on the listening they do in class by using the Audio CD, the Online Workbook, and the Presentation Tool CD-ROM.

Developing Speaking Skills

Every section of *Pathways Listening, Speaking, and Critical Thinking* provides opportunities for classroom speaking and discussion, often in pairs or in small groups. The Exploring Spoken English sections focus entirely on speaking. Striking images and brief stories about real people and places often provide the content for engaging interactions.

Accurate Speech

Clear and succinct grammar lessons give students a single language structure to concentrate on for each Exploring Spoken English section. The grammar points lend themselves to discussion of the unit theme and can be recycled throughout the unit.

Fluent Speech

Frequent classroom discussions and interactions prepare students to participate in class and succeed in an academic setting. Language Function boxes address the situations in which stock expressions or target grammatical structures are commonly used, increasing the students' level of comfort and confidence in dealing with common speaking situations.

Speaking activities are designed with a scaffolding approach. They progress from controlled activities to guided activities and free activities. Early confidence-building motivates students to attempt activities that increase in difficulty, taking them to their ultimate goal—participation in authentic speaking activities such as classroom presentations, formal discussions, and debates.

Presentation Skills boxes appear at points where students give presentations, so they provide immediate practice of skills needed for planning and delivering successful oral presentations.

Student to Student boxes provide tips and expressions to help students develop the informal, one-on-one speaking skills they will need for class work and in their day-to-day exchanges.

Engage is a consolidating speaking activity. It is a task or project involving collaboration with a partner or a group as well as an oral presentation of results or ideas.

Using Videos in the Language Classroom

The video clips in *Pathways Listening, Speaking, and Critical Thinking* come from the award-winning *National Geographic* film collection and act as a bridge between Lesson A and Lesson B of each unit. The videos consolidate content and skills from Lesson A and illustrate a specific aspect of the unit theme in a visually dynamic way.

What is the Lesson A and B Viewing section?

The Viewing section features a video on a theme related to the whole unit. All video clips are on the Online Workbook and the Presentation Tool CD-ROM, as well as on the classroom DVD.

Why teach video-viewing skills?

In daily life, non-fiction videos can be found on television, on the Internet, and in movie theaters in the form of documentaries. Just as *Pathways* provides a wide variety of listening passages to build students' listening skills, the series also builds viewing skills with videos from *National Geographic*. *Pathways* promotes visual and digital literacy so learners can competently use a wide range of modern media.

Videos differ from listening texts in important ways. First, students are processing information by viewing and listening simultaneously. Visual images include information about the video's setting as well as clues found in nonverbal communication, such as facial expressions and body movements. The video may also include animated maps and diagrams to explain information and processes. The soundtrack contains narration, conversations, music, and sound effects. Some contextual words may appear on screen in signs or as identification of people or settings. In addition, full English subtitles (closed captions) are available as a teaching and learning option.

What are the stages of viewing?

Before Viewing prepares students for the video, engages their background knowledge about the topic, and creates interest in what they will watch. Effective ways of previewing include:

- brainstorming ideas and discussing what the class already knows about the topic;
- using photographs and the video's title to predict the content;
- pre-teaching key vocabulary essential to understanding the video content;
- and skimming the summary reading.

While Viewing may occur multiple times and at different speeds while:

- picking out and understanding the main ideas of the video;
- watching and listening closely for detail;
- or watching and listening for opinion and inference.

After Viewing activities include:

- describing the main points and the sequence of events in the video;
- completing the cloze summary with provided target vocabulary;
- and answering discussion questions that relate the video to the students' own lives or experiences.

How should teachers use the videos to teach?

The narration on each video has been carefully graded to feature vocabulary items and structures that are appropriate for students' proficiency level. Here are techniques for using video in class:

- Have students preview the video by reading the transcript or the summary paragraph.
- Pause, rewind, or fast-forward the video to focus on key segments or events.
- Pause the video midway to allow students to predict what will happen next. Resume the video so students can check their predictions.
- Have students watch the video with the sound off so they can focus on what they see. If this approach is used, follow-up discussion helps students share their ideas about the content of the video. Then play the video with the sound on for students to check their ideas.
- Have students watch without subtitles after which they discuss what they hear; then play with subtitles for students to check their ideas.
- Have students follow the script as they listen to the video to help with intonation, pitch, and stress. Stop and replay key phrases for students to repeat.
- Have students watch the video independently and complete the comprehension questions on the Online Workbook.
- To extend viewing skills to speaking and writing skills, have students make a presentation or create a written report about a short video of their choice, using language they have learned from the Student Book and video narration.

All video scripts are printed at the back of the Teacher's Guide. Teachers have flexibility in how or whether they want students to use the scripts. See individual units in this Teacher's Guide for specific teaching suggestions for each video.

Features of the *Pathways* Teacher's Guide

The *Pathways* Teacher's Guide contains teaching notes, answer keys, and the audio and video scripts. There are also warm-up activities to help teachers present the material in the textbook and overviews of the unit theme and the video clip to help turn teachers into "instant experts."

Academic Pathways Boxes

Each unit in the Teacher's Guide begins with a preview of the Academic Pathways. A description of each pathway is then given at the point where it occurs in the unit along with helpful information for the teacher. Teachers should also direct students to the online and the Assessment CD-ROM with Exam*View®* resources that will help to reinforce and assess the skills learned for each pathway.

Ideas for ... Boxes

Throughout the *Pathways* Teacher's Guide, you will find boxes with ideas to help both novice and experienced teachers. There are four types of *Ideas for ...* boxes:

- **Ideas for Presenting Grammar** boxes provide a variety of ways to introduce grammatical structures and utilize the grammar charts.

- **Ideas for Checking Comprehension** boxes remind teachers of the need to continually assess students' comprehension during every class session.

- **Ideas for Expansion** boxes suggest ways to expand on the content of the book when students need extra instruction or when they have a high level of interest in a topic.

- **Ideas for Multi-level Classes** boxes provide techniques to use in mixed-ability classrooms, where learner diversity can benefit everyone in the class. On the other hand, providing the right kind of help for all the students in any classroom can be a balancing act. When different types of instruction are needed for different learners, teachers must be careful not to embarrass lower-level learners in any way or detract from the learning experience of higher-level learners.

Tips

Tips for instruction and classroom management are provided throughout the *Pathways* Teacher's Guide. The tips are especially helpful to less experienced teachers, but they are also a resource for more experienced teachers, providing new ideas and adding variety to the classroom routine.

Urban Challenges

Academic Track
Interdisciplinary

Academic Pathways:
Lesson A: Listening to a Lecture
Discussing Pros and Cons of Tourism
Lesson B: Listening to a Conversation between Classmates
Presenting a Problem and Proposing Solutions

Unit Theme

More people are living in cities than ever before. As more people move to urban areas, cities all over the world are facing new challenges.

Unit 1 explores the topic of urban life as it relates to:
– tourism
– solving urban problems
– daily life
– laws and rules

Think and Discuss *(page 1)*

5 mins

Graffiti is writing or drawing on the walls of buildings. Graffiti is usually done illegally and can be humorous, rude, or political. Recently, graffiti has developed into an art form. Brazilian graffiti art, for example, has inspired graffiti artists all over the world.

- Ask students to describe the photo. *What are these people doing? What is the mural about? How can graffiti and street art affect people's lives?*

- Discuss the questions as a class. On the board, make a list of problems that modern cities face. Ask students to brainstorm a list of positive aspects of city living.

- Ask for students' opinions about living in a city. If students live in a city, ask them to explain what they like or dislike about it. If students don't live in a city, ask them to explain what could persuade them to move to an urban area.

Exploring the Theme: Urban Challenges *(pages 2-3)*

15 mins

The opening spread features a world map showing the location of the largest cities in each country.

Exercise A.

- Before discussing the questions, ask students to look at the map key and scan the pages to familiarize themselves with the map.

- Explain the meaning of *urban agglomeration* (a collection of densely populated areas, e.g., smaller towns that have joined together to make large cities).

- Discuss the questions about the map and compare answers as a class.

Answer Key *(Answers may vary.)*

1. Mumbai, Tokyo, Mexico City, New York City, and Rio de Janeiro are some of the largest cities shown on the map.
2. All of the cities are near large bodies of water.
3. Cities will be larger, and there will be fewer small cities.

Exercise B. | Ask students to look at the photos. Discuss the questions with the class. Make a list of answers to each question. Encourage students to share their personal experiences with these urban issues.

 TIP Divide the class into two groups. Ask one group to list answers to question 1 of exercise B while the other group lists answers to question 2. Have members from each group present their answers to the class.

Building and Using Vocabulary *(pages 4-5)*

30 mins

WARM-UP

The Lesson A target vocabulary is presented in the context of ways that cities are meeting the challenges of increased population and pollution.

- Ask students to look at the three photos and brainstorm ideas about how cities are coping with overcrowding, pollution, and lack of space.

Building Vocabulary

Exercise A. | Meaning from Context Play the audio while students listen and read the text. Ask students to identify the main idea of each paragraph.

track 1-2

TIP Before students read the paragraphs in exercise A, play the audio as they listen with their books closed. Then ask students to point out the main idea of each paragraph.

IDEAS FOR... Checking Comprehension

Ask some general comprehension questions about the texts in exercise **A**. For example:

Why do people like living in micro-homes?
How does this cement reduce pollution?
Where is the High Line urban park?

Exercise B.

- Allow time for students to refer back to exercise **A** and work out the meanings of the target vocabulary words.

- Review answers by asking volunteers to read out a completed sentence.

Answer Key

1. c 2. j 3. f 4. h 5. e 6. a 7. i 8. d 9. g 10. b

TIP Before students do exercise B, ask them to cover the second column and try to complete the sentences using their own ideas. Then they can compare their answers with the sentences given.

Using Vocabulary

Exercise A. | Using a Dictionary

- Explain that learning different word forms can help students expand their vocabulary. Go over the first row of the chart as an example.

- Allow time for students to complete the chart individually. Draw the chart on the board and invite volunteers to write their answers.

Answer Key *(Answers shown are in order of noun, verb, adjective.)*

1. challenge, challenge, challenging
2. convert, convert, converted
3. finance, finance, financial
4. generation, generate, generated
5. innovation, innovate, innovative
6. maximum, maximize, maximum
7. regulation, regulate, regulatory
8. resident, reside, residential
9. restoration, restore, restorative
10. structure, structure, structural

Exercise B. | Suggest that students read through the text to get an overview before attempting to fill in the answers. Go over the answers by asking volunteers to read parts of the text aloud.

Answer Key

1. challenge	5. structures	9. generates
2. maximize	6. restoration	10. Financial
3. convert	7. innovative	
4. residents	8. regulations	

IDEAS FOR... Checking Comprehension

Ask students to summarize exercise **B** by listing the challenges faced by the city of Venice (*city is sinking, regular floods, buildings damaged by water*) and two problems that may be caused by the water barrier (*very expensive, may make the city less beautiful*).

Pronunciation Note

acqua alta: **ah**-kwa **al**-ta
MOSE: **moe**-zay

Developing Listening Skills

45 mins

(pages 6-7)

Before Listening

Predicting Content | Ask students to look at the photo and brainstorm answers to the questions.

Listening: A Lecture

Critical Thinking Focus: Identifying the Lecture Topic | Go over the information in the box. You may want to represent this information visually in the form of a flow chart. (See page 215 of the *Independent Student Handbook* for an example.)

 Exercise A. | Play the audio. Take a class vote on the correct answer. Ask students how they were able to choose the correct answer.

track 1-3

Answer Key	**3.** Problems caused by tourists

 Exercise B. | Listening for Main Ideas

track 1-4

- Go over the chart and help students identify what kind of information is missing.

- Play the audio. Remind students to use short forms and abbreviations where possible.

Exercise C.

- Allow time for students to compare answers in pairs.

- Go over the answers as a class. Since student notes will likely vary during a note-taking activity, accept any answers that correctly identify the main ideas.

Answer Key *(Student notes may vary.)*

Problems of Tourism:

1. can't handle so many people **2.** food **3.** rent **4.** housing **5.** getting smaller

Benefits of Tourism:

1. revenue **2.** restoration **3.** tourism

 Exercise D. | Listening for Details

track 1-4

- Allow time for students to read the questions.

- Play the audio while students choose their answers. Ask volunteers to call out the correct answers.

Answer Key	**1.** b **2.** c **3.** a **4.** c **5.** b

IDEAS FOR...   **Checking Comprehension**

Ask these additional questions or write them on the board.

1. *What is* acqua alta? (regular floods)

2. *What is* MOSE? (a project to build water barriers to stop flooding)

3. *Who can afford houses in Venice?* (only rich people or those who have inherited homes from their families)

4. *What are three suggestions for reducing damage from tourism?* (limiting tourists, taxing tourists, and asking tourists to avoid the busy seasons)

After Listening

Exercise A. | Making Inferences

- Remind students that inferences are conclusions that are not directly stated in the lecture.

- Ask students to discuss the questions in pairs. Encourage students to use examples from the lecture to explain their opinions. Ask each pair to share their ideas with the class.

TIP At the beginning of a course, it's important that students get to know each other. Encourage students to change partners for subsequent pair exercises so that they have a chance to work with several of their classmates.

Exercise B. | After students have worked in groups for a few minutes, ask groups to share their ideas with the whole class. Take a vote on the funniest caption.

IDEAS FOR...   **Expansion**

Students can work in groups to develop a questionnaire about tourism in their city. Have them interview friends or neighbors and report their results to the class.

Pronunciation Note

Rialto (Market): ree-**al**-toe

Exploring Spoken English
(pages 8-10)

45 mins

Language Function: Introducing a Topic

- Go over the information in the box.

- Ask students to suggest different ways to finish these sentences. For example: *To begin with we are going to review some of the problems caused by tourism.*

track 1-5 **Exercise A.**

- Ask students to read the sentences and try to remember the missing phrases from the lecture.

- Play the audio while students fill in the missing words. Pause if necessary.

Answer Key

1. what I want to do today is

2. to begin with

3. Let me add that

4. Another point I want to make is

Exercise B.

- Allow a few minutes for students to write their answers.

- Draw the chart on the board and have students tell you which phrases to write in each column.

Answer Key

Introducing a Topic at the Beginning of a Talk:
To begin with . . .
I'd like to focus on . . .
Today's topic is . . .
Today, we're going to cover . . .
What I want to do today is . . .

Introducing a Topic Later on in a Talk:
Let's move on to . . .
Let me add that . . .
Another point I want to make is . . .

Exercise C.

- Allow a few minutes for students to review the materials and make notes before speaking in pairs.

- Walk around the classroom and take notes of good examples of the target language that you hear students using.

TIP Another way to organize exercise C is to have half of the class prepare notes for Student A while the other half prepares notes for Student B. Students can work in groups to develop their ideas. This will give students a chance to cooperate on planning their explanations. Then match up pairs of students from each half of the class.

Grammar: The Passive Voice

- Go over the language in the box. Ask volunteers to read the examples aloud.

- You may want to remind students that only transitive verbs can form the passive. Transitive verbs are verbs that have an object. Intransitive verbs (e.g., *happen, arrive*) do not have an object and cannot form the passive.

IDEAS FOR... **Presenting Grammar**

- Give some additional examples and ask students to identify the tense used. For example: *Serious problems have been caused by the flooding in Venice.* (present perfect)

- Give examples in the present tense and ask students to change them to the past or future tense.

- Review the past participles of common irregular verbs.

Exercise A. | Allow time for students to complete the sentences. Remind them to use the correct tense. Ask volunteers to read their answers aloud.

Answer Key

1. was, damaged	**4.** can be avoided
2. was flooded	**5.** will be held
3. are, being rebuilt	**6.** are held

IDEAS FOR... **Expansion**

Ask students to look at the photo on page 9 of their Student Books and describe it. Students should try to form sentences that use the passive voice. Brainstorm some suitable verbs (e.g., *flood, destroy, damage, ruin, lose, hurt, injure, kill*). Review the past participles of common irregular verbs before you begin.

Exercise B.

- Ask students to look at the diagram and to identify and label the main parts of the barrier (*gates, lagoon, sea, city*).

- Read the explanation aloud and invite students to ask questions about it.

- Review the formation of questions in the passive voice.

- Allow time for pairs to complete the question and answers.

- Ask volunteers to read the questions and answers aloud in pairs.

Answer Key

1. will be constructed

2. will . . . consist, will consist

3. will . . . be attached, will be attached

4. will . . . be raised, is predicted

5. will . . . be raised, will be pumped, will force

6. will . . . be completed, will be completed

Exercise C. | Understanding Visuals

- Have students practice the conversation from exercise **B** in pairs.

- Ask students to look at the diagram and read the explanation again and discuss how the new flood barrier works and whether it will be effective. Encourage students to use the passive voice.

- Take notes of any common errors and provide feedback.

TIP Review exercise C by asking students to explain the diagram without looking at the explanation.

 Speaking *(page 11)*

30-45 mins

Discussing Pros and Cons of Tourism

Exercise A. | Critical Thinking

- Do the first item as an example. Ask students the following question: *How does tourism affect public transportation?* Provide some example answers:

Information has to be written in several languages. Maps must be easy to understand. Some routes will be much busier than others.

- Organize students into groups. Give each group a large piece of paper or ask them to work in their notebooks. Have groups choose one of the topics and write it in the center of the page. Then have them write ideas about the topic in a scattered fashion around it. Encourage students to use a graphic organizer such as the model below:

- Ask a member of each group to present their ideas to the class.

IDEAS FOR... **Multi-level Classes**

Assign each group just one of the topics, giving easier topics (e.g., culture or tourist attractions) to lower level students. Groups that finish early can move on to additional topics.

Student to Student: Apologizing for Interrupting | Go over the information in the box before starting exercise **B**. Inform students that these expressions are a polite way to apologize for interrupting a partner or group member.

Exercise B. | Organizing Ideas

- Explain that this chart will help students to group their ideas in an organized way. They may want to use some of their brainstorming ideas from exercise **A**.

- Allow time for groups to work on their charts. Members of each group should discuss with each other what to write in the chart.

Exercise C. | Discussion

- When most groups have completed their charts, ask them to stop writing. Ask each member of the group to choose one effect to speak about. They can add details to support their point of view. They can evaluate whether this point has more negative or more positive effects.

Viewing: Tuareg Farmers
(pages 12-13)

30 mins

Overview of the Video | This video presents some problems that Tuareg farmers are having with elephants that want to eat their crops. The video shows some ways in which the farmers are trying to correct the problem without harming the elephants.

Before Viewing

Exercise A. | Predicting Content

- Ask students to look at the map and describe the location of Mali. Ask them to describe the photos on pages 12 and 13. Ask what the photos tell us about life in Mali.

- Ask students to discuss the questions, but emphasize that there are no correct answers at this stage. They will find out if their guesses are correct by watching the video.

Exercise B. | Using a Dictionary

- Ask students to tell you which words they already know. Ask: *What kinds of contexts have you heard these words used in?*

- Allow time for students to use their dictionaries to find the answers.

- Practice the pronunciation of these words if necessary.

Answer Key   1. c 2. e 3. d 4. a 5. b

While Viewing

4:23

Exercise A. | Refer students back to their answers in exercise **A** in the Before Viewing section to see which of their guesses were correct.

4:23

Exercise B. | Viewing for Main Ideas

- Allow time for students to read the sentences silently before playing the video again.

- Check students' answers by taking a class vote on each sentence.

Answer Key   1. Yes 2. Yes 3. Yes 4. No 5. No 6. No

IDEAS FOR...   Checking Comprehension

Play the video again (if necessary) and ask students to work in groups to write questions about the video. You can give each group a different section of the video. Afterwards, organize a competition in which teams try to answer each other's questions.

After Viewing

Exercise A. | Ask students to work individually to complete the sentences. Instruct students to look back on the grammar box on page 9 if they need help forming the passive voice.

Answer Key

1. is shared
2. is carried
3. are attracted
4. were destroyed
5. has been repeated

Exercise B. | Critical Thinking   Ask students to evaluate the ideas in exercise **B** in the While Viewing section. If time allows, ask one member from each group to report to the class on their discussion.

IDEAS FOR...   Expansion

Ask students to choose a large city shown on the map on pages 2 and 3 of their Student Books. Instruct students to research some facts about the city for homework. Students should identify a challenge that residents of the city are facing. They can share the information with the class in the next lesson.

30 mins

Building and Using Vocabulary *(pages 14-15)*

WARM-UP

The Lesson B target vocabulary is presented in the context of life in Singapore. Instruct students to look at the photos and say what they know about Singapore. Ask: *Where is Singapore? What languages are spoken there? What ethnic groups live there?*

Building Vocabulary

Exercise A. | Using a Dictionary

- Encourage students to use their dictionaries and ask questions about these words.

- Remind students that the word class noted in parentheses can help them figure out the definitions.

- Discuss related words if there is time.

Answer Key	1. f 2. j 3. a 4. h 5. c 6. b 7. i 8. e 9. g 10. d

track 1-6

Exercise B.

- Advise students to read through the whole text to get an overview before attempting to fill in the missing words.

- Play the audio so that students can check their answers.

Answer Key

1. economy	5. enforced	9. conform
2. dominated	6. prohibited	10. debatable
3. unique	7. internalized	
4. ethnic	8. compatible	

IDEAS FOR... Checking Comprehension

Ask students to evaluate the information in the text by saying what they think they would find good or bad about living in Singapore.

Using Vocabulary

Exercise A. | Using a Dictionary

- Check students' answers by drawing the chart on the board and inviting volunteers to come and write their answers.

Answer Key *(Chart answers are in order of noun, verb, adjective.)*

Chart:
1. debate, debate, debatable
2. enforcement, enforce, enforceable
3. economy, economize, economical
4. prohibition, prohibit, prohibitive

Sentences:
1. prohibited
2. debate
3. enforceable
4. economize

Exercise B. | Ask students to complete the quiz in pairs and check their answers. Ask which statements they found most surprising and why. Ask students to identify the word class of each word in blue.

Answer Key

1. T 2. F (The largest ethnic group in Singapore is Chinese.) 3. F (It had the second-highest growth rate.) 4. F (It is not prohibited.) 5. T

Exercise C. | Self-Reflection

- Set a time limit for students to discuss the questions in groups. Ask students to develop additional questions using the new vocabulary. They can write questions in their notebooks and then ask their group.

TIP When giving feedback on exercise C, give feedback on the content of the ideas expressed as well as on correct use of the vocabulary. These ideas may be personal, so avoid judgment and respect all student answers. Share your own answers to encourage participation.

Developing Listening Skills
(pages 16-17)

45 mins

Before Listening

Predicting Content | Ask students to work in pairs to discuss the questions. Then discuss the answers as a class. Ask students which countries are near Singapore and what industries and occupations might be found there. Ask students to describe the statue in the photo. *(It is half lion and half fish.)*

Listening: A Conversation between Classmates

track 1-7

Exercise A. | Listening for Main Ideas

- Read the statements aloud and ask students if they can guess the answers before they listen.

- Play the audio once for students to get the main ideas.

Exercise B. | Have students compare answers in pairs and revise the false statements before going over the answers as a class.

Answer Key

1. T **2.** F **3.** F **4.** T **5.** F **6.** T

The false statements should be revised as follows:

2. Singapore <u>does not have many</u> natural resources.

3. The people of Singapore belong to <u>many</u> different ethnic groups.

5. The spirit of *kiasu* means "<u>afraid to lose</u>."

track 1-7

Exercise C. | Listening for Details Allow time for students to read the sentences. Play the audio again. Ask volunteers to read their answers aloud.

Answer Key

1. fishing	**5.** second
2. 1819	**6.** 50
3. 270	**7.** lose
4. 100	

TIP Another way to check the answers in exercise C is to read the sentences with incorrect answers aloud and ask students to correct you. For example: *Singapore started off as a farming village.* (No, it was a <u>fishing</u> village.)

IDEAS FOR... **Checking Comprehension**

Ask these additional questions or write them on the board.

1. *Why did the man borrow Linda's notes?* (because he was sick and he missed a class)

2. *Why is the merlion the symbol of Singapore?* (Singapore means "lion city" and it started as a fishing village.)

3. *What special laws do they have in Singapore?* (You can get fined for spitting on the street or forgetting to flush the toilet in a public bathroom.)

After Listening

Discussion | Ask students to discuss the questions in pairs. Recommend that they give examples from their own experiences. Then compare answers as a class.

track 1-8

Pronunciation: Pronouncing the letter *t*

- Go over the information in the box and play the audio. Ask students to repeat after the audio.

- If students have trouble hearing the *t* in *not now* or *what really*, explain that the final *t* merges with the following consonant so that it almost disappears.

track 1-9

Exercises A and B. | Encourage students to read the phrases aloud in order to decide which sound is correct. Play the audio. Ask students to raise their hands for which sound they hear. (You can identify them as sounds *1*, *2*, and *3*.)

Answer Key	**1.** ch **2.** d **3.** d **4.** no air
	5. ch **6.** ch **7.** d **8.** no air

Exercise C. | After students have practiced the dialogs, ask them to tell you which sound occurs in each example. *(1. ch, 2. no air, 3. ch, 4. no air, 5. d)*

Pronunciation Note | kiasu: key-**ah**-sue

30 mins

Exploring Spoken English
(pages 18-19)

Language Function: Agreeing or Disagreeing

- Go over the information in the box and demonstrate the difference in intonation between mild and strong disagreement.

- Make up a few sentences expressing your opinions and ask individual students to agree or disagree with you using these expressions. For example: *I think pizza is delicious. I think cell phones are horrible.*

track 1-10 **Exercise A.** | Play the audio, pausing to allow time for students to write their answers.

Answer Key

1. I think you're right.

2. Actually, no, I don't think so.

3. I'm not so sure about that; I agree. . .

Exercise B. | Ask students to work in pairs to practice these exchanges, using different expressions from the box. Point out when students use appropriate intonation.

Exercise C.

- Ask two students to read the sentences in the speech bubbles aloud. Point out that the second person adds a supporting argument to his or her reply. Encourage students to add similar supporting facts or statements to their replies.

- Ask volunteers to present their exchanges to the class.

Grammar: Using an Agent in Passive Voice Sentences

Go over the information in the box. Review the past participles of common irregular verbs.

> **IDEAS FOR...** Presenting Grammar
>
> Write some examples of passive sentences on the board and ask students to identify an agent and decide if an agent is necessary. Have students explain why or why not. For example:
> *Tea is grown in India.* ("by farmers"—agent is redundant)
> *His wallet was stolen yesterday.* ("by someone"—agent is unknown)

Exercises A and B. | Allow time for students to read silently and underline the passive voice forms in the paragraph. Refer students back to the grammar box to explain answers.

Answer Key

Exercise A.

1. Rivers in many cities ⟨were polluted⟩ by harmful chemicals and raw sewage. . .

2. Even fish that require very clean water to live . . . ⟨are being caught.⟩

3. A couple of reasons ⟨have been suggested.⟩

4. Not all the rivers ⟨have been cleaned up⟩. . .

Exercise B.

Even fish that require very clean water to live . . . are being caught.
Missing Agent: *by fisherman*
Reason: Agent is understood.

A couple of reasons have been suggested.
Missing Agent: *by experts*
Reason: Agent is unknown or too general.

Not all the rivers have been cleaned up . . .
Missing Agent: *unknown*
Reason: could be several different agents

Exercise C. | Discussion

- If appropriate, brainstorm names of landmarks in your town or city with students before they start this discussion.

> **IDEAS FOR...** Expansion
>
> Ask students to make additional passive voice sentences about exercise **A**. For example:
> *Rivers have been cleaned up.*

Engage: Presenting a Problem and Proposing Solutions *(page 20)*

45 mins

WARM-UP

- Bring in local newspapers or news articles that are about problems in your city. If you prefer, you can bring in some photographs to illustrate current local issues.

- Brainstorm a list of local issues in your town or city. Ask students which issues affect them most and why.

Exercise A. | Read the information in the box aloud. Ask students to work in pairs to discuss which issues they feel strongly about.

Exercise B. | Using a Graphic Organizer

- Draw a Spider Map on the board and demonstrate what to write in the center bubble and on the lines. Use an example from the warm-up or use the example of river pollution from page 19 of the Student Book to demonstrate how to complete a Spider Map.

- Tell students to draw a Spider Map in their notebooks. Make sure each student draws a Spider Map with enough space to write.

- Allow time for students to work on their Spider Maps, providing support when needed.

- Encourage students to think creatively about solutions to local problems.

Exercise C. | Planning a Presentation

- Advise students to divide up their information equally. They can alternate points, or one student can present the causes while the other presents the solutions.

- Set a time limit for the presentation (e.g., three minutes) so that students can practice in pairs.

- Remind students to use the passive voice and language from page 8 for introducing a topic.

Exercise D. | Presentation

- Ask volunteers to read the examples in the speech bubbles aloud. Ask them to underline phrases they can use in their own presentations.

- Review the information in the Presentation Skills box.

- Ask pairs to come to the front of the class to give their presentations.

- Remind students to look at the audience and only refer to their notes occasionally.

TIP After each presentation, invite the other students to give positive feedback to the presenters by saying what they liked about it. Because this is the first presentation of the course, students may feel nervous—positive feedback will help them to feel more confident.

Presentation Skills: Making Eye Contact

- Demonstrate reading without making eye contact by reading the information in the box without lifting your eyes from the text. Contrast this by reading the information again, alternately glancing down at the book and then up at the audience.

- Ask why it is important to maintain eye contact. Explain: *Giving a presentation is different from reading aloud. It involves interacting with the audience and speaking to them directly. Eye contact makes the presentation more personal and more interesting.*

IDEAS FOR... Expansion

- Ask students to bring in articles about an urban challenge from newspapers or magazines. Have students explain the issue in small groups or to the class.

- Review the unit by asking students what they learned and what they found most interesting and helpful.

Protecting Our Planet

Academic Track
Life Science

Academic Pathways:
Lesson A: Listening to a Guided Tour
Brainstorming Ideas about Conservation
Lesson B: Listening to a Student Debate
Participating in a Debate

Unit Theme

Many species of animals and plants on our planet are endangered. It is important to find ways of protecting them before they disappear.

Unit 2 explores the topic of environmental conservation as it relates to:
– wildlife conservation
– plant-life conservation
– legalized hunting
– keeping animals in zoos

Think and Discuss *(page 21)*

5 mins

Turtles have been on the earth for more than 200 million years. Several species of turtles can live to be over 100 years of age. There are approximately 300 species of turtles. Turtles live on every continent except Antarctica. The shell of a turtle is made up of 60 different bones all connected together. Sea turtles can swim up to 35 miles per hour. Species such as the sea turtle are becoming endangered as their habitats are threatened by pollution, global warming, and the increase in human population.

■ Ask students to tell you what they know about turtles. (You may wish to share the introduction above with students.) Ask students to respond to the photo and caption on page 21: *How does the photo make you feel? What about the caption?*

■ Discuss the questions as a class. For question 2, make a list of reasons for changes in the scene during the last 50 or 60 years on the board. For question 3, encourage students to agree and disagree about who should be responsible for protecting endangered species and why.

Exploring the Theme: Protecting Our Planet *(pages 22-23)*

15 mins

The opening spread features a picture of an African lion in its natural habitat. African lions, along with many other big cats, are in danger of extinction.

■ Ask students how important they think it is to protect endangered species such as this African lion. Encourage them to support their arguments with examples and facts.

■ Ask students to look at the photos and describe how they illustrate destruction of the environment.

■ Discuss the questions in exercises **A** and **B** as a class. Brainstorm possible reasons why some of these species are endangered.

TIP You may find it useful to introduce terms such as *ecosystem* (all the animals and plants in a particular area and how they interact) and *ecology* (the way in which plants and animals interact with each other) at the start of this discussion.

IDEAS FOR... Expansion

Ask students to choose an endangered species and research some interesting facts about the species for homework. They can share their facts with the class in the next lesson.

Building and Using Vocabulary *(pages 24-25)*

30 mins

WARM-UP

The Lesson A target vocabulary is presented in the context of how to protect the endangered whale population. Ask students to look at the photo. Ask what they know about whales and why they think they are endangered.

Building Vocabulary

track 1-11

Exercise A. | Meaning from Context Play the audio while students listen and read the text. Then ask some general comprehension questions: *Why did people hunt whales in the past? What are the dangers to whales now? How can we help whales to survive?*

> **TIP** To make exercise A more challenging, play the audio while students listen with their books closed. Then ask them for the main ideas.

Exercise B. | Allow time for students to refer back to the text and work out the meanings of the target words.

> **TIP** Check the answers to exercise B by asking one student to read a definition aloud and another student to reply with the corresponding word.

Answer Key	1. c 2. i 3. g 4. b 5. a 6. h 7. e 8. d 9. j 10. f

> **TIP** If students have not already done so, encourage them to start a vocabulary journal and use it throughout the course. Refer students to page 208 of the *Independent Student Handbook* for more information on starting a vocabulary journal.

Using Vocabulary

Exercise A. | Using a Dictionary

- Complete the first row of the chart as an example. Allow time for students to fill in the rest of the chart individually.

- Draw the chart on the board and invite volunteers to write their answers in it. As they do so, ask students to suggest sentences for each word.

- Remind students that the dictionary definition is sometimes different from the meaning in a given context.

Answer Key *(Answers below are in order of noun, verb, adjective.)*
1. exploitation, exploit, exploitable, exploited
2. threat, threaten, threatened
3. recovery, recover, recoverable, recovered
4. indication, indicate, indicative

Exercise B.

- Explain that a mangrove is a special kind of tree that grows near salt water and sends out roots from its trunk and branches. These roots provide a home for creatures such as shellfish. If possible, use the Internet to locate photos or diagrams of mangroves and share these with the class before completing this activity.

- Suggest that students read through the whole text to get an overview before attempting to fill in the blanks.

- Go over the answers by asking volunteers to read completed parts of the text aloud.

- Check comprehension by asking how mangroves benefit the environment.

Answer Key
1. status **2.** Evidence **3.** indicates **4.** exploitation **5.** Ongoing **6.** recover **7.** strategies **8.** violate

---

IDEAS FOR... **Checking Comprehension**

Have students close their books and ask some general questions about the text:
How do mangrove forests benefit the environment?
Why are mangrove forests being destroyed?
What are some suggestions for protecting these forests?

Exercise C. | Discussion

- Allow time for students to discuss the questions in pairs. Compare answers as a class.

Developing Listening Skills

(pages 26-27)

45 mins

Before Listening

Exercise A. | Predicting Content

- Gather ideas from the whole class after students have discussed the questions in groups.

- For question 1, make a list of types of habitats for birds (grasslands, forests, mountains, coast, rivers, wetlands). For question 2, make a list of possible causes of extinction (pollution, disease, loss of habitat, etc.).

Note-Taking

- Go over the information in the box. Ask for some examples of abbreviations and symbols that students already use.

- Explain that *indenting* (starting the line in from the margin) is one way of showing that the information is an example.

Exercise B.
track 1-12

- Refer students to the notes and ask them to identify the features mentioned in the Note-Taking box (key words, abbreviations, symbols, and indentation).

- Play the audio and ask comprehension questions: *What was the habitat of this bird?* (wetlands of Merritt Island, Florida) *What caused it to become extinct?* (poisoned by chemicals used to kill mosquitoes, loss of habitat)

Exercise C. | Have students take turns explaining each of the main points of the introduction.

Listening: A Guided Tour

Note-Taking
track 1-13

- Allow time for students to read through the notes and identify what kind of information is missing.

- Play the audio while students complete the notes.

- Check the answers by asking students to read their notes aloud. Discuss possible variations with the class.

Answer Key *(Student notes may vary.)*

Endangered Species Act (ESA) - 1973
  Protects animals and their **habitats**
    Ex.: **steelhead trout in Washington state**
  Ongoing conflict between **landowners** and **government**
    Ex: **gray wolf in Wyoming and Idaho**
  ESA protects **land**; ranchers feel law violates **their rights**
Endangered Species today
  Situation today is **worse** than in 1973
  1. > **1300** species listed as **endangered** or **threatened**
  2. Since 1973 only **39** species removed from list
  3. BUT only **14** removed because they recovered; **9** became extinct, others listed by accident
  4. **300** more species may soon be added to list
Conclusion
  Even w/ ESA in place, **not making much progress**

IDEAS FOR... Checking Comprehension

Ask these additional questions or write them on the board.

1. *What are three reasons that species are endangered?* (habitat loss, deforestation, and overfishing)

2. *Which two species may soon be added to the Endangered Species list?* (the Las Vegas buckwheat and the Miami blue butterfly)

After Listening

Exercise A.

- Have students work individually to answer the questions. Remind students to read all answer choices carefully before selecting each answer.

Answer Key   1. b 2. a 3. b

TIP   When giving feedback on multiple-choice questions, make sure to explain why answer choices were incorrect.

Exercise B. | Discussion   Ask pairs of students to come up with as many ideas as possible on ways the dusky seaside sparrow could have been saved.

Exploring Spoken English

(pages 28-30)

Language Function: Introducing Examples

- Go over the information in the box.

- Read the example sentences aloud using appropriate intonation. Ask students to repeat the sentences.

track 1-14

Exercise A.

- Play the audio and pause after each item to allow students time to write their answers.

- Go over the answers by asking volunteers to read their completed sentences aloud.

Answer Key
1. For example
2. for instance
3. such as
4. including

IDEAS FOR... Expansion

Have students look at the photo of the Miami blue butterfly on page 28 and discuss why it would matter if this species became extinct. Ask students to research more about this butterfly and why it is endangered. Students can share information in groups during the next class session.

Exercise B. | Collaboration

- Introduce the topic by asking what students already know about bees and bats. Ask why the animals might be endangered.

- Tell students to work in pairs and choose one animal each—either bees or bats.

- Monitor students while they are talking to make sure they are using all the expressions in the Language Function box on page 28.

- After they have finished, ask students what facts they found most interesting or surprising.

IDEAS FOR... Multi-level Classes

- If students need more practice with introducing examples, have them write sentences using the target language and the information in the chart on page 29. Then students can work with a partner, discuss the sentences they wrote, and correct any errors together.

- For students who finish early, ask them to close their books and talk about a topic of their choice with a partner. Encourage students to use the phrases for introducing examples.

Exercise C. | Self-Reflection

- Allow a few minutes for students to complete the sentences before sharing them with their partner.

- Ask volunteers to tell the class about one of their partner's ideas.

Grammar: Restrictive Adjective Clauses

- Go over the language in the box.

- Nominate students to read aloud the examples.

- Point out that the relative pronoun *that* in the second example can be omitted because it refers to an object.

IDEAS FOR... Presenting Grammar

Write several sentence starters on slips of paper. Distribute the slips and ask students to complete them with their own ideas.

Examples:

I like people who . . .
The music that I like best is . . .
The Web sites that I visit most are . . .

Have students walk around the room and try to find students with similar answers.

Exercise A.

- Allow time for students to combine the sentences individually.

- Ask volunteers to read their answers aloud or have them write their sentences on the board.

- Note that in sentence 2, *whom, who,* and *that* are all possible answers (*whom* is more formal), and the relative pronoun can be omitted because it refers to an object.

Answer Key *(Answers may vary.)*

1. The police discovered the body of a deer that / which had been killed illegally.
2. The woman whom / who / that I met yesterday belongs to a bird-watching club.
3. I know a woman who keeps two tigers as pets.
4. I think it was a grizzly bear that / which tore open all my trash bags.
5. There are too many people who / that don't care about endangered species.

Exercise B. | Collaboration

- Model an example sentence, such as: *I'm fascinated by animals that hibernate.*

- Allow time for students to complete the sentences individually.

- Encourage students to think of as many alternative endings as possible.

- Invite volunteers to share their most interesting ideas with the class.

Speaking *(page 31)*

30-45 mins

Brainstorming Ideas about Conservation

- Go over the information in the box.

- Explain that brainstorming is something that is normally done in a group, but it can also be done individually. It is a helpful technique for gathering ideas before writing an essay or before starting a project. When working in a group, it is important to accept all ideas and not evaluate them until later.

Exercise A. | Brainstorming

- Have students work in groups. Assign one person in each group to be the secretary who will complete the chart.

- Alternatively, ask all group members to note down their own ideas first and then add them to a combined group chart.

Exercise B. | Discussion

- Ask two students to read the examples in the speech bubbles aloud.

- Remind students to use the target language for introducing examples in their group discussions.

TIP Give each student in the group responsibility for one of the habitats from the chart. The student can lead the discussion for their habitat and can present the main points while other group members present additional points.

Viewing: Crocodiles of Sri Lanka (pages 32-33)

30-45 mins

Overview of the Video | The video discusses the mugger crocodile, an endangered crocodile that lives mostly in Sri Lanka. The crocodile was once common throughout India, but the growth of the human population has caused the mugger habitat to shrink.

Before Viewing

Exercise A. | Predicting Content

- Ask students to look at the map and describe the location of Sri Lanka. Ask them what they know about India, Sri Lanka, and crocodiles.

- Ask students to discuss the question in pairs and make notes of their ideas.

Exercise B. | Using a Dictionary

- Allow time for students to use their dictionaries or other clues in the context to find the answers.

- Remind students that words often have multiple meanings. Encourage students to pay attention to the context to work out which meaning is correct. For example, in sentence 1, *in the wild* suggests something about animals. In sentence 2, *die out* suggests something that is gone and will not come back.

> **Answer Key.**   1. b 2. a 3. b 4. b

While Viewing

Exercise A. | Note-Taking

9:08

- Go over the words in the box. Ask students to explain the words they are familiar with by giving definitions.

- Play the first two minutes of the video and allow time for students to write their answers. Ask volunteers to read their sentences aloud.

> **Answer Key**
>
> 1. human, habitat 2. crocodiles 3. mugger
> 4. farms 5. captive 6. India

Exercise B. | Note-Taking   Play the next two minutes of the video. Check students' answers by playing the video and pausing after the correct answer.

9:08

> **Answer Key**
>
> 1. subcontinent 2. a few thousand 3. 30 years ago
> 4. Rom Whitaker 5. wild

Exercise C. | Refer students back to their notes from exercise **A** in the Before Viewing section to find out how many ideas they were able to predict.

Exercise D. | Note-Taking

9:08

- Read the questions aloud. Play the rest of the video while students take notes.

- Check the answers as a class and ask for any additional information students may have picked up.

> **TIP**   Give feedback on how well students were able to use note-taking techniques such as abbreviations and symbols.

> **Answer Key** (Student notes may vary.)
>
> 1. It's not a well-studied species.
> 2. Rom is observing them at night because the shining of their eyes makes it easy to see them. He is counting them by shining a flashlight at them.
> 3. They don't often fight. In mating season, males fight for territory and the right to choose females. They are sometimes killed, but not usually.

After Viewing

Exercise A. | Collaboration   Encourage all students to write at least four questions. For example: *Why are you interested in crocodiles?*

Exercise B. | Ask students to work in groups to interview Rom using their questions from exercise **A**.

> **IDEAS FOR...   Expansion**
>
> Ask students to research Web sites on the Internet that give information about mugger crocodiles or about the Madras Crocodile Bank. Have students discuss their findings in groups.

Building and Using Vocabulary *(pages 34-35)*

30 mins

WARM-UP

The Lesson B target vocabulary is presented in the context of an interview with a fish biologist. Ask students to look at the photo and describe what they think this person does in her job. Ask: *What could be interesting or difficult about her job?*

Building Vocabulary

track 1-15

Exercise A. | Meaning from Context Play the audio while students read the text. Ask if they can suggest meanings for any of the words in blue.

Exercise B. | Using a Dictionary

- Allow time for students to write their answers.
- Remind students that the word class can often help them figure out the definition of the word.

Answer Key	1. g 2. j 3. i 4. e 5. f 6. c 7. h 8. b 9. a 10. d

TIP After completing exercise B, have students work in pairs. Tell Student A to close his or her book. Student B will read out a definition. Student A has to remember the correct vocabulary word from memory. Have students switch roles after five words.

IDEAS FOR... Checking Comprehension

Ask some general questions about the text:
1. *Why does this person like her job?*
2. *Would you like to do this job?*
3. *Which aspects of her job would you find most interesting?*
4. *Which of her suggestions for ways to contribute time would you be willing to follow?*

TIP Have students think of their own example sentences using these vocabulary words and write them in their vocabulary journals.

Using Vocabulary

Exercise A.

- Refer students to the photo and ask what students already know about wolves. (You may wish to point out that students heard some information about wolves in the Developing Listening Skills section of Lesson A.) Ask students if they know where Yellowstone National Park is and if any of them have ever been there.

- Encourage students to read through the whole text first to get an overview before filling in the blanks.

- Go over the answers by asking volunteers to read completed parts of the text aloud.

- Ask students to summarize the benefits and problems of restoring the wolf population.

Answer Key		
1. authorized	5. focus	9. contribute
2. funds	6. ignore	10. issue
3. sustain	7. annually	
4. Contrary	8. maintain	

Exercise B. | Critical Thinking

- Ask students to work in groups to discuss the questions.
- Ask a spokesperson from each group to share their conclusions with the class.

IDEAS FOR... Expansion

Ask students to work in groups to role play a discussion about the issues in exercise **B**. They can take the roles of scientists, environmentalists, farmers, tourists, or government officials.

Developing Listening Skills
(pages 36-37)

45 mins

Before Listening

Prior Knowledge

- Direct students' attention to the photo and ask if they or anyone they know has ever hunted animals or birds. Ask: *What is your opinion of this activity? Are some kinds of hunting more acceptable than others? Do you know if hunters need a license to hunt animals in our area?*

- Ask students to work in pairs to discuss the questions.

Listening: A Student Debate

Critical Thinking Focus: Evaluating Arguments in a Debate

- Go over the information in the box.

- Explain the differences between a debate and a discussion: *A discussion is a conversation where participants can interrupt each other and respond more spontaneously to each other's arguments. A debate is more formal. In a debate, speakers usually argue for or against an issue. One side presents their arguments first. The other side then presents the opposing arguments.*

track 1-16

Exercise A. | Listening for Key Concepts

- Make sure students understand the term *legalized hunting* (hunting with a state or government license).

- Play the audio once for students to get the key concepts.

Answer Key

The woman (Yumi) is in favor of hunting.
The man (Raoul) is against hunting.

track 1-16

Exercise B. | Note-Taking

- Play the audio again while students take notes in the chart.

- Draw the chart on the board and call on students to fill it in. Invite the rest of the class to suggest improvements to the notes.

Answer Key *(Student notes will vary.)*

Yumi's Arguments for Hunting
Hunting helps to control animal pops.
Hunters license fees help pay for animal conservation.
Yumi's Responses to Raoul
Natural predators also eat cows and sheep.
Cows also suffer when they are killed for food.
Most hunters are law abiding and kill only what they can eat.
Raoul's Arguments against Hunting
Some hunters are irresponsible.
Hunting is cruel and causes pain and suffering to animals.
There is a lot of illegal hunting.
Raoul's Responses to Yumi
Tourists can also pay to raise money for animal conservation.

Exercise C. | Tell students to work in pairs to discuss the arguments for and against hunting. Play the audio again if necessary.

Exercise D. | Discussion Encourage students to evaluate the arguments on the audio. Ask students to compare their own opinions with those on the audio.

After Listening

Critical Thinking

- Ask students to discuss these questions in groups. Encourage them to give examples from their own experience.

- Discuss opinions as a class.

Pronunciation: Pronouncing -s endings

track 1-17
track 1-18

Exercises A and B. | Go over the information in the box and play the audio. Ask students to raise their hands to indicate which sound they hear.

Answer Key	1. /s/ 2. /z/ 3. /ɪz/ 4. /z/ 5. /s/ 6. /z/ 7. /s/ 8. /ɪz/

Exercise C.
track 1-19

- After students have practiced, ask them to tell you which sound occurs in each example. Going down each column, students should identify the following sounds:

  1. /s/   3. /z/   5. /ɪz/   7. /z/
  2. /s/   4. /ɪz/   6. /s/   8. /ɪz/

30 mins

Exploring Spoken English
(pages 38-39)

Language Function: Responding to and Refuting Argument

- Emphasize that this language function has three parts:
  1. Acknowledge the other person's opinion.
  2. Use a contrast word.
  3. Express your opinion / refutation.

- Make up a few opinion statements and ask individual students to disagree with you using the expressions from the box.

Track 1-20 **Exercise A. |** Play the audio, pausing to allow time for students to write their answers.

Answer Key

1. That's a good argument but
2. OK, but
3. You are right

Exercise B. | Ask students to work in pairs to practice these exchanges. They may substitute different expressions from the box.

Exercise C.

- Encourage students to continue each argument with their partner as long as possible.

- Ask volunteers to present their exchanges to the class.

> **IDEAS FOR...** **Expansion**
>
> Have pairs of students create sentences similar to those in exercise **C**. The sentences can be about another topic that relates to the unit theme. Each pair can exchange sentences with another pair of students and practice responding to and refuting arguments.

Grammar: Non-Restrictive Adjective Clauses

- Go over the information in the box. Ask volunteers to read the sentences aloud using appropriate pauses for commas.

> **IDEAS FOR...** **Presenting Grammar**
>
> Point out these main differences between restrictive and non-restrictive adjective clauses:
> 1. Restrictive clauses give essential information. They cannot be removed or the meaning of the sentence will change. Non-restrictive clauses give extra information. They *can* be removed and the sentence still retains meaning.
> 2. Non-restrictive clauses have commas, or pauses in speech, while restrictive clauses do not.
> 3. Non-restrictive clauses do not use *that* and the pronoun cannot be omitted.

Exercise A. | Write the example sentence on the board and show how the word order changes and the relative pronoun replaces the subject pronoun. Allow time for students to write their answers individually.

Answer Key

2. Sting, who is a British celebrity, works to protect the Amazon.
3. Whales, which are the largest animals on earth, were hunted to near extinction.
4. Wolves have been introduced into Yellowstone, which is America's oldest national park.
5. The hippopotamus, which lives in African rivers, is not an endangered species at this time.
6. Businessman Ted Turner, whose ranch is very large, allows elk hunting on his land during part of the year.

Exercise B. | Collaboration

- Ask students to work in pairs. Encourage them to think of as many different endings for the sentences as possible.

Engage: Participating in a Debate *(page 40)*

45 mins

WARM-UP

Direct students' attention to the photo and ask them to describe what is happening. Bring in information about local zoos and encourage students to discuss whether they look interesting to visit.

Exercise A. | Evaluating Arguments

- Brainstorm a few arguments for and against keeping animals in zoos.

- Allow time for students to read the statements and write their answers.

- Monitor students as they work to see if they have any problems evaluating the arguments. If any sentences cause difficulty, discuss them as a class. Identify context clues that can help students evaluate difficult sentences.

Answer Key	1. F 2. F 3. A 4. A 5. F 6. F 7. A 8. A

Exercise B.

- Remind students of the target language for refuting an argument on page 38 and write the phrases on the board for reference.

- Ask students to work in pairs to discuss each of the statements in exercise **A**.

Exercise C. | Organizing Ideas

- Have students draw a T-chart in their notebooks. (Instruct students to look at the example T-chart on page 214 of the *Independent Student Handbook*.) In one column, students should list arguments supporting their position. In the other column, students should list ways to refute the opposing side's arguments.

- Divide the class into two groups. One half will be for keeping animals in zoos and one half will be against keeping animals in zoos.

Exercise D. | Presentation

- Pair students up with someone from the opposite group (see the following Tip). Allow time for students to practice in pairs.

- Go over the information in the Presentation Skills box.

- Organize groups of six so that each pair in the group can make a presentation to the rest of the group. (Or, if time permits, ask pairs to come to the front of the class to give their presentations.)

- Review the language in the Student to Student box so that students can encourage each other before they start.

> **TIP** To organize pairs for exercise D, assign one half of the class the letter *A* and the other half the letter *B*. Everyone in favor of zoos is A, and everyone against zoos is B. Then ask all students to stand up. Every A has to find a B and sit down together with them.

Presentation Skills: Speaking with Confidence

- Demonstrate giving a presentation by someone who hasn't organized their notes, doesn't use body language appropriately, and talks too fast without pausing.

- Discuss tips for using body language such as standing up straight, looking at the audience, and holding your arms still so that they are not distracting. Encourage students to record the presentation on audio or video or practice in front of a friend to help build their confidence.

Student to Student: Expressing Encouragement

- Practice the phrases using the appropriate intonation. Discuss other ways to show encouragement during and after presentations such as by smiling, nodding, and saying *Well done!* or *Good job*! at the end of the talk.

> **IDEAS FOR... Expansion**
>
> Ask students to summarize the points from this section by writing a paragraph or short essay outlining the arguments for and against keeping animals in zoos.

Beauty and Appearance

Academic Track
Sociology, Aesthetics

Academic Pathways:
Lesson A: Listening to a News Report
Conducting a Survey
Lesson B: Listening to an Informal
Conversation
Giving a Group Presentation

Unit Theme

Ideas about beauty and appearance change over time and often depend on cultural and social influences as well as personal opinion.

Unit 3 explores the topic of beauty and appearance as it relates to:
– the modeling industry
– cosmetic surgery
– ideas of beauty around the world
– eco-fashion
– innovative fashion design

 ## Think and Discuss *(page 41)*

5 mins

Fashion is a multi-billion dollar industry. Designers promote their images of beauty and lifestyle through advertising, glossy magazines, fashion shows, and other types of promotion such as movies and celebrity events. This particular photo is an advertisement for the Armani fashion house. Ideals of beauty and appearance are an important part of our social identity, yet they are constantly changing. The fashion industry plays a big role in determining what we perceive as beautiful.

- Discuss different types of advertising and where you find advertising (e.g., on the Internet, in emails, on billboards).

- Ask students to describe their response to the photo and discuss questions 1–3.

- Discuss students' opinions of advertising. Ask: *Is advertising necessary? Does it persuade you to buy things? What effect does it have on our ideas about beauty? Do models in fashion ads represent how ordinary people look?*

 ## Exploring the Theme: Beauty and Appearance *(pages 42-43)*

15 mins

The opening spread features a photo of jewelry and sandals for sale in Colombia.

- Ask students what fashions are most popular at the moment. Ask what kinds of accessories and body decoration (e.g., earrings, hair ornaments) and what kinds of beauty treatments (e.g., spas, facials, manicures) are popular today.

- Ask students to look at the main photo and discuss why fashion is important in our culture. Ask: *Is fashion an important part of our identity? Is it something we choose individually or are we usually influenced by the media or by our surroundings?*

- Ask students to look at the photos and discuss the questions in exercise **A**. Compare answers as a class.

- Ask students to look at the chart and discuss the questions in exercise **B**. Discuss reasons why people would want cosmetic surgery.

TIP After students suggest answers for exercise B, question 2, you may want to provide the following information to confirm if their predictions were correct. The next countries with the largest number of cosmetic surgery procedures are as follows: 6. Japan, 7. South Korea, 8. Germany, 9. Italy, and 10. Russia.

Building and Using Vocabulary *(pages 44-45)*

30 mins

WARM-UP

The Lesson A target vocabulary is presented in the context of an article about the changing world of modeling.

- Ask students to look at the photo. Ask: *What is happening in this photo?* (a model is walking down the runway at a fashion show) *Who might be in the audience?* (designers, journalists, actresses)

- Ask students what they know about fashion designers and fashion models.

Building Vocabulary

track 1-21

Exercise A. | Meaning from Context

- Play the audio while students listen and read along.

- Ask some general comprehension questions. For example: *What is the main topic of the article?* (the physical appearance of fashion models) *How is modeling changing?* (Fashion designers are starting to use models with different body types.)

> **TIP** Give students three minutes to write as many comprehension questions as they can about the text. For example: *What do models usually look like? Why are some models unhealthy? What did they do in Australia? Why are people's opinions starting to change?* Then ask students to close their books. Have volunteers ask other students their questions. Each question can only be asked once.

Exercise B. | Allow time for students to refer back to the text and work out the meanings of the words.

> **TIP** Another way to do exercise B is to have students cover the text of exercise A. Then play the audio again while students try to work out the answers by listening to the audio. Then they can uncover the text and check on any vocabulary words that they missed.

Answer Key

1. envision	5. classic	9. disturbed
2. evolving	6. constitutes	10. perception
3. consistently	7. variations	
4. ratio	8. random	

Using Vocabulary

Exercise A.

- Direct students' attention to the photo and discuss what kind of surgery this woman might be having and why.

- Encourage students to read through the whole text before they try filling in the missing words.

- Go over the answers by inviting volunteers to read completed parts of the text aloud.

Answer Key

1. disturbs 2. evolved 3. constitute 4. envision 5. classic

IDEAS FOR... **Checking Comprehension**

Have students close their books and ask some questions about the text:

1. *How many cosmetic surgeries were completed in 2009?* (8 million)
2. *What is liposuction?* (surgery to remove fat from the body)
3. *What is the average price of liposuction?* ($3000)
4. *What is the price of a hair transplant?* ($4500)

Exercise B. | Self-Reflection

- Ask students to work in groups and discuss the questions.

- Ask a spokesperson from each group to summarize the group's answers to one of the questions for the class.

Developing Listening Skills

(pages 46-47)

45 mins

Before Listening

Discussion

- Introduce the topic by asking students what they think makes a face beautiful.

- Tell students to work in pairs and try to agree on the most beautiful photo in each row. If students in a pair disagree, ask them to explain why.

- For question 2, ask students to explain their choices if they are different from those that researchers found were most common.

- Ask students if they noticed anything interesting about the photos here (all 12 are of the same person). Inform students that they will hear more about this study in the news report.

Listening: A News Report

track 1-22

Exercise A. | Listening for Main Ideas

Allow time for students to read through the research results before playing the audio.

Answer Key	1. b 2. c 3. d 4. a

track 1-22

Exercise B. | Listening for Details

- Ask students to read the questions. Play the audio again.

- Check the answers by asking students to raise their hands according to which answer they chose.

- Ask which fact or facts students found most surprising. Ask students to share some ideas about why ideas of beauty might differ between cultures.

Answer Key	1. b 2. a 3. b 4. c

TIP To make exercise B more challenging, you can write the questions on the board without the answer choices. Have students close their books and take notes as they listen. After listening, students can use their notes to complete the exercise.

IDEAS FOR... Checking Comprehension

Ask these additional questions or write them on the board:

1. *What do these expressions mean? Beauty is only skin deep.* (A person who is beautiful on the outside is not always beautiful inside.) *Beauty is in the eye of the beholder.* (Each person's idea of beauty is different.)

2. *What were the differences between the images that people were asked to compare?* (There were different distances between the eyes and the mouth.)

3. *What do Mayan people consider beautiful?* (people with crossed eyes)

4. *What do some African tribes consider beautiful?* (people with scars)

5. *What do Maori people consider beautiful?* (women with tattooed blue lips; point out the photo at the bottom of page 47)

After Listening

Critical Thinking

- Have students work in groups to discuss the questions.

- Ask a spokesperson from each group to report to the class.

- Ask students if there are aspects of beauty (physical beauty or fashion) in their culture they disagree with.

IDEAS FOR... Expansion

Ask students to choose one aspect of fashion (for men or for women) and research about how it has evolved over the centuries, or about how it differs between different cultures. Some aspects they may choose to research could include hats, shoes, makeup, jewelry, and hairstyles. Ask students to find two or three photos on the Internet of these items over the years. They can share this information with other students in the next class.

Pronunciation Note
(Judith) Langlois: Lang-**wah**

Exploring Spoken English
(pages 48-50)

45 mins

Language Function: Paraphrasing

Go over the information in the box. Give some example sentences and ask students to paraphrase them using the expressions in the box. You can use ideas from the previous listening exercise. For example: *People from the same culture usually envision beauty in the same way.* (To put it another way, people from the same culture often have the same idea of beauty.)

track 1-23
Exercise A.

- Play the audio and pause after each item to give students time to write their answers.

- Check the answers by asking volunteers to read their sentences aloud.

Answer Key

1. In other words **2.** That is to say **3.** To put it another way

Critical Thinking Focus: Understanding Quotations | Go over the information in the box. Ask if students have a favorite quotation, or mention some of your favorites.

Exercise B.

- Ask students to read the quotations individually and write their own interpretations.

- Walk around the classroom as students are writing to provide help if they are having difficulty. The information they write will be used in exercise **C**.

IDEAS FOR... Expansion

Read or dictate some additional quotations and ask students to write their interpretations. Compare the results as a class by having students read their results aloud or by putting all the interpretations on a poster display.

Exercise C. | Paraphrasing

- Read the example in the box aloud. Ask students to work in pairs to use their answers from exercise **B** to practice paraphrasing.

- Ask two or three volunteers to read their answer for each one aloud. Discuss and compare any differences in interpretations.

IDEAS FOR... Multi-level Classes

Prepare quotations on slips of paper, some of them easier and some more difficult. Distribute the slips of paper according to the level of the students. Ask students to paraphrase their quotations to a partner.

Grammar: Compound Adjectives

Go over the information in the box. Ask volunteers to make sentences using these phrases.

IDEAS FOR... Presenting Grammar

Ask students to paraphrase the example phrases. For example: *A kind-hearted man is a man who has a kind heart. In other words, he helps people and is generous.*

Exercise A. | After students have completed the exercise, ask them to identify which kind of compound adjective is used in each example. (See answers in the answer key below.)

Answer Key

1. poorly-built (adverb + past participle)

2. often-quoted (adverb + past participle)

3. highly-motivated (adverb + past participle)

4. rose-colored (noun + past participle)

5. sugar-free (noun + adjective)

6. good-looking (adjective + present participle)

Exercise B. | Ask two students to read the examples in the speech bubbles aloud. Have students work in pairs to practice using compound adjectives. Have volunteers read their answers aloud.

Answer Key

1. I have an interview for a part-time job.
2. The chef is preparing a mouth-watering meal.
3. I gave Elena the hand-made vase.
4. I can't wear this sweat-soaked shirt.
5. I'm going to buy a four-foot-tall bookshelf.
6. If you are a good-looking person, you might be able to have a career as a model.
7. The world-famous author is visiting my university.
8. In an emergency, it's good to know that we have a cool-headed babysitter.

Exercise C. | Discussion

- Allow time for students to discuss the questions in groups. Ask a spokesperson from each group to summarize the answer to one question for the class.

Speaking *(page 51)*

30-45 mins

Conducting a Survey

Exercise A.

- Explain that each student will conduct a survey by asking some of his or her classmates questions on the topic of beauty. Preview the exercise as described below.

- **Step 1: Choosing questions**
  Demonstrate how to evaluate the questions in the box. For example: *What kind of answers would you expect for each question? Will the answers be very different or similar? What can be learned from the answers? What additional questions can be asked?* Allow time for students to choose their questions and make up two more of their own.

- **Step 2: Preparing a chart**
  Monitor students as they prepare their charts, providing help if needed. Make sure they leave enough space to write answers and extra notes in their charts.

- **Step 3: Conducting a survey**
  Ask students to stand up and move around the classroom to conduct the survey. Set a time limit for each interview so that all pairs can change partners at the same time.

TIP You may want to review the information in the Student to Student box before having students complete the survey.

Exercise B. | Have students work in groups. Have them take turns telling the rest of the group about the results of their survey. They should try to interpret the results by giving possible reasons for the answers, and by saying why they found the results interesting or surprising. Ask volunteers to share the most interesting results with the class.

Student to Student: Asking about Personal Opinions

- Go over the information in the box. Explain that conducting a survey means asking about people's opinions and listening carefully to their answers. It's not always helpful to give your own opinion when you are conducting a survey because it may discourage people from saying what they think.

- You may want to discuss cultural differences in asking about personal opinions. *What topics are not OK to ask about?* (e.g., religion, politics)

IDEAS FOR... **Expansion**

Ask students to conduct a survey of their friends or family using one or more of the questions from this page. They can prepare a brief oral or written summary of the results for the next class. They can present their results by answering the following questions:
1. *What results did I expect?*
2. *What results did I get? Were they different or similar to my expected results?*
3. *What did I learn?*

Viewing: Skin Mask

30 mins

(pages 52-53)

Overview of the Video | This video shows an unusual type of modeling—how a perfect replica of a model's face can be created using silicone. This process is often used to create special effects for movies and television shows.

Before Viewing

Exercise A. | Using a Dictionary

- Discuss the meaning of the word *mask* and the different contexts in which it might appear.

- Ask students to work individually. Then discuss the words and definitions as a class.

- Ask students to predict how these words might relate to the topic of the video.

Answer Key	**1.** silicone **2.** gooey **3.** mummy **4.** special effects **5.** inject

Exercise B. | Predicting Content

- Ask students to look at the photos on pages 52 and 53. Encourage students to describe each photo by saying what they think is happening and what each mask is used for.

- You may want to make a list on the board of questions that the students would like answered in the video.

While Viewing

Exercise A.

2:55

- Allow time for students to read the questions.

- Play the video and ask students to compare answers in pairs.

- Play the video again if necessary.

- Ask volunteers to read their answers and explain why they chose them.

Answer Key	**1.** b **2.** a **3.** c

Exercise B. | Sequencing Events

2:55

- Ask students to pencil in their idea of the correct sequence.

- Play the video again while students check their answers.

- Go over the answers by asking different students to read each step in the sequence.

Answer Key	**a.** 6 **b.** 8 **c.** 1 **d.** 4 **e.** 7 **f.** 2 **g.** 9 **h.** 5 **i.** 3

After Viewing

Critical Thinking

- Encourage students to evaluate the information in the video. They can brainstorm answers for each question and try to come up with as many different answers as possible.

- If students have difficulty with question 2, suggest one possible use for skin masks by pointing out the photo on page 52. This photo shows an eye that is being created by a doctor for use by a patient who has lost an eye.

> **TIP** You could make the After Viewing exercise into a competition to see which pair of students can come up with the highest number of acceptable possible answers.

Answer Key *(Answers will vary. Sample answers are below.)*
1. to disguise an actor as someone else; to make an actor look older or younger by applying makeup to the skin mask; to be used in a stunt by a body double in dangerous scenes
2. for medical reasons when someone has serious injuries to their face; to disguise someone in order to protect their identity, especially if they are in danger; to be used as part of a costume

30 mins

Building and Using Vocabulary *(pages 54-55)*

WARM-UP

The Lesson B target vocabulary is presented in the context of eco-fashion—fashion that is safe and healthy for the environment. Ask students to look at the photo and think of some adjectives to describe this dress such as *creative, imaginative, strange, eccentric,* or *artistic*. Ask students: *What other kinds of materials could be recycled to create fashion?*

Building Vocabulary

track 1-24

Exercise A. | Using a Dictionary

- Allow time for students to work individually to complete the exercise.

- Explain that each word in parentheses gives a clue to the missing word. Remind students that the word class can often give them a clue, too.

- Play the audio so that students can check their answers.

Answer Key

1. convince	5. insert	9. transport
2. alternative	6. derive	10. definite
3. exhibit	7. integrate	
4. textile	8. considerably	

Exercise B.

- Allow time for students to read the article. Advise them to read the whole text before choosing their answers.

- Check the answers by asking two students to read the conversation aloud.

- Inform students that another word for *second-hand* in American English is *used.* These words are often used interchangeably (e.g., *second-hand clothing, a used car, a used bookstore*).

Answer Key

1. transported 2. textiles 3. integrate
4. derived 5. exhibited 6. insert

Using Vocabulary

Exercise A.

- Refer students to the photo and ask them to describe it. Ask: *What is the Cargolifter balloon being used for?*

- Encourage students to read through the whole text first to get an overview before writing their answers.

- Check the answers by asking volunteers to read out parts of the text. Ask students which idea they found most innovative or most useful.

Answer Key

1. convince 2. considerably 3. transport
4. integrated 5. exhibited 6. alternative 7. insert

Understanding Suffixes | Go over the information in the box. Ask students if they can think of any other suffixes that make adjectives such as *-al, -ious, -ful, -less,* or *-able*. Refer students to page 209 of the *Independent Student Handbook* for more information about suffixes.

Exercise B. | Using a Dictionary

- Encourage students to guess the correct word first before checking in the dictionary.

- Go over the answers and practice pronunciation if necessary, paying special attention to syllable stress.

Answer Key

1. Cooperative 2. definitive 3. addictive
4. active 5. constructive 6. Derivative

IDEAS FOR... Expansion

For homework, ask students to find five more adjectives ending in *-ive* or *-ative* and write example sentences that illustrate their meaning. You can use the sentences to make an activity like the one in exercise **B**.

Developing Listening Skills
(pages 56-57)

Before Listening

Predicting Content | Direct students' attention to the photos. Ask them to describe each item and guess what it is for. They do not need to write their predictions at this stage.

Listening: An Informal Conversation

track 1-25

Exercise A. | Listening for Main Ideas

- Play the audio all the way through so that students can understand the main ideas.

- Tell them to write their answers below the photos in the previous exercise. Ask volunteers to read their answers aloud. Ask if anyone predicted the correct answers.

Answer Key

1. antigravity jacket
2. Kevlar vest
3. wearable electronics

track 1-25

Exercise B. | Note-Taking   Play the audio again while students complete the notes. Write the notes on the board in one color and ask students to come to the board and write their answers in another color.

Answer Key

Antigravity jacket: part **balloon** and part **jacket**

Kevlar: **man-made** fiber, stronger than **steel**

- used in **bullet-proof vests** and **ropes**
- developed in **1960s**

Biosteel made from **spider-silk** protein produced in **goat milk**

- possible uses: **transport objects**

Wearable electronics integrate **clothes** and **electronics**

Ex.: GPS sneakers allow parents to **track children**

Exercise C. | Listening for Specific Information
track 1-25

- Play the audio again while students take notes of their answers. Ask students to compare answers in pairs before checking them as a class.

Answer Key

1. daydreams **2.** Kevlar vest **3.** Spiders eat each other.
4. It's innovative and useful.

IDEAS FOR...   **Checking Comprehension**

After listening, have students close their books and answer the following questions.

1. *What is Kevlar used in?* (in bullet-proof vests for police officers)
2. *What is special about spider silk?* (It is five times as strong as steel.)
3. *What kind of jacket did the woman think was useful?* (a jacket with a cell phone right in the collar)

After Listening

Critical Thinking | Ask students to discuss these questions in pairs. Then have them discuss their opinions with the class.

track 1-26

Pronunciation: Pronouncing /n/ and /ŋk/
Go over the information in the box and play the audio. Model these sounds for students:

/n/ as in *thin*   /ŋ/ as in *sing*   /ŋk/ as in *blink*

Explain that the difference between these sounds can alter the meaning of a word. For example:

win—wing—wink   thin—thing—think

track 1-26

Exercise A. | Play the audio and pause it for students to repeat the words.

Exercise B. | Collaboration

- Explain that students will first think of words and then make up questions using the words. Suggest a target of 6–8 words.

- When they have finished, invite volunteers to write their words on the board. Ask other volunteers to ask someone in the class a question using one of the words.

Exploring Spoken English

(pages 58-59)

30 mins

Language Function: Asking for Clarification

Go over the information in the box. Ask for clarification by modeling these expressions. For example: *What does* eco-fashion *mean? What do you mean by* biosteel?

track 1-27 **Exercise A.** | Play the audio, pausing to allow time for students to write their answers. Play the audio again and pause after each key expression for students to repeat with the appropriate intonation.

Answer Key

1. What exactly is
2. Sorry, what does…mean
3. What do you mean by

Exercise B. | Have students work in pairs to practice asking for clarification. They may use different expressions from the box.

IDEAS FOR... **Multi-level Classes**

While students are doing exercise **B**, walk around the classroom and monitor the level of support students need. Students who need more support can switch roles and repeat the exchanges in exercise **B**. Higher-level students can make up their own exchanges using other technical terms that they know.

Grammar: Tag Questions

- Go over the information in the box. Ask volunteers to read the questions aloud.

- Explain that tag questions are a way of eliciting a response from the other person by asking them to confirm some information. It is usually something the speaker doesn't know or isn't sure of.

IDEAS FOR... **Presenting Grammar**

Ask students to write two things about their partner that they are not sure of.
For example:
Your favorite color is blue.
You went to Spain for your last vacation.

They will use tag questions to ask their partner about these pieces of information.
For example:
Your favorite color is blue, isn't it?
You went to Spain for your last vacation, didn't you?

Their partner will answer each question using an appropriate positive or negative response.

Exercise A. | Have students write their answers first and make sure they are correct. Then students can practice the exchanges with their partner.

Answer Key

2. **Q:** We've already discussed eco-fashion, **haven't we**?
   A: Yes, **we have**.
3. **Q:** You'd like to learn more about wearable electronics, **wouldn't you**?
   A: No, **I wouldn't**.
4. **Q:** You're not going to wear a wool sweater today, **are you**?
   A: Yes, **I am**.
5. **Q:** It's not possible to make textiles from plastic bottles, **is it**?
   A: Yes, **it is**.
6. **Q:** You had a good time at the fashion show, **didn't you**?
   A: No, **I didn't**.

Exercise B. | Role-Playing Ask students to work in pairs. Encourage them to think of as many questions as possible. Ask volunteers to present their interview to the class.

IDEAS FOR... **Expansion**

For exercise **B**, students may want to use the information about fashion designers that they heard about on the audio. Or, they can base the role play on fashion designers that they know.

Engage: Giving a Group Presentation *(page 60)*

45 mins

Lesson Preparation Note | This presentation exercise requires students to do some research on the Internet or in the library. You may want to assign this research for homework or arrange to have Internet or library access available during the lesson.

WARM-UP

- Have students look at the photos and ask them to compare the clothing fashions in these two places.

- Bring in (or ask students to bring in) advertisements and photos from fashion magazines that illustrate different types of fashion. Ask students which ones they prefer and why.

- Ask students what criteria they use to choose their clothes (e.g., style, comfort, cost) and what makes them buy a new item of clothing. Make a list of students' ideas on the board.

Exercise A. | Discussion

- Read the task in the box aloud. Ask students to work in groups to make a list of different fashion trends in their city or country. They can draw pictures to illustrate the styles or use photos or illustrations from magazines if available.

Exercise B. | Brainstorming

- Students can choose to talk about fashion in the city they are in or in another city they know well.

- Explain that the chart will help students to consider all aspects of fashion including hairstyles, clothing, and accessories. Explain that *accessories* are handbags, belts, scarves, gloves, hats, jewelry, etc.

- Ask students to work in groups to complete the chart. If necessary, allow extra time for groups to do research outside of the classroom. Set aside time in class so students can discuss their research findings before continuing on to exercise **C.**

Exercise C. | Planning a Presentation

- Advise students to assign one part of the presentation to each group member so that everyone has an equal role.

- Tell students to refer to page 211 of the *Independent Student Handbook* for more information on organizing group presentations. They may want to make one person the group leader.

- Review the information in the Presentation Skills box about preparing notes before students begin to plan their presentations.

Exercise D. | Presentation

- Students can give their presentation to another group or to the whole class.

- Encourage other students to ask questions and give positive feedback at the end of each presentation.

> **TIP** To make the presentations more lively, you can ask students to bring in items of clothing that illustrate the fashions they are talking about. They can display the clothing during the presentation. Similarly, groups can create a visual aid that includes photos or illustrations of each type of fashion.

Presentation Skills: Preparing Your Notes | Go over the information in the box. Give some examples of notes using key words and short sentences that are suitable for a presentation.

> **IDEAS FOR... Expansion**
>
> Ask students to write a description of one of the fashions they learned about during another group's presentation. Have students share their descriptions in small groups.

Energy Issues

Academic Track
Interdisciplinary

Academic Pathways:
Lesson A: Listening to a Guest Speaker
Role-Playing a Town Meeting
Lesson B: Listening to a Study Group Discussion
Creating and Using Visuals
in a Presentation

Unit Theme

Finding clean, safe, and renewable sources of energy is a challenge that all countries face today.

Unit 4 explores the topic of energy as it relates to:
– energy disasters
– production of energy
– alternative energy sources

Think and Discuss *(page 61)*

5 mins

More than 30 countries in the world operate nuclear power plants, and several other countries are planning to start a nuclear power program in the future. France is the only country that uses nuclear power as its primary source of electricity. In fact, around 75 percent of its energy is derived from nuclear power. The first nuclear power plant in France was opened in 1963. There are now 59 nuclear power plants in France. After some recent nuclear disasters, however, some European countries have decided to close down older reactors and phase out the use of nuclear power.

■ Ask students to describe their reactions to the photo and discuss the questions.

■ Make a list of different types of energy sources and ask which sources of energy students use most frequently.

■ Discuss students' opinions of nuclear energy. Ask: *Do you think nuclear power is necessary? Is it safe? What alternatives are there?*

■ Discuss whether attitudes to energy use are changing nowadays and why. Ask students to list all the ways they use energy every day.

Exploring the Theme: Energy Issues *(pages 62-63)*

15 mins

The opening spread features a photo of a wind farm in Abilene, Texas.

■ Ask students for their reaction to the photo. Discuss the possible advantages and disadvantages of wind farms.

■ Ask students to look at the two smaller photos and read the captions. Discuss why energy use is increasing and why it is important for everyone to have electricity.

■ Discuss the questions in the Exploring the Theme box with the class.

IDEAS FOR... Expansion

Ask groups of students to research energy statistics for their region or country. Brainstorm questions with the class and assign questions to different groups. For example: *How much energy is used? What different types of energy are used? What types of energy are produced? How has energy use/production changed in recent years?* Students may want to present their information in the form of a pie chart or bar graph. Refer students to page 216 of the *Independent Student Handbook* for more information on how to create a chart or graph.

Building and Using Vocabulary (pages 64-65)

30 mins

WARM-UP

The Lesson A target vocabulary is presented in the context of the Deepwater Horizon oil spill in the Gulf of Mexico.

- Ask students to look at the map and identify the location of the oil spill. Ask students to look at the photo and list all the kinds of damage that can result from an oil spill. For example, birds and fish as well as tourism and fishing industries are affected.

- If possible, bring in a photo or diagram of an oil rig to show how it drills for oil under the ocean floor.

Building Vocabulary

track 2-2

Exercise A. | Meaning from Context

- Play the audio while students listen and read along.

- Ask some general comprehension questions. For example: *What was the Deepwater Horizon?* (an oil rig in the Gulf of Mexico) *What caused the explosion?* (a buildup of pressure that caused natural gas to shoot up from the ocean floor) *How much oil was spilled?* (5 million barrels)

- Ask if students remember hearing about this disaster in the news. If so, ask them what other details they can remember about the disaster.

Exercise B. | Allow time for students to refer back to the text and work out the meanings.

> **TIP** To make exercise B more challenging, ask students to cover the text in exercise A and the column of vocabulary words in exercise B so that they can try to remember the words from memory.

| Answer Key | 1. d 2. e 3. g 4. b 5. f
6. i 7. j 8. c 9. h 10. a |
| --- | --- |

Using Vocabulary

Exercise A.

- Ask students what connection they think there could be between coal mining and earthquakes.

- Ask them to read the text and fill in the missing words. Remind them to use the correct form of each word.

- Ask volunteers to write their answers on the board.

| Answer Key | 1. experts 2. triggered 3. react
4. controversy 5. abandon |
| --- | --- |

Exercise B.

- Ask students to work in pairs to practice the conversation.

- Monitor the pairs for correct pronunciation and intonation.

> **IDEAS FOR... Checking Comprehension**
>
> Tell students to close their books. Ask some questions about the text:
> 1. Where was the earthquake? (in Newcastle, Australia)
> 2. When was the earthquake? (in 1989)
> 3. How deep was the mine? (2297 feet)
> 4. How deep was the earthquake? (6 miles)
> 5. What was the controversy? (Some people thought the earthquake was caused by the mine, but others didn't agree.)

Exercise C. | Discussion

- Ask students to work in groups to discuss the questions.

- If groups finish early, ask them to focus on one question and make notes about their answers to present to the class.

- Ask volunteers to share the most interesting ideas with the class.

> **TIP** Advise students to write their own example sentences for the new vocabulary words in their vocabulary journals.

Developing Listening Skills

(pages 66-67)

45 mins

Before Listening

Predicting Content

- Introduce the topic by asking students what they know about the nuclear disaster in Chernobyl.

- Ask students to look at the map and describe the exact location of the Chernobyl Nuclear Power Plant. Ask students to explain what they can learn from the diagram.

- Ask students to find definitions for the words in question 1 in their dictionaries. Ask students to infer how each word might be related to the topic of a nuclear disaster. For example: Containment *means keeping something under control. What needs to be kept under control in a nuclear plant?* (the reactor)

Listening: A Guest Speaker

Critical Thinking Focus: Using an Outline to Take Notes   Go over the information in the box. Draw a blank outline template on the board and show students how to use numbers and letters to organize the outline as described in the box.

Exercise A.
track 2-3

- Play the audio while students read the outline.

- Encourage students to ask you questions about the outline. Point out the use of abbreviations and symbols in the outline and remind students to use these as they take notes.

Exercise B. | Discussion

- Refer students to the outline in exercise **A**. Ask them to identify the main topics and the details.

- Discuss how the outline structure can help when you review your notes.

Exercise C. | Listening for Main Ideas
track 2-4

- Allow time for students to read the questions. Play the audio.

- Go over the answers by asking students to raise their hands for each correct answer choice.

Answer Key	1. a, c, d 2. a 3. b

Exercise D. | Outlining
track 2-4

- Play the audio again while students complete the outline.

- Replay any difficult parts of the audio, if necessary.

Answer Key *(Student notes may vary.)*

C. The Chernobyl plant today
  1. Still extremely **radioactive**
  2. There are plans to build a **concrete shell**
D. Radioactivity
  1. Many areas are still contaminated with cesium **137**
  2. Half-life of **30** years
E. The exclusion zone today
  1. **400** people live there
  2. Animals have returned, for ex., **wild horses, deer, wolves, eagles, bears**

IDEAS FOR...   Checking Comprehension

Ask these additional questions or write them on the board.
1. *What did city officials tell people to do at first?* (stay indoors and close the windows)
2. *Why did the radioactive material spread so quickly?* (It spread through the smoke from the fire that burned for 10 days.)
3. *How many people were forced to leave their homes?* (300,000)
4. *How did children become ill?* (They drank contaminated milk.)

After Listening

Discussion

- Have students work in pairs to discuss the questions.

- Ask volunteers to share their ideas with the class.

 TIP   To check comprehension, ask students to take turns giving a lecture about the Chernobyl disaster to their partner using the completed outlines from page 66 and page 67.

Pronunciation Note
Pripyat: **Prip**-it
Belarus: Bel-uh-**roose**
cesium: **see**-zee-uhm

Exploring Spoken English

45 mins

(pages 68-70)

Language Function: Emphasizing Important Information

- Go over the information in the box.

- Give some example sentences and ask students to repeat them using one of the phrases in the box.
  T: Nuclear energy has many risks.
  S: Don't forget that nuclear energy has many risks.

Exercise A.

track 2-5

- Play the audio and pause after each item to allow students time to write their answers.

- Go over the answers by asking volunteers to read their sentences aloud.

Answer Key

1. I want to emphasize that

2. it's important to remember that

3. Let me stress

IDEAS FOR... Expansion

Discuss the wild horses in the photo on page 68 of the Student Book. Ask students to suggest reasons why they are able to live in this region and not in the wild.

Exercise B.

- Ask students to form groups of three. Each student should choose one of the pictured forms of energy (oil, coal, or wind).

- Ask a volunteer to read the example in the speech balloon to the class.

- Point out how the speaker in the example uses details and his personal experience to support the argument.

- Walk around the classroom while students are working and take notes of any language problems.

TIP If class size requires you to have more than three students in a group, ask two students to share one topic. Make sure that both students get a chance to speak.

IDEAS FOR... Multi-level Classes

If groups finish exercise **B** quickly, ask them to switch roles and do the exercise again. Higher-level students can try to do the exercise again without looking at the book, by using their own ideas, or by selecting a different energy form not pictured here (e.g., nuclear, solar).

IDEAS FOR... Expansion

Ask students to do a class survey of the types of energy used by students in the class and what students think are advantages of each type of energy.

Grammar: The Future Perfect

- Go over the information in the box.

- Explain that the future perfect shows that an event will occur before another event in the future. The future perfect also shows that something will happen before a specific time in the future.

- Practice the pronunciation of the examples. Explain that the word combination *will have* is often contracted in speech to the contraction *will've* (pronounced *willuv*).

- Give some examples from your own life that illustrate aims you will have accomplished by some future date.

IDEAS FOR... Presenting Grammar

Ask students to draw a time line like the one on page 215 of the *Independent Student Handbook*. The time line should illustrate different goals that students hope to have achieved over the next 10 years. Students can share their time line with a partner and answer more detailed questions about their plans.

Exercise A.

- Allow time for students to discuss the answers in pairs.

- Invite volunteers to read their answers aloud.

Answer Key

1. will have increased
2. will have returned
3. will have changed
4. will have, replaced
5. will have built

Exercise B. | Self-Reflection

- Organize students into groups of three.

- Ask two students to read the examples in the speech balloons aloud.

- Encourage students to continue the discussion of each point by asking further questions as in the example.

- Ask a volunteer from each group to tell the class about another person in their group.

Speaking *(page 71)*

30-45 mins

Role-Playing a Town Meeting

Exercise A.

- Ask if students have ever attended a town meeting. Ask: *What was it about? What happened?*

- Discuss the kinds of topics that are usually raised at town meetings and what the aim of such meetings might be.

- Ask three students to read the situation and the role cards aloud.

- Organize students into groups of four. Students should choose their roles so that they have two group members for each role.

Exercise B. | Ask pairs of students to work together on gathering ideas to support their arguments.

Exercise C. | Role-Playing

- Read the information in the Student to Student box before starting exercise **C**.

- Read the examples in the speech balloons.

- Monitor students during the discussion and take notes of any language problems.

Student to Student: Conceding a Point

- Go over the information in the box.

- Explain that conceding a point shows that you are open to different points of view.

IDEAS FOR... **Expansion**

Ask students to role play a town meeting about the construction of an oil rig off the coast of their region. Help students to brainstorm some advantages (employment, cheaper energy) and some risks (environmental impact, risk of an oil spill) before starting the role play.

Viewing: Solar Power
(pages 72-73)

30 mins

Overview of the Video | This video presents some recent developments in the use of solar energy.

Before Viewing

Exercise A. | Understanding Visuals

- Ask students to look at the photo and tell how they think solar energy works.

- Ask students to read the information and label the diagram individually.

- Go over the answers by drawing (or asking a student to draw) the diagram on the board and inviting students to write the labels.

Answer Key

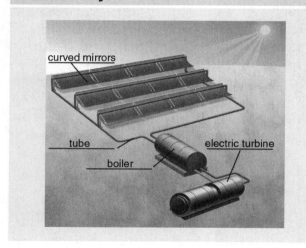

curved mirrors

tube

boiler

electric turbine

While Viewing

Exercise A.
2:53

- Allow time for students to read the text. Point out that the answers can be one or two words.

- Play the video as students write answers.

- Ask students to compare answers in pairs.

- Ask volunteers to read sections of the text aloud. Write the answers on the board.

Answer Key
1. energy 2. our sun 3. year
4. electricity 5. solar energy 6. reliable

Exercise B.
2:53

- Ask students to pencil in their ideas based on their first viewing of the video before watching again.

- Play the video again while students check their answers.

TIP Go over the answers by asking students to tell you which numbers to write on the board.

Answer Key

Students should check statements 2, 4, 5, 6, and 8.

Exercise C. | Viewing for Specific Information
2:53

- Allow time for students to read the questions.

- Play the video again while students choose their answers.

- Go over the answers by asking students to raise their hands for each answer option they think is correct.

Answer Key 1. b 2. a 3. c 4. a

After Viewing

Critical Thinking | Ask students to work in pairs. Encourage students to evaluate the information in the video by looking for arguments for and against the programs mentioned.

IDEAS FOR... Expansion

- Ask students to research other solar energy systems such as the photovoltaic system. They can give a three minute presentation about their findings in the next lesson. If possible, ask students to bring in diagrams from magazines or the Internet to show the class.

- Ask students to research availability of solar panels in your city or region. Instruct students to find answers to the following questions: *How much do they cost? How many different types are available? How much energy do they produce?*

Building and Using Vocabulary *(pages 74-75)*

30 mins

WARM-UP

The Lesson B target vocabulary is presented in the context of information about alternative energy sources.

Ask students to look at the two photos. Ask if they have any experience with alternative energy sources. Ask: *Have you ever visited a hydroelectric dam? Do you know where any hydroelectric dams are located in the United States or in another country?*

Building Vocabulary

track 2-6

Exercise A. | Meaning from Context

■ Play the audio while students listen and read along.

■ Ask students to identify the main idea of each paragraph.

■ Ask students if they can explain the meaning of any of the words in blue before looking at exercise **B**.

> **TIP** To make exercise A more challenging, ask students to listen with books closed and identify the main idea of each paragraph.

Exercise B.

■ Allow time for students to work individually, using dictionaries if necessary.

■ Remind students that the word class can often help identify the correct definition.

Answer Key

1. abundant	5. pursuing	9. renewable
2. enthusiasm	6. disadvantage	10. shortages
3. incentives	7. principle	
4. layers	8. utilize	

IDEAS FOR... Checking Comprehension

Ask students to answer these questions about the listening:

1. *What disadvantages of oil are mentioned?* (It's difficult to find; there are shortages; it's expensive; it creates pollution.)

2. *What two types of alternative energy are mentioned?* (wind and hydroelectric energy)

3. *What two incentives to encourage alternative energy use are mentioned?* (money and tax breaks)

4. *What is the difference between a renewable and a non-renewable energy source?* (Renewable energy is sustainable; it will not run out.)

Using Vocabulary

Exercise A.

■ Have students look at the photo and ask them to describe it. Ask which country they think it could be and where they think geothermal energy might be found. (Note: This photo is of a hot spring in Iceland.)

■ Ask students to work in pairs to discuss their answers. Make sure they cover the answers at the bottom of the page as they do so.

■ Read aloud the answers at the bottom of the page.

Answer Key

1. T **2.** T **3.** F (Other sources such as coal are more abundant.) **4.** F (The government offers incentives to install solar systems, but not geothermal.) **5.** T **6.** F (Geothermal energy has been used for thousands of years.)

Exercise B. | Self-Reflection
Ask students to discuss the questions in pairs. Encourage students to use new vocabulary words in their answers.

IDEAS FOR... Expansion

Encourage students to have a mini-debate in groups of three or four. Each person in the group should choose an energy source and explain why it is better than the others.

Developing Listening Skills

45 mins

(pages 76-77)

Before Listening

Understanding Visuals | In pairs, each student will describe one diagram while their partner asks questions. Suggest that students start by describing what each labeled item in the diagrams is for. Write some useful verbs on the board for reference: *turn, lead (to), connect (to), send, store, generate,* and *produce.*

Listening: A Study Group Discussion

 track 2-7

Exercise A. | Listening for Key Concepts

- Discuss what a study group is and what the purpose of the discussion could be.

- Allow time for students to read the sentences.

- Play the first part of the discussion. Ask volunteers to explain the reasons for their answers. For example: *Sentence 1 is false because they have been meeting for nearly three months.*

Answer Key	1. F 2. T 3. T 4. T

 track 2-8

Exercise B. | Using a Graphic Organizer

- Preview the graphic organizer by asking the following questions: *How many types of energy will be presented? What kind of information is in each column?*

- Ask students to read over the notes briefly and try to predict the missing information.

- Play the discussion while students complete the notes.

- Check the answers as a class.

> **IDEAS FOR...** **Checking Comprehension**
>
> Ask students to work in groups of three. Each person should choose one type of energy from the audio and use their notes to summarize its advantages and disadvantages for the other group members.

Answer Key *(The missing words for each graphic organizer are listed below.)*

Solar Power

1. pollution
3. renewable

1. cells
2. Clouds and darkness
3. Battery

Wind Power

2. no air / water pollution
3. almost nothing
4. financial incentives

1. ugly
2. noise
3. energy
4. storing power

Hydroelectric Power

1. abundant
2. much maintenance
3. pollution
4. very cheap

1. environment
2. animal habitats
3. to move

After Listening

Critical Thinking | Encourage groups to evaluate the information on the audio. Ask if they can think of any additional advantages or disadvantages of these alternative energies.

 track 2-9

Pronunciation: Stressing Two-Word Compounds

- Go over the information in the box. Play the audio, pausing to allow time for students to repeat the examples.

 track 2-10

Exercise A.

- Complete item 1 as a class. Use underlining to show that stress on the first word would mean a teacher of English (a compound noun), but equal stress would mean a teacher who is English (adjective + noun).

- Play the audio while students choose the correct phrases.

Answer Key

1. a teacher who is English 2. juice made from oranges
3. a van in motion 4. a small stove for keeping food warm
5. a coat

Exercise B. | After students have practiced, invite volunteers to read the sentences aloud. Ask the rest of the class to identify the meaning.

Exploring Spoken English
(pages 78-79)

Language Function: Expressing Approval and Disapproval

Go over the information in the box. Ask students for some suggestions to complete these expressions.

rack 2-11
Exercise A.

- Play the audio, pausing to allow time for students to write their answers.

- Play the audio again and pause after each sentence for students to repeat with the appropriate intonation.

Answer Key

1. disapprove of; it's fine to
2. it's wrong; it's not right

Exercise B.

- Allow time for students to complete the chart individually.

- While students are working, encourage them to think of reasons why they approve or disapprove of each issue.

Exercise C. | Discussion

- Remind students to use expressions for approval and disapproval in their discussion.

- Wrap up the activity by taking a vote on each issue to see where the class stands.

Grammar: The Future Perfect Progressive

- Go over the information in the box. Ask volunteers to read the examples aloud.

- Explain that the future perfect progressive involves talking about actions that will be in progress before a specific time in the future.

- You may want to contrast this verb tense with the future perfect from page 70, which is used to talk about completed actions and events in the future.

IDEAS FOR... Presenting Grammar

Give some example sentences to describe activities you or your class will have been doing by the end of this year. Write the beginning of the sentences on the board and supply verbs so that students can finish them.

By the end of December, we . . . (study English)
By the end of December, we will have been studying English for one year.

By the end of this year, I . . . (live in New York)
By the end of this year, I will have been living in New York for two years.

Exercise A. | Have students complete the exercise individually. Invite volunteers to read their sentences aloud.

Answer Key

1. will have been living 2. will have been selling 3. will have been driving 4. will have been producing 5. will have been working 6. will have been using 7. will have been meeting

Exercise B. | Ask students to work individually. Go over the answers by asking volunteers to read parts of the text aloud.

Answer Key

1. will have been working 2. will have submitted 3. will have received 4. will have been teaching 5. will have been giving

Exercise C. | Discussion

- Ask students to work in pairs. Walk around the classroom and take notes of any language problems. Give feedback to the class on how well they used the target tenses.

IDEAS FOR... Expansion

Choose one of the technologies from exercise **C** and ask students to stand in a line according to who has been using this technology the longest.

Engage: Creating and Using Visuals in a Presentation

(page 80)

45 mins

Lesson Preparation Note | This presentation exercise requires students to do some research on the Internet or in the library. You may want to assign this research for homework or arrange to have Internet or library access available during the lesson.

WARM-UP

Discuss with the class what sources of energy are most widely used in your region or in their home countries. Direct students' attention to the photo and ask them their opinion of this form of energy production. Ask: *Do you think this energy is cost-effective? Is it good for the environment?* Ask students if they know about any other unusual sources of energy.

Exercise A. | Discussion

- Read the task in the box and the list of energy sources aloud. Ask what students already know about any of these energy sources.

- Assign topics or ask groups to choose topics so that all topics are covered.

> **IDEAS FOR... Multi-level Classes**
>
> If you have students at different levels, you may consider assigning easier topics (e.g., ethanol, tidal power, or ocean power) to the lower-level students. These topics will likely be easier to research and will have information readily available.

Exercise B. | Researching

- Discuss with students where and how they can complete their research. Ask groups to brainstorm key words that might help them with their research.

- If possible, take your class to the library or computer lab to do their research. Otherwise, assign this step for homework.

- Remind students to find clear visuals to support their presentation. Advise them to bring in a variety of different visuals so that they can choose the best ones with their group. Instruct students to look back at the photos and diagrams in this unit for some examples.

Exercise C. | Planning a Presentation

- Advise students to assign one part of the presentation to each student so that everyone has an equal part. Students may appoint a group leader who makes sure all points are covered and everyone has a chance to speak.

- Refer students to page 211 of the *Independent Student Handbook* for more information on organizing their presentation.

> **TIP** If students prepare a poster, remind them to choose visuals that are large enough for the audience to see. Help them to think about layouts and headings and draw a couple of different possible layouts on the board. If students are preparing a slideshow, this may be a good opportunity for students to learn about how to create special effects using the tools of PowerPoint.

Exercise D. | Presentation

- Review the information in the Presentation Skills box before students give their presentations.

- Students can give their presentation to another group or to the whole class.

- Encourage other students to ask questions and give positive feedback at the end of each presentation.

> **TIP** Give feedback on overall presentation skills such as having a clear and audible voice volume, using eye contact and body language effectively, and using notes appropriately.

Presentation Skills: Fighting Nervousness

- Go over the information in the box.

- Brainstorm any other tips or techniques for fighting nervousness such as deep breathing or visualization.

Migration

Academic Track
Life Science, Biology

Academic Pathways:

Lesson A: Listening to a Radio Show
Talking about Your Family History

Lesson B: Listening to a Conversation
between Friends
Doing a Research Presentation

Unit Theme

Migration means to move from one place to another. Animal migration (including the migration of birds, fish, and insects) is usually seasonal and involves moving to a warmer climate for the winter months. Human migration can be seasonal—as when workers migrate for seasonal work—or permanent—as when people move to another country to find a new home (emigration or immigration).

Unit 5 explores the topic of migration as it relates to:
– migration of early modern humans across the world
– scientific research about DNA
– migration of animals, insects, and fish

Think and Discuss *(page 81)*

5 mins

Snow geese live in Greenland, Canada, Alaska, and the northeastern tip of Siberia during the period from May to August. In the winter, the geese migrate to warm parts of North America and as far south as Mexico.

- Ask students to describe their reaction to the photo and the theme of migration. Ask: *In what different contexts could the word* migration *be used? How does it relate to animals and to humans?*

- Discuss the questions.

- Ask if students know anyone who has migrated and why they did so. Invite volunteers to talk about their personal experiences.

TIP People migrate for various reasons: economic hardship, natural disasters, or war and persecution. Because these issues may evoke painful memories for students, only call upon volunteers who are willing to share their experiences.

Exploring the Theme: Migration *(pages 82-83)*

15 mins

The opening spread features a map showing the migration of early modern humans and how they spread throughout the world.

- Ask students to look at the map and try to identify the sequence of human migration. Ask: *Where were the earliest humans? Where did they migrate to?*

- Discuss the questions in the Exploring the Theme box. Ask some general questions that relate to the unit theme. For example: *How did humans travel during these migrations? What kind of evidence could have helped scientists discover the path of human migration?*

IDEAS FOR... Expansion
Ask students to brainstorm a list of animals, birds, or fish that migrate annually. They can choose one species and find out where its members migrate from and to. They can present their information to the class in pairs or in groups. Examples include elephants, buffalo, reindeer, Canada geese, snow geese, whales, sea turtles, and eels.

Building and Using Vocabulary *(pages 84-85)*

30 mins

WARM-UP

The Lesson A target vocabulary is presented in the context of human migration.

■ Ask students to look at the photo and brainstorm ideas for how DNA material could help trace the first human migrations.

■ Discuss reasons for voluntary and involuntary migration.

Building Vocabulary

track 2-12

Exercise A. | Meaning from Context

■ Play the audio while students listen and read along.

■ Ask a few general comprehension questions. For example: *Why did people leave their birthplace voluntarily? What kind of involuntary migration is discussed? What have DNA researchers discovered?*

Exercise B. | Allow time for students to refer back to the text and work out the definitions of the words in blue.

Answer Key

1. implications	5. migrations	9. linked
2. subsequently	6. immense	10. assume
3. incredible	7. declined	
4. encountered	8. absorbed	

TIP To make exercise A more challenging, ask students to listen to the text first with their books closed. Then ask some general comprehension questions.

Using Vocabulary

Exercise A. | Using a Dictionary

■ Discuss the illustration. Ask: *What are these people doing? What animals did they hunt?*

■ Ask students to read the text before trying to fill in the missing words in order to familiarize themselves with the passage.

■ Remind students to use the correct form of each word as they complete the paragraph.

■ Ask volunteers to write the answers on the board.

Answer Key

1. migrated
2. Subsequently
3. assumed
4. absorb
5. implication

TIP Ask students to summarize the main idea of the text by answering this question: *What theory did scientists change their minds about?*

Exercise B. | Discussion

■ Have students work in pairs to answer the questions. Ask volunteers to summarize their ideas for the class.

Exercise C. | Choosing the Right Definition

■ Remind students that a dictionary may have several definitions for one word; it is important to read all the definitions to identify which one is correct for the given context.

■ Ask students to work individually to write their answers.

■ Ask students to tell you the correct answers as you write them on the board.

■ Ask in what way these three definitions are similar.

Answer Key   a. 2 b. 3 c. 1

IDEAS FOR... Expansion

Choose another vocabulary word from page 84 and ask students to find additional definitions or synonyms for it in the dictionary. For example, *decline* can mean to lose strength, to become smaller, or to say no. Have students list these additional definitions in their vocabulary journals.

Pronunciation Note
Neanderthals: nee-**an**-der-thals

Developing Listening Skills
(pages 86-87)

45 mins

Before Listening

Predicting Content

- Ask students to describe the people in the photos. Ask: *Where do you think these people are from? How old are they?*

- Ask students to tell you their guesses and then have them look at the answer at the bottom of the page.

- Discuss questions 2 and 3. Ask students to share their own experiences.

Listening: A Radio Show

Critical Thinking Focus: Understanding Scientific Theories

- Go over the information in the box. Refer back to the text on page 85 if necessary.

- Ask students for other examples of scientific theories. Ask: *What kind of evidence could be used to support those theories?*

 Exercise A. | Listening for Key Concepts
track 2-13

- Allow time for students to read the questions.

- Play the audio while students choose their answers.

- Go over the answers as a class.

Answer Key	1. b 2. a 3. c

 Exercise B. | Note-Taking Direct students'
track 2-13
attention to the time line. Explain that this type of visual organizer is a useful way of taking notes or of organizing notes for review purposes.

Answer Key *(Answers for boxes from left to right)*

Box 2: Group of ppl. **left Africa** & arrived in **the Middle East**

Box 3: 2 grps. reached **Central Asia** & **Southern Europe**

Box 4: **ppl. from Siberia crossed over to North America**

Exercise C. | Listening for Details
track 2-13

- Allow time for students to read the sentences before you play the audio.

- Suggest that students pencil in their answers before listening again.

- Play the audio and pause after each answer.

Answer Key	1. b 2. d 3. a 4. c

IDEAS FOR... Checking Comprehension

Refer students back to the map on pages 82 and 83. Have them work in pairs to explain in their own words how the migration of humans took place. They should ask questions to clarify details or make a list of other questions they would like to ask about this topic.

After Listening

Critical Thinking

- Have students work in pairs to discuss the questions.

- Ask a spokesperson from each group to summarize their ideas for the class.

Answer Key *(Answers may vary.)*

1. Small genetic mutations that occur over a long period of time could cause people to look different from one another

2. It implies that they did not become part of the group. Perhaps they were killed, or they died from other causes.

3. Answers will vary.

IDEAS FOR... Expansion

Ask students to research information about the earliest humans. Tell students to research the following questions: *Where was the earliest human skeleton found? What do scientists know about it?* Have students share their findings with the class.

---

45 mins

Exploring Spoken English
(pages 88-90)

Language Function: Expressing Surprise

- Go over the information in the box.

- Emphasize the importance of intonation in expressing surprise. Explain that flat intonation can make these expressions sound sarcastic or insincere.

track 2-14

Exercise A. | Play the audio and pause after each item to allow students time to repeat the phrases. Give feedback on intonation.

> **TIP** Demonstrate correct intonation by writing the expressions on the board and drawing arrows above the words to show the correct pitch direction.

track 2-15

Exercise B.

- Play the audio and pause after each item for students to write their answers.

- Write the correct answers on the board.

- If you have time, play the audio again and ask students to repeat the interviewer's responses using correct intonation.

Answer Key

1. Imagine that!
2. That's really quite surprising.
3. That's incredible!

Exercise C.

- Ask volunteers to read the dialog in the speech balloons aloud.

- Ask students to write down three surprising things about themselves and tell them to their partner.

IDEAS FOR... Expansion

Ask students to write one surprising thing about themselves on a slip of paper. Collect the slips and put them in a bag. Ask each student to pick out a slip at random. Have students walk around the room and find the person who wrote the statement by asking questions. For example, if the slip says, "I climbed Mount Kilimanjaro," the conversation will be as follows:

S1: Have you climbed Kilimanjaro?
S2: No, I haven't. / Yes, I have.
S1: That's amazing! When did you do that?

Exercise D. | Discussion

- Explain that one person in each pair will choose one topic and tell their partner some amazing facts about it.

- Ask two volunteers to read the dialog in the speech balloons aloud.

- Remind students to use expressions for showing surprise with the appropriate intonation. They should try to add a sentence or two about why they were surprised as in the example.

IDEAS FOR... Multi-level Classes

Higher-level students who finish early can work on writing some more animal facts to tell their partner. Lower-level students can repeat the exercise by switching roles.

Grammar: Using Past Modals to Make Guesses about the Past

- Go over the information in the box.

- Remind students how to form the past tense of modals (modal + *have* + past participle).

- Practice the pronunciation of the example. Explain that *have* is often contracted in speech to *could've, may've,* or *might've.*

- Ask volunteers to read the example exchanges.

IDEAS FOR... Presenting Grammar

Refer students back to the texts on pages 84 and 85 and ask them to create similar exchanges about early human migration. They should try to use the target language in their conversations. For example:

S1: Did early humans migrate to find food and water?

S2: They might have. Or they might have needed to find more space to live.

Exercise A.

- Organize students into groups of three.

- Ask three volunteers to read the example answers for the first item aloud.

- Monitor students as they are speaking and take notes of any common errors.

- Give feedback on the correct use of the target grammar.

Answer Key *(Answers will vary. Possible answers are below.)*

2. He might have sprained his ankle.

3. She might have started an aerobics class.

4. They may not have been able to find work in their own countries.

TIP Use your notes from exercise A to write examples of common student errors on the board. Ask students to correct them.

Exercise B. | Discussion

- Have students work in pairs.

- Ask two volunteers to read the dialog in the speech balloons aloud.

- Remind students to use the past modal forms of *could, may,* and *might.*

TIP Before starting exercise B, encourage students to pair up with a classmate they have not worked with before. One way to do this is to give each student a letter: *A* or *B*. Then ask all students to stand up and walk around until all As have found a B to pair up with.

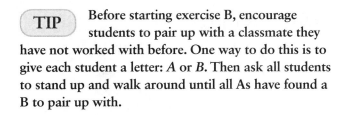# Speaking *(page 91)*

30-45 mins

Talking about Your Family History

Exercise A. | Using a Graphic Organizer

- You may want to introduce this topic by talking about your own family history. Ask students to draw the diagram in their notebooks and complete it with your information. Encourage them to ask you questions.

- Allow time for students to complete the diagram with their own information.

Exercise B.

- Go over the information in the Student to Student box before doing this activity.

- Organize students in groups of three. Each person should take a turn to talk about their family history while the others express interest and surprise as appropriate.

- Remind students to use past modals to make guesses about the past and write a few examples on the board as reference.

- When students have finished, ask a spokesperson from each group to tell the class about the most interesting or surprising information.

Student to Student: Expressing Interest

After you have gone over the information in the box, practice saying these phrases with appropriate intonation.

Viewing: Wildebeest Migration *(pages 92-93)*

30 mins

Overview of the Video | This video presents some information about the migratory habits of the wildebeest.

Before Viewing

Exercise A. | Understanding Visuals

- Direct students' attention to the photo. Ask: *What does a wildebeest look like? Can you describe it?* (It is a large antelope with high shoulders, thin legs, and two large curving horns.)

- Have students look at the map and discuss questions 1 and 2 as a class.

- Ask students to follow the arrows and explain the direction of the wildebeest migration. For example: *First, they move south to Ndutu. Then they go toward the Maswa Game Reserve.*

- Note that the map uses several abbreviations that may be unfamiliar to students. Inform students about the meaning of the abbreviations in the map: *GR* means *Game Reserve.* *NCAA* is an abbreviation for *Ngorongoro Conservation Area Authority.*

Pronunciation Note
Ngorongoro: en-**gor**-ong-gor-oh

Answer Key
1. Kenya and Tanzania
2. Answers will vary according to the time of year.

Exercise B. | Using a Dictionary

- Ask if students know any of these words and ask them to define or explain each word they are familiar with. Then they can check their answers in a dictionary.

- Point out that the plural of *calf* is *calves.*

Answer Key | 1. d 2. e 3. a 4. b 5. c

IDEAS FOR... Expansion

Ask students to try to use the words from exercise **B** to describe the photo on page 92. For example: *The photo shows a **herd** of wildebeest crossing a river. They may be trying to find somewhere to **graze**.*

While Viewing

Exercise A. | Sequencing Events
3:07

- Discuss what is happening in the photo on page 93. Discuss why people enjoy visiting national parks.

- Play the video. Ask volunteers to read the sentences aloud in the correct order. Write the answers on the board.

Answer Key	a. 4 b. 1 c. 3 d. 2 e. 5

Exercise B. | Note-Taking
3:07

- Allow time for students to read the notes.

- Play the video again while students complete the notes.

Answer Key
• 2 mil. animals travel **2,000** miles
• At beginning of yr., all wildebeest give **birth** in same month
• Calves can run **as fast as their mothers** two days after birth
• Nobody knows what triggers **the migration**
• 200,000 of the **weakest** wildebeest will die from starvation, disease, and overexertion
• Others die from predators; cat tries to separate calf from **its mother**
• Kenya's Masai Mara: **rains** create huge area of **grazing**
• In **November**, the wildebeest head south again to the **Serengeti.**

After Viewing

Critical Thinking | Ask students to work in pairs. Encourage students to think of as many answers as possible.

Building and Using Vocabulary *(pages 94-95)*

30 mins

WARM-UP

The Lesson B target vocabulary is presented in the context of the migration of monarch butterflies.

Ask students to look at the photo. Ask: *What do you already know about the migration of monarch butterflies? What do you know about the life cycle of butterflies?*

Building Vocabulary

track 2-16

Exercise A. | Meaning from Context

- Play the audio while students listen to the interview.

- Ask students to explain what they find most interesting or surprising about the job of a butterfly expert.

- Ask students to paraphrase the sentences containing words in blue. For example: *She has dedicated herself to the study of butterflies. In other words, she has spent all her time studying them.*

> **TIP** Write the words in blue on the board. Ask students to close their books and try to remember the context of these words in the interview.

IDEAS FOR... Checking Comprehension

Give students five minutes to write as many questions as they can about the text. Remind students that all questions should have an answer that is found in the text. Then ask students to work in pairs. Have students close their books and answer their partner's questions about the text.

Exercise B. | Self-Reflection
Allow time for students to work in pairs before discussing the answers as a class.

Using Vocabulary

Exercise A.

- Ask students to describe the photo. Ask: *Have you ever done any fishing? Have you ever eaten salmon? What do you know about salmon?*

- Allow time for students to read through the text and choose their answers.

IDEAS FOR... Checking Comprehension

Check the answers to exercise **A** by asking comprehension questions. Encourage students to use a vocabulary word in their answers.

1. *How many tons of salmon are caught each year in the Pacific?* (**approximately** 800,000)
2. *How does the writer describe the challenges salmon are facing?* (They are facing **overwhelming** challenges.)
3. *Why do dams on rivers cause a problem?* (They **interfere** with migration.)
4. *What have many countries done to stop drift nets?* (They have made them **illegal**.)
5. *What have farmers done to raise salmon in different ways?* (They have **established** salmon farms.)
6. *What has farm-raised salmon done to wild salmon in restaurants?* (It has **displaced** it.)
7. *What have some countries done to raise young salmon?* (They have **invested** money.)
8. *Why do salmon need to be protected?* (To **ensure** they survive)

Answer Key

1. approximately **2.** overwhelming **3.** interfere **4.** illegal **5.** established **6.** displaced **7.** invested **8.** ensure

Exercise B. | Critical Thinking

- Ask students to discuss the questions in pairs.

- Encourage students to think of arguments for each side of the issue.

IDEAS FOR... Expansion

Ask students to role play a discussion between two people with opposing points of view on the issue in exercise B. Instruct students to list all the arguments for and against this issue in a T-chart to help them prepare for their role play.

Developing Listening Skills
(pages 96-97)

45 mins

Before Listening

Prior Knowledge | Ask students to discuss the questions in groups. Ask: *Why are tourists interested in visiting the Serengeti National Park? What kinds of jobs might this kind of tourism provide for the local community?*

Answer Key

1. The photos were taken in Tanzania, near the Serengeti National Park.
2. Tourists will likely be filming or photographing animals and natural landscape scenes.
3. Answers will vary.

Listening: A Conversation between Friends

track 2-17
Exercise A. | Listening for Main Ideas

■ Allow time for students to read the questions. Play the audio.

■ Go over the answers by asking volunteers to read the correct sentences aloud.

Answer Key   1. b 2. a 3. b 4. b

track 2-17
Exercise B.

■ Ask students to pencil in their answers before playing the audio again.

■ Go over the answers by asking students to explain why the false sentences are wrong. For example: *For item 1, Larry—not Sandy—went to Tanzania, and Larry had probably not been there before.*

Answer Key   1. F 2. T 3. F 4. T 5. F

Pronunciation Note
Mara: **muh**-rah
Ikoma: ih-**kom**-ah
Robanda: row-**bahn**-dah

IDEAS FOR...   Checking Comprehension

Ask these additional questions or write them on the board:

1. *Why did the Ikoma people have to move?* (so they would not hunt the animals; so the animals could have a protected area in the Serengeti National Park)

2. *How has the eco-tourism company tried to help the Ikoma people?* (by building schools, drilling wells, and providing job training)

After Listening

Critical Thinking | Encourage pairs to evaluate the information on the audio. Remind them to use examples from their own experience to support their arguments. Discuss students' answers as a class.

track 2-18
Pronunciation: Using Question Intonation

■ Go over the information in the box. Review the difference between *yes / no* and *wh-* questions.

track 2-19
Exercises A and B.

■ Play the audio for the first item and do it as a class. Go over the answers by writing the question on the board and inviting volunteers to come and draw the intonation lines.

Answer Key

1. Have you ever tried bush meat? Would you like to?
2. Why do animals migrate? What about humans?
3. Is migrating dangerous for animals?
   What are the risks?
4. How many tourists visit Tanzania each year?
5. Do you enjoy photography?
6. Should the people of Robanda be forced to move?

Exploring Spoken English

(pages 98-99)

Language Function: Expressing Hopes

Go over the information in the box. Ask students to talk about their own hopes using these expressions.

 Exercise A.

- Play the audio, pausing to allow time for students to write their answers.

- Play the audio again and pause after each sentence for students to repeat with the appropriate intonation.

Answer Key

1. It would be ideal if
2. I really hope
3. It would be great

Exercise B. | Role-Playing

- Allow time for students to read all three scenarios. Read the example dialog in the speech balloons aloud.

- Remind students to use expressions for agreeing and showing interest, too.

Grammar: Using Past Modals to Make Inferences

Go over the information in the box. Ask volunteers to read the examples aloud. You may want to contrast the use of past modals to make inferences with the use of past modals to make guesses.

IDEAS FOR... Presenting Grammar

Bring in some interesting and unusual pictures of people in different situations or give some short descriptions of unusual behavior. Ask students to use *must have* or *can't have* to make inferences to explain their behavior.

For example:

T: A man is standing on a street corner looking at a map.

S: He must have gotten lost.

T: A woman is coming home, and her hair is wet.

S: She must have gone out in the rain.

T: A man is holding a lottery ticket, but he looks unhappy.

S: He can't have won any money.

T: Several people are looking at a house with a broken window.

S: Someone must have broken in.

Making Inferences.

- Have students work in pairs.

- Monitor students as they are working to make sure they are using the correct grammar forms and have understood the meaning of the target language.

- Discuss the answers to the questions.

- Give feedback to the class on any common errors.

IDEAS FOR... Expansion

Direct students' attention to the photo at the bottom of the page. Ask: *How were scientists able to create this model? What did they base their model on?* Remind students to use modals in their answers.

Engage: Doing a Research Presentation *(page 100)*

45 mins

Lesson Preparation Note | This presentation exercise requires students to do some research on the Internet or in the library. You may want to assign this research for homework or arrange to have Internet or library access available during the lesson.

WARM-UP

Review what you have learned about animal migration in this unit. Brainstorm a list of other animals that migrate and write them on the board.

Exercise A. | Getting Background Information

- Read the task in the box aloud. Organize students into groups to discuss the questions.

- Point out that these questions refer to migration in general, not to the specific animal that they will research later.

Exercise B. | Researching

- Discuss where and how students should carry out their research. Discuss ways to verify information obtained on the Internet.

- Ask groups to select an animal and then to brainstorm key words that might help them in their search.

- If possible, take your class to the library or computer lab to do their research. Otherwise, assign this step for homework.

- Remind students to bring in a visual to accompany their talk.

Exercise C. | Organizing Information

Students can complete the chart while doing their research and compare their answers as a group in class. Alternatively, they can allocate sections of the chart to be completed by each member of the group.

Exercise D. | Presentation

- Go over the information in the Presentation Skills box before doing this activity.

- Advise students to decide what information will be presented by each member of the group and to practice the entire presentation before giving it to the class. They can time their presentation to see how long it takes.

- Advise students to make a list of possible audience questions.

- Invite groups to come to the front of the class to give their presentation.

- Encourage the class to ask questions.

TIP Give feedback on overall presentation skills such as having a clear and audible voice, using eye contact and body language effectively, and using notes appropriately. Also provide feedback on students' ability to answer audience questions.

Presentation Skills: Preparing for Audience Questions

- Go over the information in the box.

- Explain that thinking about the audience's point of view can help with planning a good presentation. Students should think about what is going to be most interesting for the audience and what they would be most interested in learning.

IDEAS FOR... Expansion

Ask students to write a description of their animal and its migratory habits for homework. They can display it (with a photo) on the class wall or class Web site.

Tradition and Progress

Academic Track
Interdisciplinary

Academic Pathways:
Lesson A: Listening to a Student Presentation
Interviewing a Classmate
Lesson B: Listening to a Study Group
Discussion
Evaluating Web Sources

Unit Theme

There are many reasons why tradition and progress may seem to be in conflict. Progress often means modernization and can cause traditional ways of life to disappear.

Unit 6 explores the topic of tradition and progress as it relates to:
- the Hadza people of Tanzania
- the country of Bhutan
- the Amish
- restoring farmland
- saving languages
- Native Americans

Think and Discuss (page 101)

5 mins

The native people of Alaska have traditionally hunted walrus to make their living. They use the walrus for food, fuel, and clothing. Melting sea ice and overhunting have resulted in fewer areas for walrus to breed and to feed. As a result, the native people of Alaska will end up having to leave this traditional job in favor of more modern jobs in the cities.

■ Ask students to describe their response to the photo and the questions. Ask: *Is progress positive, negative, or both? How has technology changed the traditions of people living in Alaska?*

IDEAS FOR... Expansion

Use the answers from questions 1–3 to create two word maps related to the unit's theme: tradition and progress. (Refer to page 208 of the *Independent Student Handbook* for an example.) Write the words *tradition* and *progress* in the center of each word map. Then ask students to suggest related words to add to the word maps. Have students copy down the word maps in their vocabulary journals.

Exploring the Theme: Tradition and Progress (pages 102-103)

15 mins

The opening spread features a map showing places where progress is changing people's traditional ways of life.

■ Ask students to look at the map and describe life in these different countries. Ask: *What are your ideas based on?* (Students may mention news articles, or personal experiences.)

■ Ask students to look at the photos and read the captions. Discuss questions 1–3.

■ Discuss some general questions related to the theme. For example: *Is progress always good? Is it important to preserve traditions? Why? What traditions do you value in your own culture?*

IDEAS FOR... Expansion

Ask students to choose one tradition from their culture and give a short presentation to the class about it. If possible, they should bring in a photo associated with the tradition. If all students share the same culture, ask them to choose a tradition from another culture they know well.

Building and Using Vocabulary (pages 104-105)

 30 mins

WARM-UP

The Lesson A target vocabulary is presented in the context of the lifestyle of the Hadza people of Tanzania.

- Ask students to look at the map and identify the exact location of Tanzania.
- Direct students' attention to the photo and ask them to describe the landscape. Ask: *What do you think life is like in this area?*

Building Vocabulary

 track 2-21

Exercise A. | Meaning from Context

- Play the audio while students listen and read the text.
- Ask a few general comprehension questions. For example: *Do the Hadza people raise animals? How do they survive? How do they make money? What is threatening their way of life?*

Exercise B. | Allow time for students to refer back to the text and work out the meanings of the vocabulary items.

Answer Key

1. anticipate	5. displaying	9. reject
2. domestic	6. agriculture	10. transition
3. consequences	7. isolated	
4. contradiction	8. period	

 TIP — Check the answers to exercise B by asking a question about each word. For example:

T: What are domestic animals?
S: They are animals that are not wild. They are kept on farms or as pets.

Using Vocabulary

Exercise A. | Discussion Have pairs of students discuss the questions. Encourage students to make guesses if they are not sure about an answer.

Answer Key *(Answers will vary.)*

1. Bushmen of the Kalahari, the Navajo (Native Americans), and the Amish reject the modern world.
2. People could set up more permanent homes. They could have more possessions. They plant food. Communities became more organized and more hierarchical.
3. They could communicate through gestures, pictures, or an interpreter.

Exercise B. | Using a Dictionary

- Ask students to work in pairs to complete the chart.
- Point out that the word class for each word is given.

 TIP — Ask volunteers to come to the board and let the class tell them what to write.

Answer Key *(Missing word forms and definitions are listed below.)*

2. agricultural (adj.): relating to agriculture
3. consequently (adv.): as a result of
4. contradict (v.): to tell someone what he or she says isn't true; contradictory (adj.): having information that disagrees with other information
5. display (n.): an arrangement of things for people to view
6. domestic (adj.): relating to a country (Note that this is the same word form with a different definition.)
7. isolate (v.): to keep one person or thing separate from another; isolation (n.): the state of being separated from others
8. periodic (adj.): happening from time to time
9. rejection (n.): the act of saying or showing that you do not want something or someone

Exercise C. | Self-Reflection

- Ask students to work in groups to discuss the questions.
- Ask a spokesperson from each group to tell the class about the most interesting points of their group's discussion.

Pronunciation Note

Hadza: **hadh**-zuh
Hadzane: hadh-**zuh**-nay

Developing Listening Skills

(pages 106-107)

45 mins

Before Listening

Predicting Content | Ask students what they already know about Bhutan. Direct students' attention to the map, flag, and fast facts. Discuss questions 1–4.

TIP An optional activity is to discuss any questions students would like to ask about Bhutan. For example: *What system of government does it have? What is the weather like?* Make a list of students' questions on the board. After the audio, discuss which questions were answered and ask students to research the remaining questions for homework.

Listening: A Student Presentation

track 2-22

Exercise A. | Listening for Main Ideas

- Allow time for students to read the questions in exercise **A**.

- Play the audio while students choose their answers.

- Go over the answers by asking volunteers to explain their answer choices.

Answer Key 1. b 2. a 3. a 4. c

track 2-23

Exercise B. | Completing an Idea Map

- Direct students' attention to the idea map and ask them to pencil in anything they can remember from the audio.

- Play the audio so that students can complete the idea map. This audio track contains a selected excerpt of the student presentation so that students may focus directly on the information that pertains to the note-taking exercise.

- Draw the idea map on the board and ask students to come and write their answers in the blanks.

- Discuss the advantages of using this kind of graphic organizer for note-taking. For example, it may be easier to remember the information by visualizing the idea map.

Answer Key *(Answers are listed for each row of bubbles from left to right.)*

First Row: Gross National **Happiness**

Second Row: **good** government; sustainable **development, environmental** protection; **cultural** preservation

Third Row: **king** puts needs of **the country** first; government will keep **68 percent** of the land covered in **forests**; government has banned **TV channels** that it thinks are **harmful**

TIP To check comprehension and accurate note-taking, ask students to paraphrase this section of the audio in their own words.

IDEAS FOR... Checking Comprehension

Ask these additional questions or write them on the board.

1. *What is another name for Bhutan?* (Druk Yul or Land of the Thunder Dragon)

2. *What type of government did it have in the past?* (an absolute monarchy)

3. *When did Bhutan get TV?* (in 1999)

4. *What was one negative effect of the isolation?* (The education system fell behind.)

5. *What are two positive effects of opening up the country?* (Communication technology and art have moved ahead.)

After Listening

Critical Thinking

- Have students look at the photo. Ask: *Where are these children? Who are they? What are they doing?*

- Have students work in groups to discuss the questions. Ask a spokesperson from each group to summarize their ideas for the class.

Student to Student: Congratulating the Group | Practice these expressions and encourage students to use them later when they give a group presentation.

Pronunciation Note
Bhutan: Boo-**than**

Exploring Spoken English
(pages 108-110)

Language Function: Using Fillers

- Go over the information in the box.

- Demonstrate how to use these expressions by starting to give an explanation or a definition for a word and then pausing as if to remember the right words.

Exercise A.
track 2-24

- Play the audio. Pause after each item to allow students time to repeat the phrases.

- If you have time, play the audio again and ask students to repeat using the correct intonation.

Answer Key   1. let me think 2. um

Exercise B. | Ask students to practice the sentences in pairs using other expressions from the box.

Exercise C. | Self-Reflection

- Ask volunteers to read the examples in the speech bubbles aloud.

- Model one or two additional exchanges on the same topic with one or two students.

IDEAS FOR...   Expansion

Write some vocabulary words or phrases from this unit on slips of paper. Give one slip to each student. Ask students to stand up and walk around the classroom. When you give the signal, all students should stop walking, turn to their nearest neighbor, and ask them to explain the word or phrase they have on their slip. The other student should reply and use fillers as needed.

Exercise D.

- Read the directions for the exercise with the class. Ask volunteers to read the definition of each word. For each word, ask questions related to the topic. For example:

  1. *Do you have a blog? Do you read any blogs? Which ones?*
  2. *What are the main differences between a* brick-and-mortar *company and an Internet company that is only online?*
  3. *Give some examples of* climate change. *What aspects of* climate change *are you most worried about? What do you think we should do about it?*
  4. *Have you done anything recently to* go green? *Do you have any plans to* go green? *How can we encourage more people to* go green?

- Ask students to work in pairs to complete and continue the conversations.

- Remind students to use fillers when they explain the buzzwords.

Answer Key *(Filler expressions will vary. Buzzword answers are below.)*

1. climate change
2. the blogosphere
3. go green
4. brick-and-mortar

IDEAS FOR...   Multi-level Classes

Lower-level students can refer back to the box when explaining the buzzwords. Higher-level students can challenge themselves by covering the box and using their own ideas to continue the discussion in exercise **D**.

Grammar: Verb + Gerund

- Go over the information in the box.
- Remind students of the difference between gerunds and infinitives.
- Ask students to try and make example sentences with each of these verbs.

IDEAS FOR... **Presenting Grammar**

Give some example sentences for students to rephrase using the target verbs. For example:

T: He says he forgot his homework.
S: He admitted forgetting his homework.

T: It's wonderful to have your help.
S: I appreciate having your help.

Students can continue this exercise in pairs.

Exercise A.

- Ask students to look at the photo. Teach the phrase *horse-drawn carriage*. Ask for some ideas for why this person is driving a horse-drawn carriage.
- Ask students to work individually to underline the verbs followed by a gerund in the article.
- Go over the answers as a class.
- Some students may underline *accustomed to riding* in this exercise. Point out that *accustomed to* is an adjective followed by a preposition and a gerund and therefore, does not follow the verb + gerund format. Encourage students to refer to their dictionaries if they are unfamiliar with a word or its word form.

Pronunciation Note

Amish: **Ah**-mish

> **TIP** Check the answers to exercise A by reading the text aloud and having students raise their hand when they hear a verb followed by a gerund. Then pause and ask students to repeat the phrase.

Answer Key *(Verbs are underlined.)*

<u>enjoy</u> living simply
<u>stop</u> attending school
<u>resist</u> using technologies
<u>like</u> having their picture taken
<u>keeps</u> growing
<u>recommend</u> separating oneself
<u>avoid</u> going out into the modern world
<u>risk</u> living near people

Exercise B. | Collaboration   Have students work individually to write five sentences. Then encourage students to work together and ask questions about each of their partner's sentences.

Speaking *(page 111)*

Interviewing a Classmate

Exercise A. | Go over the instructions with the class. During this discussion, students' answers should be brief, giving an opinion based on their own judgment. More detailed discussion will take place in exercise **B**.

Exercise B. | Discussion

- Explain that some questions may need further discussion to clarify their exact meaning. Go over the first question as a class. *Does the government respond to the needs of the people?* Tell the class to consider questions such as: *What are the needs of the people? How does the government find out about the needs of the people? How does it respond?*
- Remind students to take notes on their partner's answers so that they will be able to share the information in exercise **C**.

Exercise C. | Invite volunteers to share the results of their discussion with the class.

IDEAS FOR... **Expansion**

Discuss what questions students would add to the questionnaire. Ask them to design another pillar and more questions for the chart.

Viewing: Farm Restoration
(pages 112-113)

30 mins

Overview of the Video | This video presents information about a project aimed at returning farmlands to their traditional and natural state.

Before Viewing

Exercise A. | Meaning from Context

- Ask students to describe the photo of a farm silo surrounded by grasslands and woods. Explain the meaning of the word *creek* (a small stream).

- Ask students to read the sentences aloud and suggest some possible ways to paraphrase the words in blue before looking at exercise **B**.

Pronunciation Note
Okabena: Oh-ka-**bee**-nah

Exercise B. | Using a Dictionary
Ask students to try to match the words with their definitions. Then they can check their answers in a dictionary.

Answer Key   1. d 2. f 3. a 4. e 5. c 6. b

While Viewing

3:09

Exercise A.

- Allow time for students to read the questions.
- Play the video.
- Ask volunteers to read their answers aloud. Write the answers on the board.

Answer Key   1. b 2. c 3. a 4. b

3:09

Exercise B.

- Allow time for students to read the sentences.
- Play the video again while students write their answers.
- Ask students to tell you the missing words and phrases and write them on the board.

Answer Key

1. generation farmer
2. the creek *or* Okabena Creek
3. five years
4. cover for animals
5. wildlife music
6. happier

After Viewing

Critical Thinking | Ask students to work in groups. Encourage students to evaluate the information in the video. Ask: *Does the video present one side of the issue or more than one side? Are there are other ways of looking at the Reinvest in Minnesota project?*

IDEAS FOR...   Expansion

- Ask students to work in pairs to role-play an interview with this farmer. One student will be Dale Aden and one will be a local news reporter. Have students brainstorm some questions together before they begin their role-play.

- Ask what students know about farming in the United States or in their country. Ask: *What problems do farmers have and what is being done to help solve them?* Students will learn more about this topic in Unit 10.

Building and Using Vocabulary *(pages 114-115)*

30 mins

WARM-UP

The Lesson B target vocabulary is presented in the context of saving languages that are dying out.

- Ask students if they know of any languages that are no longer spoken (e.g., many Native American languages, Latin, classical Arabic, and classical Gaelic). You may want to differentiate between languages that are no longer spoken or written from those that exist only in written form.

- Ask students to discuss why it is important to preserve language variety. Ask: *What happens when a language becomes extinct? Is language an important part of a community's culture? Why?*

Building Vocabulary

Exercise A. | Using a Dictionary

- Ask students to work individually. When checking the words they know, ask them to visualize the context in which they hear each word, or think of example sentences to accompany each word.

- As students check their dictionaries, encourage them to explore additional meanings and word forms.

Answer Key

1. grant	5. perspective	9. portion
2. found	6. regain	10. undertake
3. enable	7. highlight	
4. objective	8. federal	

track 2-25

Exercise B.

- Ask students to read the interview silently and try to predict the missing words.

- Play the audio while students write their answers.

Answer Key

1. found	5. objective	9. highlight
2. portion	6. perspective	10. grant
3. federal	7. regain	
4. undertake	8. enable	

IDEAS FOR... Checking Comprehension

Ask students to summarize the interview by asking these questions: *What is this person's job? Why are some languages dying out? What can be done to save them?*

Using Vocabulary

Exercise A.

- Ask students to describe the photo. Ask students what they know about Native American traditions and way of life.

- Ask students to read the whole text before writing their answers. Remind students that they may have to change the word form.

- Have volunteers read their completed sentences aloud.

Answer Key

1. granted 2. federal 3. founded 4. enabled
5. portion 6. undertake 7. regained

Exercise B. | Choosing the Right Definition

Explain that dictionaries often have several meanings for one word. It is important to look at the context to work out which one is the right definition.

Answer Key   a. 3 b. 1 c. 2

Exercise C. | Discussion

- Ask students to form groups and appoint one person as a secretary to take notes of their discussion.

- Ask a spokesperson from each group (not necessarily the secretary) to report to the class.

Pronunciation Note
Huilliche: well-**ich**-eh

45 mins

Developing Listening Skills
(pages 116-117)

Before Listening

Prior Knowledge

- Ask students to discuss questions 1 and 2 in pairs. If time permits, ask students to make a T-chart listing information they know and information they would like to know about Native Americans.

- Point out that while only a few Native American groups are labeled on the map, there are several hundred Native American groups. Ask students to research the names of three to five additional groups and where they are (or were) located in the United States. Students can share this information with the class during the next session.

Listening: A Study Group Discussion

track 2-26
Exercise A. | Listening for Main Ideas

- Discuss how students would go about reviewing for an exam in a study group.

- Play the audio. Go over the answers as a class.

Answer Key	1. b 2. a 3. c

Critical Thinking Focus: Evaluating Numbers and Statistics | Go over the information in the box. Review some statistics from earlier in the unit to practice these questions. For example: *The government of Bhutan wants to keep 68 percent of the land covered in forests* (page 107). *A recent survey counted 230,000 Amish people* (page 110).

track 2-26
Exercise B. | Note-Taking

- Ask students to read the outline. Play the audio again while students write their answers.

Answer Key *(Words missing from the outline are listed below.)*

Background: reservations, language and traditions, west, agriculture, businesses, improve land/buy land

InterTribal Sinkyone Wilderness Area: coast, limited, ceremonies

Big Cypress Swamp: Florida, animals, plants

IDEAS FOR... Checking Comprehension

Ask students to summarize the main changes on Native American reservations. Ask: *What were reservations like before and after the Native Americans were granted the right to run businesses on their land?*

After Listening

Discussion | Encourage pairs to relate the information on the audio to their own personal experience. Have students share their ideas as a class.

track 2-27
Pronunciation: Linking Consonants to Vowels | Go over the information in the box. Play the audio, pausing for students to repeat.

track 2-28
Exercise A. | Play the audio for the first item and repeat it together. Play the rest of the audio. Ask students to repeat each phrase as a group and then individually.

1. click on
2. out again
3. an opinion
4. an offer
5. and improved
6. isn't easy

track 2-29
Exercise B. | After students have practiced in pairs, play the audio. Go over the answers by writing the sentences on the board and drawing lines to show the linked words.

Answer Key

1. Click on the file to open it.
2. You should speak out again.
3. He doesn't have an opinion.
4. The car dealer made an offer.
5. This car is new and improved.
6. Land conservation isn't easy.

Pronunciation Note
Navajo: **nah**-vah-hoh
Apache: ah-**patch**-ee
Sioux: sue
Sinkyone: **sink**-ee-own
Seminole: **Sem**-uh-nohl

Exploring Spoken English
(pages 118-119)

30 mins

Language Function: Expressing a Lack of Knowledge

- Go over the information in the box.

- Ask students to use these expressions to talk about things they found surprising in the previous listening about Native American reservations.

Exercise A.
track 2-30

- Play the audio, pausing to allow students to write their answers.

- Play the audio again and pause after each sentence for students to repeat with the appropriate intonation.

Answer Key

1. I had no idea that, I wasn't aware that

2. I didn't realize that

> **IDEAS FOR... Expansion**
>
> Refer students to the text on page 114 about dying languages. Ask them to use the expressions from page 118 to say what they found surprising in this interview.

Exercise B.

- Direct students' attention to the first photo and read the first sentence of the text that accompanies it.

- Then ask two volunteers to read the sentences in the speech bubbles aloud.

- Remind students to use a variety of expressions from the box in their conversations.

- Point out that *neither did I* is a way of agreeing with a negative statement.

Grammar: Verb + Object + Infinitive

- Go over the information in the box. Ask volunteers to read the examples aloud.

- You may want to contrast these verbs with those that are followed by a gerund (see Grammar on page 110).

> **IDEAS FOR... Presenting Grammar**
>
> Give some example sentences for students to rephrase using the target verbs. For example:
>
> T: Don't stay up late tonight.
> S: She advised me not to stay up late tonight.
>
> T: Please come to dinner tomorrow.
> S: She invited me to come to dinner tomorrow.
>
> Students can continue this exercise in pairs.

Exercise A. | Collaboration   Students may want to work individually at first. When they have finished, have students exchange sentences for peer review.

> **IDEAS FOR... Multi-level Classes**
>
> Pair up lower-level and higher-level students. Pairs can work on writing sentences together. Then pairs can exchange with another pair for peer review.

Exercise B. | Self-Reflection

- Ask two volunteers to read the example sentences in the speech bubbles aloud.

- Explain that students should think of personal examples from their own lives. This will help them to remember the target structure.

- Advise students to write some key sentences in their notebooks.

Presentation Skills: Varying Your Voice Volume

- Go over the information in the box.

- Demonstrate how to vary your voice volume by reading the information and emphasizing certain words for more dramatic effect.

Engage: Evaluating Web Sources *(page 120)*

45 mins

Lesson Preparation Note | This presentation exercise requires students to do some research on the Internet or in the library. You may want to assign this research for homework or arrange to have Internet or library access available during the lesson.

WARM-UP

- Discuss the differences between using print and Web resources. Ask students to suggest some reasons why Web sites might be less reliable than print resources. (One major difference is that anyone can publish a Web site. Also, information found online is not always carefully checked. The authors and their affiliations are not always shown. Information can often be incorrect, misleading, or out-of-date.)

- Ask students: *What kinds of Web sites do you visit when you want to do research? Why do you choose those Web sites?*

- Ask for some examples of types of Web sites that might be misleading or inaccurate (e.g., Web sites that advertise a product, Web sites where anyone can edit or add information).

- Ask students to suggest ways of checking the reliability of Web sites. Make a list of their ideas on the board.

Exercise A.

- Read the task aloud. Brainstorm some possible traditions to research. These may be popular holiday traditions in different countries such as Thanksgiving (U.S.), Guy Fawkes Night (U.K.), Fasching (Germany), Mardi Gras (U.S.), Inti Raymi (Peru), Day of the Dead (Mexico), or Songkran (Thailand). Alternatively, students may want to research other types of traditions such as marriage ceremonies, tea ceremonies, or birthday celebrations.

- Have students work individually to complete their form, either in class or for homework.

Exercise B. | Ask students to share their information in pairs. Suggest that pairs come up with some criteria for describing whether a Web site is useful for research. Such criteria might include whether it is accurate, easy to use, or objective. Students might also want to consider if it covers a wide range of topics.

Exercise C.

- Ask each pair of students to join another pair of students. Each group member will present their Web site to the group.

- Ask a spokesperson from each group to summarize the main points of their discussion and to explain how they ranked their Web sites.

 Ask the class for feedback on what they have learned in this lesson and how it will affect their research in the future.

IDEAS FOR... **Expansion**

After the class has completed exercise **C**, ask students to make a list of Web sites that are useful for general research. Next to each Web site, have students write why they think the site is useful and reliable. Compile the annotated list and share it with all members of the class.

Money in Our Lives

Academic Track
Economics

Academic Pathways:
Lesson A: Listening to a Radio Interview
Discussing Values
Lesson B: Listening to a Conversation
between Friends
Preparing a Budget

Unit Theme

Money is an important part of society today. Money can influence our lives in many positive and negative ways.

Unit 7 explores the topic of money as it relates to:
- debt
- the effect of money on happiness
- average spending habits
- the global financial crisis
- personal finance tips

Think and Discuss *(page 121)*

5 mins

One of the first cultures in the world to make coins was the Lydian culture in BC 700. They lived in present-day Turkey. Some of the earliest known paper money dates back to China, where it was used from about AD 960 onwards. In Europe, the first bank to issue paper money was in Sweden in 1661. Other European countries soon followed. In 1694, the Bank of England began to print "running cash notes," which were originally receipts for cash deposited with the bank. Later, these notes were issued for fixed amounts and were used as currency.

- Ask students to describe the photo.

- Discuss questions 1 and 2.

- Discuss some other customs associated with money. At the New Year, Chinese parents and grandparents give money to the children of the family in a red envelope. Ask students if they are familiar with similar money-related customs.

IDEAS FOR... Expansion

Ask students to research a question they have about the history of money. For example: *What did people use before money? What was used before coins and bills?* Students should take brief notes and report back to the class in the next lesson.

Exploring the Theme: Money in Our Lives *(pages 122-123)*

15 mins

The opening spread features a photo of piles of fake money for sale in Hong Kong.

- Ask students to look at the two smaller photos and read the captions. Discuss questions 1–3.

- Ask students to talk about how they pay for goods and services. Ask: *Do you use checks, credit cards, debit cards, or cash? Do you ever give or receive money as a gift? When and why? Is it a good idea?*

- Discuss some general questions related to the theme. For example: *Do you think a cashless economy is a good idea? Do you think money brings happiness?*

- Ask students to look at the chart and read the captions. Explain that *public debt per person* means the debt of a country divided by the number of people who live in that country.

Answer Key

1. Of the countries shown in the chart, Japan has the largest public debt per person. Kenya has the smallest.

2.-3. Answers will vary.

Building and Using Vocabulary *(pages 124-125)*

30 mins

WARM-UP

The Lesson A target vocabulary is presented in the context of credit card debt.

- Ask students to look at the first photo and suggest what it might represent. Ask what they think the woman is doing in the second photo and why.

- Discuss the relative advantages and disadvantages of using a credit card. Ask: *Is it a good idea to have several credit cards? What are some different rules and policies that credit cards have? What happens if you don't pay back your debt?*

Building Vocabulary

track 3-2

Exercise A. | Meaning from Context Play the audio while students listen and read along in their books.

Exercise B. | Allow time for students to refer back to the text and work out the meanings of the words in blue.

Answer Key

1. ceased	5. promote	9. commitment
2. demonstrate	6. obviously	10. statistics
3. purchase	7. errors	
4. component	8. major	

TIP Go over the answers to exercise B by asking students to rephrase the sentences from the text using the definitions in exercise B. For example:

T: Credit card debt is a *major* problem.
S: Credit card debt is an *extremely important* problem.

IDEAS FOR... Checking Comprehension

Ask a few general comprehension questions. For example: *Why did Kelly Jones need a debt-management plan? Why do people cut up their credit cards? What does the display of cut-up cards demonstrate? What do you think are other components of the process to help people pay their bills?*

Using Vocabulary

Exercise A. | Remind students to use the correct form of each word. After checking the answers, ask students if they agree with the statements in 1, 2, 3, and 6. Ask them to explain their opinions.

Answer Key

1. Purchasing 2. error 3. promotes
4. obviously 5. statistics 6. cease

Exercise B. | Discussion

- Ask students to work in pairs to discuss the questions.

- Ask volunteers to share their ideas with the class.

IDEAS FOR... Multi-level Classes

Ask each pair of students to choose just one of the questions, whichever they find most interesting. Students can also make up their own questions using the target vocabulary, based on their level.

Exercise C. | Choosing the Right Definition

- Remind students that a dictionary may have several definitions for one word and that it is important to read all the definitions to identify which one is correct in the given context.

- Ask students to work individually to write their answers.

- Ask students to tell you the correct answers as you write them on the board. Have students tell you how these three definitions are similar.

Answer Key a. 2 b. 1 c. 3

IDEAS FOR... Expansion

Choose another vocabulary word from the text on page 124 and ask students to find various definitions for it in the dictionary. For example: *demonstrate* can mean "to show," "to prove," or "to protest." Encourage students to write these meanings in their vocabulary journal.

Developing Listening Skills

45 mins

(pages 126-127)

Before Listening

Exercise A.

- Ask students to look at the photo and describe what they think the woman is saying to her granddaughter. Ask: *Is it important to teach children about saving and spending money? Why, or why not?*

- Read the statements and ask each student to rank them individually.

Exercise B. | Discussion

- Ask students to compare their rankings in groups and come up with a group ranking of these five statements.

- Encourage students to justify their choices and try to persuade other group members to agree with them.

Listening: A Radio Interview

track 3-3

Exercise A. | Listening for Main Ideas

- Allow time for students to read the questions.

- Play the audio while students choose their answers.

- Go over the answers by asking volunteers to explain why they made their answer choices.

Answer Key	1. b 2. a 3. b 4. c 5. b

TIP Another way to present exercise A is to write the questions on the board without the answer choices. Have students close their books and take notes as they listen. After listening, they can answer the questions in their own words.

track 3-3

Exercise B. | Note-Taking

- Have students study the outline and ask them to pencil in anything they can remember from the audio or from the expansion activity.

- Play the audio again so that students can complete the outline.

- Ask volunteers to read their answers aloud. Discuss the advantages of using this kind of outline to take notes.

IDEAS FOR... Checking Comprehension

Read the following statements aloud and ask students to tell you if they are true or false:

1. *Spending money on others does not make us happy.* (false)

2. *Spending money on experiences such as language lessons can make you happy.* (true)

3. *Money is not a component of happiness.* (false)

After Listening

Critical Thinking Focus: Summarizing | Go over the information in the box. Give some examples of an opening statement (*This study is about . . .*) and a concluding statement (*This study shows that . . .*).

Exercises A and B. | Each student will summarize one study from the audio. Encourage students to relate the information on the audio to their own experiences.

Exploring Spoken English
(pages 128-130)

45 mins

Language Function: Showing That You Are Following a Conversation

Go over the information in the box. Ask a student to tell you about their weekend or their last vacation. Show that you are following them by using these expressions.

Exercise A.
track 3-4

- Play the audio. Pause after each item to allow students time to repeat the phrases.
- If you have time, play the audio again and ask students to repeat using the correct intonation.

Answer Key	1. Really 2. Uh-huh 3. Has she 4. I see

Exercise B. | Ask students to complete the questionnaire individually.

Exercise C. | Discussion

- Ask volunteers to read the examples in the speech bubbles aloud.
- Model one or two additional exchanges about the survey topics with one or two students.
- Emphasize that students should follow up with some additional questions to keep the conversation going.

Exercise D. | Critical Thinking

- Direct students' attention to the photo and the caption and ask them if they can think of any reasons to explain rising food prices.
- Encourage students to look at the survey from different points of view. For example:

   S1: I think people in Spain are most worried about getting a job.

   S2: Why?

   S1: I heard on the news that there is high unemployment in Spain right now.

- After students have finished exercise **D**, you may want to share information from the Nielsen survey results as a way to confirm students' predictions. According to the survey, rising food prices are the top concern for people in the Asia-Pacific area. Increasing utility prices are the biggest concern for Europeans. In North America, the economy is the biggest concern.

IDEAS FOR... **Expansion**

Ask students to think of another research question related to money and happiness and suggest how they would set out to research the answer.

Grammar: Using Connectors to Add and Emphasize Information

Go over the information in the box. Ask volunteers to read the examples aloud.

IDEAS FOR... **Presenting Grammar**

Give some example sentences and ask students to rephrase them using the connectors in parentheses.

T: I have a debit card. I have three credit cards. (*not only, but also*)

S: I not only have a debit card, but I also have three credit cards.

T: My rent is very expensive. I spend a lot on train fares. (*what's more*)

S: My rent is very expensive. What's more, I spend a lot on train fares.

T: I always pay my bills on time. I never get into debt. (*in fact*)

S: I always pay my bills on time. In fact, I never get into debt.

Students can continue this exercise in pairs.

Understanding Visuals

- Briefly explain the three steps of the exercise to students. First, students describe and talk about the information in the visuals. Then they relate the first graph to their own experiences. After that, students relate the second graph to their own experiences.

- Ask students to look at the graphs. Ask some general questions about the graphs. For example: *What are the differences between the two bar graphs?* (The first shows the global average of how people spend extra money. The second shows how people in Latin America intend to cut down on spending in the future.) *How many categories are there in each graph?* (nine) *What do the numbers represent?* (percentage of people) *In what order are the categories presented?* (from the highest to the lowest)

- Ask a volunteer to read the example in the speech bubble aloud. Present some other useful expressions for describing the graphs. For example: *A greater / smaller percentage of people spend money on (x) than on (y). More / Fewer people intend to cut down on (x) than on (y). Less than / More than 50 percent of people spend money on . . . . On average, people tend to spend more on . . . than on . . . .*

TIP Get feedback on this exercise by asking students what they found most surprising about the graphs and about their partner's answers to questions 2 and 3.

IDEAS FOR... Expansion

Do a class survey on the topics shown in the graphs by asking students how they spend their money and how they will spend it after the economy improves. Ask each student to choose their top spending habits for each situation. Then ask volunteers to come to the board and assemble the data by asking students to raise their hands for each category. All students can then record the information in their notebooks in the form of two bar graphs.

 Speaking *(page 131)*

30-45 mins

Discussing Values | Go over the information in the box. Ask students what their most important value is and what other values they would add to this list.

IDEAS FOR... Expansion

Brainstorm key words for personal values on the board such as *honesty, loyalty, family, friendship, respect, generosity,* and *compassion.* Ask students to choose the value that is most important to them. Then ask them to stand up and form a group with other students who chose the same word. (Make two groups for a word if necessary.) As a group, students should decide on a definition of their value and say why they chose it.

Exercise A.

- Give some examples of items, services, and experiences (e.g., a car, a necklace, an art class, a visit to a spa, a visit to a nice hotel, a meal in a fancy restaurant).

- Allow time for students to work individually to complete their lists. Encourage students to transfer their information into a Venn diagram to share with their partner. Refer students to page 214 of the *Independent Student Handbook* for an example of a Venn diagram.

Exercise B.

- Ask two students to read the examples in the speech bubbles aloud.

- Encourage students to ask questions to find out about their partners' values by asking about their lists.

- Go over the Student to Student box before doing this exercise.

Exercise C. | Critical Thinking You may want students to switch partners for this exercise. They can tell their new partner what they learned in exercise **B**.

Student to Student: Asking Sensitive Questions | Go over the information in the box. Ask students to think of different endings for these questions. For example: *Do you mind if I ask you how much money you spent on your watch?*

Viewing: The Black Diamonds of Provence *(pages 132-133)*

30 mins

Overview of the Video | This video presents some information about the harvesting and selling of truffles in the south of France.

Before Viewing

Exercise A. | Using the Dictionary

■ Ask students to look at the map and describe the exact location of Richerenches. Have students look at the photo and ask them to describe what kind of town Richerenches is.

■ Ask students to brainstorm some ideas about what the black diamonds could be.

■ Ask which of the target words students already know. Ask volunteers to read the definitions from the dictionary aloud to see if they were right about the meanings.

Pronunciation Note
Richerenches: reesh-e-**ronsh**

Answer Key	1. e 2. d 3. a 4. c 5. b

Exercise B. | Predicting Content

■ Direct students' attention to the photo of truffles. Ask: *Do you know what truffles are?* (Refer to the photo on page 133.) *Have you ever tasted one? What did it taste like?*

■ Brainstorm answers to the question and write them on the board.

While Viewing

3:09

Exercise A.

■ Allow time for students to read the questions.

■ Play the video.

■ Ask volunteers to read their answers aloud. Write the answers on the board.

Answer Key	1. c 2. a 3. b 4. c

Exercise B. | Note-Taking

3:09

■ Allow time for students to read the notes.

■ Play the video again while students write their answers.

■ Ask students to tell you the answers while you write them on the board.

Answer Key

Richerenches:

- a town in **Provence**, in southern France
- has one of the largest **truffle markets** in France

Truffles:

- are black with **white** veins
- are used a lot in France, **the United States**, and **Japan**

Possible reasons for decline:

- **fewer trees**
- **not a lot of places left for truffles to grow**

Dogs:

- have sensitive **noses**
- can **smell** truffles

After Viewing

Critical Thinking

■ Ask students to work in groups.

■ Encourage students to summarize and make inferences based on the information in the video. Remind them to base their inferences on actual information from the video.

IDEAS FOR... **Expansion**

■ Ask students to work in pairs to role-play an interview with a truffle hunter.

■ Ask students what they know about the other "luxury" foods such as caviar, saffron, lobster, foie gras, matsutake mushrooms, and bird's nest. Have students look up the cost of two or three of these foods to share with the class.

Building and Using Vocabulary *(pages 134-135)*

30 mins

WARM-UP

The Lesson B target vocabulary is presented in the context of the global financial crisis.

- Ask students to look at the photo and say what they know about the stock market. Ask: *How does the stock market work? How do people make money? Why is it important to the economy?*

- Ask what students know about the beginning of the global financial crisis.

Building Vocabulary

track 3-5

Exercise A. | Meaning from Context

- Play the audio while students read the interview in the Student Book.

- Ask students to summarize the main reasons for the global financial crisis mentioned in the interview.

Exercise B.

- Remind students to use the context in exercise **A** to work out the meanings of the words in blue.

- Go over the answers by asking students to read the sentences aloud.

Answer Key

1. Professionals	**5.** Consumers	**9.** capable
2. currency	**6.** preceded	**10.** assist
3. Sums	**7.** Criteria	
4. individuals	**8.** fee	

TIP Another way to approach these vocabulary exercises is to write the vocabulary words on the board. Then have students do exercise B. Finally, they can read and listen to the text in exercise A to check their answers.

IDEAS FOR... Expansion

Ask students how easy or difficult it is to get a loan and what kind of criteria and conditions are required.

Using Vocabulary

Exercise A.

- Ask students if they have any personal finance tips to share with the class.

- Advise students to read the whole text before writing their answers.

- Ask volunteers to read the sentences aloud.

- Ask students if they agree or disagree with these tips. Which tips do they think are the most useful?

Answer Key

1. precede **2.** fees **3.** sum **4.** professional
5. assist **6.** capable **7.** consumers

Exercise B. | Discussion

- Ask students to work in pairs.

- For question 1, have each pair of students tell the class one financial tip they both have followed.

TIP Monitor students as they work in pairs and take notes of any additional vocabulary items related to the theme that they need. Write these terms on the board when you give feedback to the class.

IDEAS FOR... Expansion

Ask students if their spending habits have changed during the course of their lives. Ask volunteers to share their experiences with the class.

Developing Listening Skills

(pages 136-137)

45 mins

Before Listening

- Go over the information in the box.
- Discuss the questions. Ask students to compare these different types of cards and say which is best and why.

Listening: A Conversation between Friends

track 3-6
Exercise A. | Listening for Main Ideas

- Discuss the photo and guess how this man could have obtained all these credit cards. Ask: *Do you think he uses all of these credit cards to buy things?*
- Allow time for students to read the questions.
- Play the audio. Go over the answers as a class.

Answer Key	1. a 2. b 3. c 4. b 5. c

track 3-6
Exercise B. | Listening for Details

- Ask students to read the sentences.
- Play the audio again while students choose their answers.
- Go over the answers by asking students to explain the reasons for their answer choices.

Answer Key	1. F 2. F 3. T 4. T

IDEAS FOR... Checking Comprehension

Ask students to draw a three-column chart in their notebook. They should summarize each person's opinions (James, Tina, and Donna) about paying by cash or credit card in each column. Whose opinion do they most agree with?

After Listening

Discussion

- Encourage pairs to relate the information on the audio to their own personal experience.
- Compare answers as a class.

track 3-7
Pronunciation: Vowel-to-Vowel Linking | Go over the information in the box. Play the audio, pausing for students to repeat.

track 3-8
Exercise A.

- Look at the first item and repeat it together. Encourage students to practice saying each item to themselves.
- Play the rest of the audio. Ask students to repeat each phrase as a group and then individually.

Answer Key	1. /y/ 2. /w/ 3. /w/ 4. /y/ 5. /y/ 6. /y/ 7. /w/ 8. /w/

Exercise B. | Self-Reflection

- Read the questions and draw students' attention to the vowel-to-vowel linking in each one.
- Remind students to pay attention to vowel-to-vowel linking in their discussions.

Exploring Spoken English
(pages 138-139)

Language Function: Digressing from the Topic

Go over the information in the box. Give a couple of examples of how to use these expressions. For example: *I don't usually like to pay for things by credit card. Oh, that reminds me, I heard about a new kind of credit card the other day . . .*

Exercise A.

- Play the audio, pausing to allow students to write their answers.

- Play the audio again and pause after each sentence for students to repeat with the appropriate intonation.

Answer Key	**1.** By the way **2.** That reminds me

> **IDEAS FOR... Expansion**
>
> Refer students to the text on page 114 about dying languages. Ask them to use the expressions for digressing to say what they found surprising in this interview.

Exercise B. | Discussion

- Ask two volunteers to read the example sentences in the speech bubbles aloud.

- Remind students to use a variety of expressions from the box in their conversations.

Grammar: Using Connectors of Concession

Go over the information in the box. Ask volunteers to read the examples aloud.

> **IDEAS FOR... Presenting Grammar**
>
> Give some example sentences that students can combine using different connectors of concession. For example:
>
> **T:** Ivan has a lot of money. He isn't happy.
>
> *Possible responses:*
>
> **S:** Ivan has a lot of money, yet he isn't happy.
>
> **S:** Although Ivan has a lot of money, he isn't happy.
>
> **S:** Ivan has a lot of money. Even so, he isn't happy.
>
> Students can continue this exercise in pairs.

Exercise A. | Collaboration

- Students may want to work individually at first. Then they can compare answers in pairs.

- Pairs of students can work on writing sentences. Then they can exchange sentences with another pair for peer review.

Answer Key	**1.** f **2.** d **3.** e **4.** a **5.** b **6.** c *(Student sentences will vary.)*

> **IDEAS FOR... Multi-level Classes**
>
> Students who finish early can work on writing their own examples. They can exchange sentences with another student for peer review.

Exercise B. | Discussion

- Ask two volunteers to read the example sentences in the speech bubbles aloud.

- Explain that students should think of ways to introduce the sentences from exercise **A** into a conversation.

Engage: Preparing a Budget

45 mins

(page 140)

WARM-UP

Discuss reasons why someone might want to consult a financial professional. If possible, bring in some information about financial advice services.

Exercise A.

- Read the directions aloud. Ask students to work in pairs and choose their roles.

- Students can prepare for their role-play by making some notes and preparing some questions.

Exercise B. | Role-Playing

- Go over the information in the budget sheet and explain any unfamiliar terms.

- Ask students to discuss the questions in pairs.

Exercise C. | Presentation

- Ask each pair of students to join another pair of students. Each pair will present their budget to the other pair.

- Ask a spokesperson from each group to summarize the best points of each budget.

Presentation Skills: Dealing with Difficult Questions |

Go over the information in the box. Practice the target language together as a group.

TIP Ask the class for feedback on what they have learned from this lesson and how it will affect their household budgets in the future.

IDEAS FOR... Expansion

- Ask students to make up a typical budget sheet for someone from their city with estimated costs for each type of expense. Have students work in groups to compare their budgets.

- **Building Computer Skills:** This may be a good opportunity for students to learn how to use a computer spreadsheet program. Ask volunteers to keep a record of the money they spend for one week (if they are comfortable doing so). They can use a data spreadsheet to create a graph or chart of their expenses. Then they can compare the results with each other and give each other advice on saving money.

- Give groups of students a fixed budget for a one-week vacation. In their group, students have to decide where to go, where to stay, and what to spend their money on. Finally, they will report to the class on how they decided to spend the money in their budget.

- Ask students to do some research on the Internet to find useful tips for saving money or cutting down on expenses. You may want to assign different topics to different groups. For example, some expenses include transportation, food, accommodation, insurance, phone, and Internet service.

Health and Fitness

Academic Track
Health and Medicine

Academic Pathways:
Lesson A: Listening to a Question-and-Answer Session
Discussing Environmental Health Concerns
Lesson B: Listening to a Conversation between Friends
Sharing Advice about Health and Fitness

Unit Theme

Keeping healthy and fit is an important part of our daily life. The food we eat, the chemicals in our environment, and our lifestyle can all affect how healthy we are.

Unit 8 explores the topic of health and fitness as it relates to:
– chemicals used in growing food
– chemicals in our environment
– medicinal plants in the rainforest
– the increased popularity of yoga
– rock climbing

Think and Discuss *(page 141)*

5 mins

Rock climbing is a sport that is both physically and mentally demanding. It is important to train beforehand and practice climbing techniques, to climb with other more experienced climbers, and to have good climbing equipment.

- Ask students to describe their reaction to the photo. Ask: *Would you like to try this type of rock climbing? What do you think motivates people to try a sport like this?*

- Discuss question 1. Make a list of mental and physical skills that would be needed for extreme sports.

- Discuss question 2. Discuss how physical and mental health are connected and how much control we have over each one.

Exploring the Theme: Health and Fitness *(pages 142–143)*

15 mins

The opening spread features a photo of a beach and a man doing yoga.

- Ask students about the photo: *Why do you think the man has chosen this place to practice yoga? How do our surroundings influence our health and state of mind?*

- Ask students to look at the top two photos and read the captions. Discuss questions 1 and 2. Ask students if they are aware of chemicals in the products they use. Ask students if they ever choose organic food products to avoid pesticides.

- Ask students to look at the third photo and read the caption. Discuss questions 3 and 4.

Answer Key *(Answers will vary.)*

1. To measure indoor air pollution
2. Chemicals could have negative effects such as causing illness. However, chemicals could also be used to help control diseases such as malaria.
3. Popular rock-climbing routes can be found in the Rockies and the Alps. Rock-climbing gear would include climbing ropes, harness, gloves, chalk (to keep your hands dry when climbing), carabiners (to connect your harness to anchors on the rock face), and more.
4. Answers will vary.

IDEAS FOR... Expansion

- Ask students to choose one sport that they enjoy and find out about its health benefits. Have students take some brief notes and share their findings with a partner.

- Ask students to research the Internet on their own and find information about chemicals in our environment and their effect on our health.

Building and Using Vocabulary *(pages 144-145)*

30 mins

WARM-UP

The Lesson A target vocabulary is presented in the context of pesticides and the rise in popularity of organic foods.

- Ask students to look at the photos and describe what is happening. Ask some general questions about the topic: *Do you think pesticides are good or bad? Do you agree that organic food is healthier? Are there some disadvantages?*

Building Vocabulary

track 3-10

Exercise A. | Meaning from Context

- Ask students if they know the song *Big Yellow Taxi* (originally sung by Joni Mitchell). Bring in a CD or suggest that students look up the lyrics on the Internet for homework.

- Write these two questions on the board: *Why have opinions about DDT changed? Why are some people choosing to eat organic food?*

- Play the audio while students read the article.

Exercise B.

- Allow time for students to read the sentences and fill in the missing words. Ask volunteers to read their answers aloud.

- Ask students to use their dictionaries to find words in the same family for each vocabulary word. For example: *accumulate* (v.) – *accumulation* (n.). Tell students to write these related words in their vocabulary journal.

Answer Key

1. constant	5. assessed	9. option
2. persists	6. pesticides	10. eliminated
3. organic	7. appreciate	
4. accumulate	8. Traces	

> **TIP** Challenge students by asking them to cover the text in exercise A while they do exercise B. They can uncover the text to check their answers.

Using Vocabulary

Exercise A. | Understanding Collocations

- Do the first part of the exercise as a class. Allow time for students to work individually to complete the sentences.

- Go over the answers as a class.

- Ask students to come up with additional examples for each collocation and record them in their vocabulary journals. For example: *He disappeared without a trace.*

Answer Key

1. without a trace	3. accumulate evidence
2. constant exposure	4. show appreciation

Critical Thinking Focus: Asking Questions for Further Research | Explain that developing appropriate research questions is an important part of conducting research. Sometimes the initial question can be very broad. Asking additional questions can help to narrow the focus. A research question should be neutral and not express an opinion. For example: *What are the harmful effects of DDT?* (The word *harmful* shows that the researcher expects a negative answer.) *What are the effects of DDT?* (This question is neutral.)

Exercise B. | Collaboration

- Refer students back to the text on page 144. Allow time for students to collaborate while writing questions.

- Ask volunteers to write their questions on the board.

- Discuss the questions and get feedback from the class about which ones are the most interesting and useful, and which ones are neutral in terms of expectation.

- Have students research the answers to the questions for homework.

Answer Key *(Research questions will vary.)*

1. Why was DDT used in the past? What was it used for?
2. Why doesn't DDT disappear? What effect does it have on the environment?
3. What is the meaning of the word *organic*? Does it mean the same thing in all countries / states?

Developing Listening Skills

45 mins

(pages 146-147)

Before Listening

Predicting Content

- Have students look at the photo. Ask: *Why do you think this testing is being carried out? What different reactions could the man have to these products? Why is it important to test products in this way?*

- Discuss questions 1 and 2. Ask volunteers to share their ideas and experiences with the class.

Listening: A Question-and-Answer Session

track 3-11

Exercise A. | Listening for Main Ideas

- Allow time for students to read the questions. Play the audio while students choose their answers.

- Go over the answers by asking volunteers to explain how they made their answer choices. Ask students if they were surprised by the answers to these questions.

Answer Key   1. b 2. a 3. b 4. c

track 3-11

Exercise B. | Note-Taking

- Direct students' attention to the outline and ask them to pencil in anything they can remember from the audio.

- Play the audio again so that students can complete the outline. Ask volunteers to write the missing words on the board.

Answer Key

PBDEs

Impact on health: High concentrations can cause cancer in **lab animals**

Dr. W. suggests: For small amounts in humans, **don't worry about them**

Lead paint

Impact on health: Small amounts of it can cause **brain damage in children**

Dr. W. suggests: **make sure paint is not chipping, move to a new home**

Answer Key *(continued)*

Mercury

Impact on health: Permanent damage to **memory and ability to learn**

Dr. W. suggests: Eat fish **in moderation**

Cell phones

Impact on health: Driving and using a cell phone can lead to **accidents**

Radiation from cell phones **could cause brain cancer**

Dr. W. suggests: **Turn off cell phones while driving, don't send text messages while driving, use a headset**

IDEAS FOR...   **Checking Comprehension**

Ask these additional questions or write them on the board:

1. *What are PBDEs and what are they used for?* (They are flame-retardants that are used to make products resistant to flames in order to decrease the risk of fire)
2. *What is a major source of mercury?* (coal-burning plants)
3. *What are we exposed to when we use cell phones?* (radiation)
4. *What will the next seminar be about?* (organic foods)

After Listening

Discussion

- Direct students' attention to the photo and discuss the caption.

- Ask students to work in groups to discuss the three questions. Discuss students' answers as a class.

IDEAS FOR...   **Expansion**

Have students take part in a debate about organic foods. They can work in pairs, groups, or in two teams. One side should gather arguments in favor of organic farming; the other side should look at the disadvantages.

Exploring Spoken English
(pages 148-150)

Language Function: Expressing Uncertainty

Go over the information in the box. Write example sentences on the board. Ask students to rephrase each example using language from the box.

T: Pesticides are harmful.
S: It seems to me that pesticides are quite harmful.

T: Cell phones could cause brain tumors.
S: It appears that cell phones could cause brain tumors.

track 3-12 Exercise A.

- Play the audio. If necessary, pause after each item to allow students time to write the phrases.

- Play the audio again and ask students to repeat each target expression.

Answer Key

1. it looks as though

2. it doesn't appear that

3. I'm not altogether sure that

Exercise B. | Discussion

- Direct students' attention to the photos. Ask a volunteer to read the example in the speech bubble aloud.

- After students have discussed the photos in pairs, have them compare their ideas as a class.

- Discuss how these photos could be related to the theme of chemicals in our environment.

Exercise C. | Discuss the answers as a class.
Ask students to think about questions for further research that are raised by these photo captions. For example: *What is chemical-free makeup made with?*

Answer Key   a. 2 b. 4 c. 3 d. 1

Grammar: Phrasal Verbs

- Go over the information in the box. Note that some phrasal verbs are intransitive (e.g., *grow up*) and therefore do not have an object.

- Give students some example verbs and ask them to come up with the phrasal verb that has the same meaning: *reduce* (*cut down*), *stop* (*give up*), *refuse* (*turn down*).

IDEAS FOR...   **Presenting Grammar**

- The grammar box discusses phrasal verbs where the particle can be moved before or after the object. Write sentences with separable and inseparable phrasal verbs on strips of paper (see the list of examples below). Make sure each sentence has an object pronoun. Cut up the sentences so that each word is on a separate slip of paper. Students can work in groups to unscramble the sentences. Monitor groups for correct placement of the phrasal verbs. As a class, discuss which verbs can be separated by an object and which ones cannot.

- Dictate a list of phrasal verbs (see the list of examples below) or write them on the board and ask students to group them into verbs that can be separated and those that cannot. See if the whole class agrees. They can check their answers in a dictionary.

Examples:

Separable verbs	Inseparable verbs
turn off	look after
cut down	get around
give up	take after
turn off	look into

Exercise A. | Using a Dictionary

- Have students look at the photo and ask who the people are (lawyer, witness, jury / jurors). Ask: *What kinds of cases are usually tried by a jury?*

- Look at the book title and ask what kind of book this is. Ask: *What does the title mean?* You may want to contrast a civil action or lawsuit with a criminal one. Encourage students to look up definitions of these terms in their dictionaries and record them in their vocabulary journals.

- Allow time for students to read the whole text and choose their answers. Instruct students to use their dictionaries to look up meanings of unfamiliar words.

- Go over the answers by reading the summary and asking students to provide the phrasal verb.

Answer Key

1. finding out **2.** got together **3.** turned down **4.** put back **5.** thrown out **6.** hold out **7.** keeping back **8.** gave in

---

IDEAS FOR... **Checking Comprehension**

Ask students to summarize the book to their partner in their own words, using the phrasal verbs in the box.

Exercise B. | Critical Thinking Ask students to discuss the questions in pairs. Discuss who should be responsible for the safety of drinking water. Ask: *Should private companies be allowed to own the water supply?*

 ## Speaking *(page 151)*

30-45 mins

Discussing Environmental Health Concerns

Exercise A.

- Read through the survey and answer questions about any unfamiliar words.

- Ask students to interview their partner using the survey. At this stage, answers do not have to be very detailed.

Exercise B. | Self-Reflection

- Ask a student to read the example in the speech bubble aloud.

- Encourage students to give reasons and examples for each of their answers.

Exercise C. | Collaboration

- Ask students to work in pairs to write their ideas. They can collaborate on the same set of sentences or help each other to develop their own ideas.

- Read the example in the speech bubble aloud. Students may want to introduce their sentences with the following phrases:
  We decided that . . .
  We agreed that . . .
  We plan / intend to . . .

IDEAS FOR...   **Multi-level Classes**

Students who finish early can make up other survey questions to ask their partner. Alternatively, they can help lower-level students develop their actions in exercise **C**.

Student to Student: Going First

- Go over the information in the box.

- Remind students to use these phrases when they are planning their next presentation.

Viewing: Paraguay Shaman
(pages 152-153)

30 mins

Overview of the Video | This video is about a scientific expedition to collect medicinal plants from a rainforest in Paraguay.

Before Viewing

Exercise A. | Prior Knowledge

- Ask students to look at the map and identify the exact location of Paraguay and the Mbaracayú Forest Nature Reserve.

- Direct students' attention to the photo and ask them to guess what kind of job a shaman has.

- Read the directions aloud and ask students to work in groups to brainstorm and write down their ideas.

- Invite volunteers to share their ideas with the class.

Exercise B. | Using a Dictionary Ask students which words they already know. Then have them look up any unfamiliar words in a dictionary.

Answer Key   1. b 2. e 3. d 4. a 5. c

While Viewing

2:33

Exercise A.

- Have students look at the photo. Ask them to guess the meaning of the word *deforestation* (the removal of forests and trees for the conversion of land into farms or towns).

- Allow time for students to read the questions.

- Play the video while students choose their answers.

Answer Key   1. a 2. c 3. a

Exercise B. | Viewing for Specific Details

- Allow time for students to read the sentences and pencil in their ideas before playing the video again.

- Go over the answers as a class. Ask pairs of students to correct the false sentences.

- The following sentences have been changed so that they are now true:
  1. There is a long tradition of using traditional herbs for healing in Paraguay.
  3. Gervasio is looking for a root.
  5. The book will help other people learn about plants. If necessary, point out the places in the video where these answers are found.

Answer Key   1. F 2. T 3. F 4. T 5. F

After Viewing

Critical Thinking

- Ask students to work in groups.

- Encourage students to make inferences based on information in the video. They should support their answers with evidence from the video. Encourage students to refer to page 205 of the *Independent Student Handbook* for more information on making inferences.

Answer Key

1. He has a "deep knowledge of local medicinal plants" that was probably passed down to him from previous shamans.
2. Yes. "Scientists published a book to help record and transmit Gervasio's forest knowledge."

IDEAS FOR... Expansion

- Ask students to role-play an interview with a scientist who is carrying out this research.
- Play the video with the sound turned off. Ask volunteers to come up to the front of the class and narrate a short portion of the video.

Pronunciation Note
Mbaracayú: **bar**-a-cay-oo
Gervasio: Har-**vay**-syõ

Building and Using Vocabulary *(pages 154-155)*

WARM-UP

The Lesson B target vocabulary is presented in the context of the increasing popularity of yoga. Ask students to look at the photos and make some suggestions as to why yoga is becoming more popular.

Building Vocabulary

track 3-13

Exercise A. | Meaning from Context   Play the audio while students read the information. Ask students if they or anyone they know have ever practiced yoga and what their experience was like.

> **IDEAS FOR... Checking Comprehension**
>
> Ask students to work in groups of three. Each member of the group should prepare comprehension questions about one segment of the text. They can take turns asking their questions to the other group members.

Exercise B. | Remind students to use the context in exercise **A** to work out the meanings of the words in blue. Go over the answers by asking students to read the sentences aloud.

Answer Key		
1. Expansion	5. Initially	9. prior to
2. attributed	6. equivalent	10. legislation
3. ultimate	7. Versions	
4. data	8. Global	

TIP   Have pairs of students test each other on the vocabulary words in exercise B. One student closes the book. The other student says the sentence with the missing word (they can say *blank* for the missing word). The student with the closed book supplies the missing word. Have one student give answers for items 1-5, then switch roles and give the sentences for items 6-10.

Using Vocabulary

Exercise A.

- Advise students to read the text all the way through before selecting their answers.

- To make this exercise more challenging, have students cover the word box and try to remember the words from the previous exercise.

Answer Key	1. attributed 2. prior to 3. initially
	4. equivalent 5. legislation

Exercise B. | Using a Dictionary   Ask students to work individually. Advise them to write their answers first and then check them in a dictionary. Write the answers on the board.

Answer Key
1. data: figures, statistics
2. global: international, overall
3. ultimate: best, maximum

Exercise C.

- Explain that synonyms do not always work equally well in all contexts.

- Ask students to work individually. Discuss why the alternative answers are not correct.

Answer Key	1. international 2. best 3. maximum
	4. figures 5. overall 6. statistics

Exercise D. | Ask students to work in pairs. Ask each pair to tell the class about their answers.

> **IDEAS FOR... Expansion**
>
> Ask students to role-play a conversation between two friends. Student A is trying to persuade Student B to try yoga. Student B is trying to persuade Student A to join a health club or gym.

Pronunciation Note

(Swami) Vivekananda: vee-vi-kuh-**nuhn**-duh
Sivananda yoga: siv-an-**ahn**-da **yoh**-guh
yoga nidra: **yoh**-guh **nih**-drah

Developing Listening Skills

45 mins

(pages 156-157)

Before Listening

Prior Knowledge

- Direct students' attention to the photo. Have students work in pairs to discuss the questions.

- Ask volunteers to summarize the main points of their discussions for the class.

Listening: A Conversation between Friends

track 3-14

Exercise A. | Listening for Main Ideas   Allow time for students to read the questions. Play the audio. Go over the answers as a class.

Answer Key   1. b 2. a 3. c 4. b

track 3-14

Exercise B. | Listening for Details

- Ask students to read the sentences and pencil in their answers.

- Play the audio again while students check their answers.

- Write the answers on the board.

Answer Key   1. b 2. a 3. d 4. c

track 3-14

Exercise C.

- Ask students to read the sentences. Play the audio again while students choose their answers.

- Go over the answers as a class. Ask students to explain why the false sentences are wrong. For example: *Item 1 is false because the man says that a half an hour of rock climbing is equivalent to about an hour of jogging.*

Answer Key   1. F 2. T 3. T 4. F 5. T 6. F 7. T 8. F

IDEAS FOR...   **Checking Comprehension**

Ask students to listen and take notes about any additional information they hear about each type of rock climbing. For example:

Indoor climbing: You can use safety ropes that catch you if you fall. The walls are not too high—and the floor is soft, so it doesn't hurt if you fall.

Bouldering: You can use ropes for extra safety.

Traditional rock climbing: You climb very high up on a rock wall—usually up the side of a hill or mountain. You connect ropes to the rock so that you don't fall off. It is usually done in pairs.

Free solo climbing: You climb very high on rock walls alone (without other people or equipment).

After Listening

Discussion | Encourage students to brainstorm different types of extreme sports and talk about their familiarity with them. Suggest students try to classify extreme sports according to different criteria such as where they take place (land, sea, or air). (Some examples of extreme sports are skydiving, caving, motocross, waterskiing, whitewater rafting, and windsurfing.)

track 3-15

Pronunciation: Dropped Syllables | Go over the information in the box. Play the audio. Ask students to repeat the words.

track 3-16

Pronunciation

- Play the audio while students cross out the dropped syllables.

- Play the audio again, pausing after each item to check the answer and have students repeat together or individually.

Answer Key

1. int*e*resting	**5.** choc*o*late	**9.** gen*e*rally
2. veg*e*table	**6.** asp*i*rin	**10.** bev*e*rage
3. diff*e*rent	**7.** hist*o*ry	**11.** cam*e*ra
4. fav*o*rite	**8.** ev*e*ning	**12.** rest*au*rant

Exploring Spoken English
(pages 158-159)

30 mins

Language Function: Showing Understanding

Go over the information in the box. Read the expressions using the appropriate intonation and ask students to repeat. Give some statements about yourself so that students can respond using these phrases.

T: I ran six miles yesterday.

S: You must have been tired / exhausted.

track 3-17

Exercise A.

- Play the audio, pausing to allow time for students to write their answers.

- Play the audio again and pause after each sentence for students to repeat it with the appropriate intonation.

Answer Key

1. That must have been fun.
2. You must be exhausted.
3. It must be pretty safe, then, huh?

Exercise B. | Role-Playing

- Ask two volunteers to read the example sentences in the speech bubbles aloud.

- Organize students into groups of four, assigning one role to each group member.

- Each student will read their information and imagine they are telling their friends about it. Encourage students to ask questions to continue each discussion. Remind them to use expressions from the box.

Exercise C. | Self-Reflection

- Ask two volunteers to read the example sentences in the speech bubbles aloud.

- This is a good opportunity for students to get to know each other and ask for help with vocabulary that is relevant to their lives.

IDEAS FOR... Expansion

Write a number of adjectives on slips of paper. Give one to each student. Students will walk around the classroom and say sentences that aim to elicit their adjective from the other person. For example, if Student A's adjective is *tired,* then the student says, *I ran ten miles this morning.* Student B responds, *You must be tired!*

Grammar: Three-Word Phrasal Verbs

- Go over the information in the box. Point out that three-word phrasal verbs cannot be separated.

- Ask students to explain the meaning of *looking forward to* and *get rid of.*

Exercise A. | Students may want to match the words and definitions individually before comparing answers in pairs. Have students go over answers in pairs.

Answer Key

1. f 2. c 3. h 4. a 5. d 6. g 7. b 8. e

track 3-18

Exercise B. | Allow time for students to complete the conversation individually. Play the audio so that students can check their answers. Have students practice the conversation in pairs.

Answer Key

1. drop in on
2. coming down with
3. gets rid of
4. come up with
5. get down to

Exercise C. | Collaboration

- Allow time for students to work through all the phrasal verbs. Ask: *Which ones were the most difficult to remember?*

- Advise students to choose the most difficult three-word phrasal verbs and think of a visual example that will help them remember its meaning. They should write example sentences and draw illustrations in their vocabulary journal.

45 mins

Engage: Sharing Advice about Health and Fitness *(page 160)*

WARM-UP

Introduce the topic by talking about several of your own real or imaginary problems such as the examples below. Ask students to give you advice. Read the language in the box.

I eat too much chocolate.
I drink too much coffee.
I don't have enough time to exercise.
I don't sleep well.

Exercise A.

- Ask students to work individually to write their ideas.

- Walk around the classroom and offer support with grammar or vocabulary as needed.

Exercise B. | Organize the class into groups
of five. Students can choose their own category. Alternatively, you can assign a random number from 1 to 5 to each category. Students will choose a number without knowing what the category is.

> **TIP** If the total number of students in your class is not a factor of five, make two or more groups of four and tell students to leave out one category.

Exercise C. | Discussion

- Each student will gather ideas from the group about their category. They will choose the most useful ideas and organize them in the most logical order for presentation.

- Go over the information in the Presentation Skills box.

IDEAS FOR... Multi-level Classes

Lower-level students can use the dictionary to help them write advice. Higher-level students can exchange sentences with one another and evaluate the ideas and grammar.

Exercise D. | Presentation

- Have groups take turns presenting their advice to the rest of the class.

- Encourage the rest of the class to ask questions and to give positive feedback at the end of each presentation.

Presentation Skills: Relating to Your Audience | Go over the information in the box. Ask for suggestions about how these ideas for relating to the audience could be included in the presentations about health advice.

> **TIP** Ask the class for feedback on what they have learned from this lesson and how it will affect their health and fitness habits in the future.

IDEAS FOR... Expansion

- Compile a class list of the best 10 health and fitness tips. Ask students to do some research on the Internet for other tips for improving health and fitness.
- Ask students to research and compile a short list of useful Web sites with reliable information about health and fitness.
- Ask students to find out about medical research that has been in the news recently. Ask: *What did the researchers find out? What conclusions can be drawn from this research? How could it affect our daily lives?* Encourage students to come up with a few questions for further research on this topic. Students can share their findings with the class or in small groups.

Mind and Memory

Academic Track
**Psychology /
Brain Science**

Academic Pathways:

Lesson A: Listening to a TV Show
Giving a Short Persuasive Speech

Lesson B: Listening to a Conversation
between Classmates
Using Memory Skills to Recall
Information

Unit Theme

There are many aspects of mind and memory that scientists still do not understand. Both mind and memory are fascinating subjects of research in both animals and humans.

Unit 9 explores the topic of mind and memory as it relates to:
– memory and creativity in animals
– human memory

– memorization techniques

Think and Discuss *(page 161)*

5 mins

Elephants, along with chimpanzees, orangutans, and dolphins, are considered to be among the most intelligent animal species. They have good memories, can learn from others, can use tools to solve problems, have a range of emotions including empathy and sorrow, and can recognize themselves in a mirror.

- Ask students to describe their reaction to the photo. Discuss questions 1–3.

- Discuss the meaning of the word *intelligence*. Ask: *Are there different kinds of intelligence? Is memory an important part of being intelligent? How would you test someone's intelligence?*

Exploring the Theme: Mind and Memory *(pages 162-163)*

15 mins

The opening spread features a computer-generated depiction of the human brain.

- Ask students what they know about the human brain and memory. Ask: *What are some facts that scientists don't know about the human brain? What things do you find easiest or most difficult to remember?*

- Ask students to look at the photos and read the captions. Discuss questions 1–3. (Note: According to research, octopuses use coconut shells for shelter, sometimes piling them up and carrying the shells around with them for future use.)

- Discuss the differences between human and animal intelligence.

Answer Key

1. Answers will vary.

2. (Answers may vary.) Chimpanzees use stone hammers to open nuts and twigs to extract termites. Gorillas use walking poles to measure water depth. Elephants use branches to scratch their backs or swat flies away. Dolphins use sponges in their beaks to uncover prey on the ocean floor.

3. (Answers may vary.) Humans use their memories in a number of ways. Some examples include learning skills, remembering people and places, and telling stories.

IDEAS FOR... Expansion

Ask students to research another animal that uses tools. Encourage them to use the Internet to find answers to the following questions: *What does the animal use the tools for? Does this animal use tools to get food, to scare predators, for shelter, or another way?* Have students take notes and share the information with the class in the next lesson.

Building and Using Vocabulary *(pages 164-165)*

30 mins

WARM-UP

The Lesson A target vocabulary is presented in the context of whether animals can show altruism.

- Ask students to look at the photo and describe what is happening. Ask: *Which animal do you think is stronger?*

- Discuss the meaning of the word *altruism* (concern for the happiness and safety of others instead of yourself). Ask: *Do you think animals can show altruism? If so, how? How do humans show altruism?* Ask students to give some examples from their own lives.

Building Vocabulary

Exercise A. | Using a Dictionary   Ask students to read the words and try to think of contexts where they have come across them before. Then students should read the definitions and try to match them with the words. Instruct students to use their dictionaries for any words they do not know.

Answer Key	1. j 2. c 3. h 4. f 5. a 6. d 7. i 8. e 9. b 10. g

track 3-19

Exercise B.

- Allow time for students to read the text and try to fill in the missing words.

- Play the audio so that students can check their answers.

Answer Key

1. philosophies	5. motive	9. illustrate
2. abstract	6. correspond	10. flexible
3. adjacent	7. underestimate	
4. interpret	8. capacity	

TIP   Check the answers to exercise B by pausing the audio after each sentence and asking students to repeat the missing word.

IDEAS FOR...   Checking Comprehension

Ask students to summarize the text by answering these questions: *Why was this scene so interesting for scientists? What did it seem to show and why was it surprising?*

Using Vocabulary

Exercise A.

- Direct students' attention to the photo. Ask: *Do you think that animals can really communicate? What are the differences between animal and human communication?*

- Advise students to read the whole text before filling in their answers.

- Remind students to use the correct form of each word.

- Ask students if they agree with current scientific thinking on animal intelligence or if they agree with the theory of behaviorism. Have students discuss any doubts or questions they have about each of these theories.

Answer Key

1. capacity 2. underestimated 3. illustrate
4. abstract 5. corresponding 6. interprets

Exercise B. | Discussion   Ask students to work in pairs to discuss the questions. Ask volunteers to share their ideas with the class.

IDEAS FOR...   Multi-level Classes

Students who finish early can make up other discussion questions using other target words from page 164. They can write their questions in their notebooks so that you can check them. Then they can discuss the questions in pairs.

Pronunciation Note
Rene Descartes: ruh-**nay** day-**kart**

Developing Listening Skills

(pages 166-167)

Before Listening

Predicting Content

- Ask students to look at the photos. Ask what they know about parrots and dogs. Ask: *Do you have a pet parrot or dog? How intelligent is your pet?*

- Discuss questions 1 and 2.

Listening: A TV Show

track 3-20

Exercise A. | Listening for Main Ideas

- Allow time for students to read the questions.

- Play the audio while students choose their answers. Go over the answers by asking volunteers to explain how they made their answer choices.

Answer Key	1. c 2. b 3. a 4. a

track 3-20

Exercise B. | Note-Taking

- Refer students to the outline and ask them to pencil in anything they can remember from the audio.

- Play the audio again so that students can complete the outline.

- Ask volunteers to write the missing words on the board.

IDEAS FOR... Checking Comprehension

Ask students to form groups of three. Each student will summarize one of the experiments in their own words (the parrot, the crow, or the dog) and tell the rest of the group what the experiment is trying to prove.

Answer Key *(Notes will vary.)*

Beliefs about animal intelligence:

- Descartes: Animals are **beings without minds**
- Scientists today believe **that animals are intelligent**
- Ex. of mental skills of animals: Good memory, **the ability to understand symbols, awareness of self, understanding others' motives, imitating voices, and showing creativity**

Diane Willberg:

- Parrots: **able to use tools**
- Shows parrot 2 green objects. Parrot says **color**
- Shows parrot 2 balls. Parrot says **shape**
- Crows Lab experiment: D.W. puts a **piece of meat** in a bottle
- The crow **makes a hook from metal wire to get meat**

Samantha Bean:

- In one room **200 objects**. In another room **200 photographs**. S.B. shows Betsy **a photo**. Betsy **gets the corresponding object.**
- S.B. believes this shows **abstract thinking.**

Matthew Leonard:

- Self-awareness **is ability to recognize self in the mirror**
- Exs: humans, **elephants, dolphins, apes**

After Listening

Critical Thinking Focus: Questioning

Results | Go over the information in the box. Give some examples of situations where research results might be biased such as a medical research study carried out a by a drug company. Ask students to brainstorm some additional examples.

Critical Thinking

- Ask students to work in pairs or groups of three to discuss the questions.

- Ask a spokesperson from each group to summarize their ideas for the class.

- Answers to question 1 could be listed on the board and could then be related back to the Critical Thinking Focus. Ask students how the source of funding might bias the results of the study and how this bias can be avoided.

Exploring Spoken English

45 mins

(pages 168-170)

Language Function: Enumerating

Go over the information in the box. Ask students to answer each of the following questions by giving you three reasons or examples. Remind students to use the expressions from the box.

How are animals similar to humans?
How are animals different from humans?
Why do scientists think animals are intelligent?

track 3-21 Exercise A. | Play the audio. Pause after each item to allow students time to fill in the phrases.

> ### Answer Key
>
> **1.** for one thing, For another **2.** First, then, and then

Exercise B. | After students have discussed their answers in pairs, compare answers as a class.

> ### Answer Key
>
> **1.** examples **2.** steps in a process

Exercise C. | Collaboration

- Direct students' attention to the photo of the circus animal on page 169. Take a class vote on who is in favor and who is against the use of animals in circuses.

- Ask students to work with a partner and choose a role. Then have each student list his or her reasons individually.

> ### IDEAS FOR... Expansion
>
> Ask students to think of steps to a process that they know well and explain it to their partner. They may find the following list of examples helpful:
> - How to write an essay
> - How to cook a favorite meal
> - How to send a photo to someone by email

> ### Answer Key *(Student examples will vary.)*
>
> *Against using animals in circuses:*
> It is cruel to animals.
> Some tricks are dangerous to animals.
> Animals are kept in cages or in poor conditions.
>
> *In support of using animals in circuses:*
> It is entertaining for children.
> Animals enjoy performing tricks.
> Animals have a good relationship with their owners.

Exercise D. | Discussion

- Ask students to work in pairs and explain their ideas from exercise **C** to their partner. Remind them to use language for enumerating.

- To wrap up the exercise, write all the arguments on the board in a T-chart.

> **TIP** Another way to organize exercises C and D is to have students form two groups. Students in one group will find reasons to support the use of animals in circuses and students in the second group will find reasons against it. Then have each member of one group pair up with a member from the other group.

Exercise E. | Enumerating

- Have students look at the photos and ask what each person is doing.

- Tell students to work in pairs. Each partner will choose one topic and read the information.

- Remind students to retell the information to their partner using the expressions from the box.

- Write the target language on the board for reference:
  First, Next, After that
  First, Then, And then
  First, Second, Third

> ### IDEAS FOR... Multi-level Classes
>
> For exercise **E**, challenge higher-level students to remember the information without looking at the text. Lower-level students can write the enumerating expressions in the text to help them prepare for their summary.

Grammar: Subject-Verb Agreement with Quantifiers

Go over the information in the box. Ask volunteers to read out the examples.

> **IDEAS FOR...** Presenting Grammar
>
> Write the example sentences on the board with the verbs missing. Ask students to decide if the missing verb should be singular or plural in each sentence.

Exercise A. | Self-Reflection

- Do the first item with the class, using information about your own parents.

- Monitor students as they work individually. Take notes of any problems.

- Ask volunteers to read their sentences aloud. Give feedback on any errors.

Answer Key *(Answers will vary.)*

Exercise B. | Discussion

- Ask volunteers to read the examples in the speech bubbles aloud.

- Give feedback to individual pairs as you walk around the classroom and listen to their discussions.

Exercise C. | Collaboration

- Ask students to work in groups. Each student in the group should write the sentences in their notebook. Ask for some example sentences from each group.

Speaking *(page 171)*

30-45 mins

Giving a Short Persuasive Speech

Exercise A. | Brainstorming

- Brainstorm two or three ideas with the whole class for each role. Then have students brainstorm more ideas in groups of three or four.

- Draw the chart on the board and invite one volunteer from each group to come to the board to fill in their group's ideas.

Answer Key *(Answers will vary.)*

> **Work:** guide dogs for blind people, horses pull wagons
>
> **Entertainment:** horse racing, animals in zoos
>
> **Pets:** cats, dogs, rabbits
>
> **Research:** mice to test new drugs, monkeys to try out new surgery methods
>
> **Food:** farming, fishing

Exercise B. | Ask each student to write one sentence. Each person in the group should choose a different role from the chart in exercise **A**. For more practice, advise students to write two or three reasons to support their statement.

Exercise C. | Presentation

- Demonstrate the three steps of giving a persuasive speech with an example: *In my opinion, animals should not be used for entertainment. First, it is cruel to the animals because they are kept in poor conditions and treated badly. Second . . .*

- Remind students to use the language for enumerating from page 168. Encourage students to add more information to support each of their three reasons and / or examples.

Exercise D. | Encourage students to give each other positive feedback on their presentations. Have students vote on which group member gave the most persuasive presentation.

Student to Student: Joining a Group

Encourage students to use this language the next time they join a new group.

Presentation Skills: Using Gestures

Ask students to think of different hand gestures that could be useful when giving a presentation. Some examples include extending your hand toward the audience when asking their opinion, or pointing toward yourself when giving your own opinion.

Viewing: Animal Minds

30-45 mins

(pages 172-173)

Overview of the Video | This video presents some information about research on animal intelligence, specifically dealing with the intelligence of rats and dolphins.

Before Viewing

Exercise A. | Using the Dictionary

- Ask students to read the sentences carefully and try to work out the meanings of the words in blue before using their dictionary.

- Ask students to find words in the same family in the dictionary such as *coercive, cognition,* etc. Have students list these additional word forms in their vocabulary journals.

Answer Key

a. revelation **b.** unconsciously **c.** deduced **d.** outsmarted **e.** cognitive **f.** coercion **g.** sophisticated

Exercise B. | Predicting Content

- Have students look at the two photos on page 172. Ask: *What do you think is the purpose of these tests?*

- Ask what they already know about the intelligence of rats and dolphins.

While Viewing

5:33

Exercise A.

- Allow time for students to read the questions. Play the video.

- Check the answers to exercise **A** by asking students to explain what was interesting about each answer.
  For example:
  T: Why was question 1 interesting?
  S: Because scientists deduced that the rat must have formed a mental map of the maze and remembered where the food was.

T: Why was question 2 interesting?
S: Because they don't use any coercion. They reinforce the behavior that they want with a whistle followed by a bucket of fish.

T: Why was question 3 interesting?
S: Because the dolphin understood that the trainer wanted it to show some new kinds of behavior.

Answer Key 1. b 2. b 3. c

Exercise B. | Sequencing Events

- Allow time for students to read the sentences and pencil in their ideas before playing the video again.

- Go over the answers and ask pairs to retell the experiment to their partner in their own words.

Answer Key 1. e 2. b 3. a 4. d 5. f 6. c

After Viewing

Critical Thinking

- Ask students to work in groups. Encourage students to analyze and evaluate the information on the video.

- Remind students to use strategies for questioning results from page 167.

IDEAS FOR... Expansion

- Brainstorm ideas for other kinds of tests that could be used to show animal creativity.
- Ask students to tell about examples of animal intelligence from their own experience.

Building and Using Vocabulary *(pages 174-175)*

30 mins

WARM-UP

The Lesson B target vocabulary is presented in the context of ways to improve human memory.

- Ask students to look at the photo and make some suggestions as to how playing cards could be used to improve memory.

Building Vocabulary

track 3-22

Exercise A. | Meaning from Context

- Play the audio while students read the information.

- Ask students for their opinion as to why some people are better at memorization than others.

Exercise B.

- Remind students to use the context in exercise **A** to work out the meanings of the words in blue.

- Go over the answers by asking students to read the completed sentences aloud.

Answer Key

1. enhance	**5.** unprecedented	**9.** dramatic
2. aptitude	**6.** method	**10.** ethical
3. framework	**7.** originated	
4. virtually	**8.** exact	

IDEAS FOR... Checking Comprehension

Ask students to describe the World Memory Championships in their own words. Ask: *Why do you think Dominic O'Brien was able to win so many times? Would you like to participate in the World Memory Championships? How long do you think it would take you to memorize the order of 54 cards?*

Pronunciation Note

mnemonic: ni-**mon**-ick
mnemonist: ni-**mon**-ist

Using Vocabulary

Exercise A. | Understanding Collocations

- Direct students' attention to the photo and ask what kind of test the chimpanzee might be taking.

- Explain that collocations are pairs of words that often occur together.

- Ask students to read the text all the way through before selecting their answers.

- To make this exercise more challenging, have students cover the word box and try to remember the vocabulary words from page 174.

TIP Another way to approach exercise A is to write the collocations on the board in scrambled order and ask students to group the words into phrases before reading the text.

Answer Key

1. dramatic **2.** virtually **3.** unprecedented **4.** method
5. exact **6.** ethical

IDEAS FOR... Checking Comprehension

Ask students to summarize the experiment in their own words and explain what the results show.

IDEAS FOR... Expansion

Ask students to use the Internet to find out more about Professor Tetsuro Matsuzawa's work or other interesting research about chimpanzees (e.g., the work of Jane Goodall) and tell the class about their findings in the next lesson.

Exercise B. | Discussion Ask students to work in pairs. Encourage groups to share their answers with the class.

IDEAS FOR... Multi-level Classes

Encourage students to write additional discussion questions using the target vocabulary words. Have students form a pair with a classmate of similar ability to revise and discuss the questions.

Developing Listening Skills
(pages 176-177)

45 mins

Before Listening

Self-Reflection

- Read the questions and ask students to discuss them in groups. Ask each group to give one answer for each question and talk about your own answers, too.

- Ask students to explain what they know about different types of memory such as long-term and short-term memory.

Listening: A Conversation between Classmates

 track 3-23 **Exercise A. | Listening for Main Ideas**

- Discuss the photo and why this person's job might be difficult.

- Allow time for students to read the questions. Play the audio. Go over the answers as a class.

Answer Key	1. b 2. a 3. c 4. a

 track 3-23 **Exercise B. | Listening for Details**

- Ask students to read the outline. Play the audio again while students fill in their answers. Go over the answers by writing the missing words on the board.

Answer Key

I. Superior Autobiographical Memory (SAM)

    A. Definition: **remembering almost everything about your own life**

    B. How SAM works: **part of brain is bigger than normal**

II. The Hippocampus (originated from words meaning **horse and sea monster**)

    A. Dr. S. Experiment: **removed a patient's hippocampus trying to stop seizures**

    B. Result: **patient lost most of his memory**

        1. Contribution to science: **gained understanding about the brain**

Answer Key *(continued)*

III. Method of Loci / The Location Method

    A. Use: **helps you to remember lists of words**

    B. Steps

        1. Picture pathway that you know well

        2. **Create an image for each word, put image at places on the path**

        3. Later, **walk down path in your mind and remember each word**

IDEAS FOR... **Checking Comprehension**

Ask these additional questions or write them on the board:

1. *What is Heather preparing for?* (a memory contest in her psychology class)

2. *What kind of questions were people with SAM able to answer?* (what they were doing on specific dates in the past)

3. *What did scientists discover about the brains of people with superior autobiographical memories?* (their hippocampus is bigger)

After Listening

Discussion | Provide some extra information about this case: *The patient's epilepsy was severe. He was unable to work because of the illness. The doctors were not sure the operation would work. The operation stopped the patient's problems with epilepsy. After Dr. Scoville realized that the surgery failed, he worked to stop the procedure from ever being done again. In fact, the patient is the only person who ever had this operation.*

track 3-24 **Pronunciation: Using Word Stress to Clarify Information**

- Go over the information in the box. Play the audio. Have students work in pairs to complete the exercise. Give feedback on intonation.

Answer Key

1. A book of *crossword* puzzles? 2. A *memory* test?
3. A *new* car? 4. A *world* champion?

Exploring Spoken English
(pages 178-179)

30 mins

Language Function: Checking Background Knowledge

- Go over the information in the box. Give some examples using topics and information from the previous lesson. For example: *Have you heard about research on the intelligence of chimpanzees?*

- Ask students to complete the examples with their own ideas.

track 3-25

Exercise A.

- Play the audio, pausing to allow students to write their answers.

- Play the audio again and pause after each sentence for students to repeat with the appropriate intonation.

> **Answer Key**
>
> **1.** Have you ever heard of
> **2.** You know about, don't you?
> **3.** What can you tell me about
> **4.** do you know about

Exercise B. | Checking Background Knowledge

Ask two volunteers to read the examples in the speech bubbles aloud. This activity gives students the opportunity to review earlier topics in the book. Advise students to refer back to earlier units if they don't remember the information. Call on a few pairs of students to repeat their exchanges for the class.

> **IDEAS FOR...** Expansion
>
> Prepare a variety of topics on slips of paper. You will need one slip for each student in your class. The topics can be from this unit or from a previous unit in the book. Put the slips in a paper bag. Have each student pick one topic out of the bag and ask their partner about it. Encourage students to share any information they know about the topic. When they have finished, they can pass the slips on to the next pair.

Grammar: Present Participle Phrases

- Go over the information in the box. Ask volunteers to read out the examples.

- Point out the possible confusion caused by using the incorrect subject in the participle clause.

> **IDEAS FOR...** Presenting Grammar
>
> Write the example sentences using participial phrases on slips of paper so that each word is on a separate slip. Students can work in groups to put the sentences together. Alternatively, give one slip to each student and have them stand in a line in the correct order of the words in the sentence.

Exercise A. | Collaboration

- Students may want to match the sentences individually at first before comparing answers in pairs.

- Pairs can work on writing sentences individually or together. Then they can exchange sentences with another pair for peer review.

> **Answer Key** *(Matching answers appear at the end of each combined sentence.)*
>
> **1.** Hearing his master's whistle, the Border collie turned to the right. (b)
> **2.** Recognizing itself in the mirror, the ape displayed self-awareness. (a)
> **3.** Seeing another bird, the jay waited to hide its food. (d)
> **4.** Taking the fish from the trainer's hand, the dolphin made a happy noise. (c)
> **5.** Using a touch screen, the orangutan communicates with people. (e)
> **6.** Living with chimps, Jane Goodall made many discoveries about chimp society. (f)

> **IDEAS FOR...** Multi-level Classes
>
> Students who finish early can work on creating their own sentences using participle phrases based on information in this lesson or the previous lesson.

Exercise B. | Self-Reflection

- Brainstorm some other ways to finish the example sentences. Encourage students to be creative and think of as many different endings as they can.

Engage: Using Memory Skills to Recall Information *(page 180)*

45 mins

WARM-UP

- Brainstorm ideas for remembering vocabulary. Try to classify the different types of memory techniques such as visual, auditory, verbal, and nonverbal.

- Tell the class about some other tips for remembering words:
  Rhymes: i *before* e *except after* c
  Acronyms: *The names of the Great Lakes can be remembered by the acronym HOMES—Huron, Ontario, Michigan, Erie, and Superior.*

Exercise A.

- Read the information in the box. Play the audio from page 176 if necessary.

- Ask students to work individually to write their lists.

Exercise B.

- Emphasize that timing is important in order for this experiment to be fair. It may be best to do this in two stages.
  1. Student A looks at Student B's list for 30 seconds. Then Student A tries to remember the words. Student B gives a score.
  2. Student B looks at Student A's list for 30 seconds. Then Student B tries to remember the words. Student A gives a score.
- Discuss what made some words easier to remember than others. Ask: *Was it the position in the sequence? Did one word stand out from the others?*

Exercise C.

- Have students exchange lists again and this time set a time limit of five minutes.
- Explain that for this method to work, students have to choose a framework with a sequence that is very familiar and images that are memorable (visual, creative, or funny).

Exercise D. | Students give back the lists and try to recall the words in sequence.

Exercise E. | Critical Thinking

- Ask students to work in groups to compare their results with the previous exercise. Encourage students to hypothesize about the results.

- If students have difficulty adapting this technique, give some suggestions such as using key words or phrases for a presentation and using headings or subheadings to remember information.

- Ask a spokesperson from each group to summarize the group's best ideas for the class.

> **TIP** Ask the class for feedback on what they have learned from this lesson and how it will affect their study habits in the future.

IDEAS FOR... **Expansion**

Ask students to do some research on the Internet for other memory techniques. Have students write a short presentation describing how to use a memory technique they learned about. Students can present their findings to a partner or to a small group.

Food Concerns

Academic Track
Interdisciplinary

Academic Pathways:
Lesson A: Listening to a PowerPoint Lecture
Role-Playing a Debate
Lesson B: Listening to an Informal
Conversation
Creating a PowerPoint Presentation

Unit Theme

Methods of producing food are changing in many countries. Traditional methods of agriculture are being modernized and improved in order to increase food production for the world's growing population.

Unit 10 explores the topic of food as it relates to:
– the decline in varieties of food
– genetically-modified food
– the Slow Food movement
– food shortages

Think and Discuss *(page 181)*

5 mins

Methods of growing and producing food are changing all over the world. Modernization and mechanization (use of mechanical harvesters and other machines) as well as increased use of pesticides, hormones, and antibiotics have changed the way food is produced and have also changed the nature of the food we eat.

Modern farming methods are more efficient and produce more food. However, not everyone agrees that they are better. For example, when chickens that are fed growth hormones and antibiotics to prevent disease are compared to chickens that are grown on free-range farms where they can roam freely outdoors, a major debate arises about which kind of chicken is safer to eat.

- Ask students to describe the photo. Ask their opinion of this method of farming. Ask: *How could this be modernized or mechanized? Would it be better?*

- Discuss questions 1 and 2.

- Discuss what kind of criteria students use when choosing the food they eat.

Exploring the Theme: Food Concerns *(pages 182-183)*

15 mins

The opening spread features a photo of several chefs preparing food in a kitchen.

- Ask students about the main photo. Ask: *Do you enjoy cooking? How do you choose the food you eat?*

- Ask students to look at the three smaller photos and read the captions.

- Explain the meanings of *disease-resistant* (able to withstand diseases), *genetically-modified* (a food whose DNA has been altered), and *antibiotics* (drugs used to prevent diseases).

- Discuss questions 1–3. Ask students how aware they are of chemicals in the food they eat. Ask if they choose organic food products over conventional products and, and if so, why.

- Discuss changes in farming and agriculture from traditional times to the present day.

IDEAS FOR... **Expansion**

Ask students to research one type of food that they like and find out some interesting facts about how it is produced. Students should take notes to answer the following questions: *Where is it grown or made? What are traditional methods of growing or making it? Have the methods of growing or making this food changed in recent years?*

Students can share their findings in small groups or with the whole class.

⏱ Building and Using Vocabulary *(pages 184-185)*

30 mins

WARM-UP

The Lesson A target vocabulary is presented in the context of modern-day farming techniques.

- Ask students to look at the graph. Ask: *What does this graph show? What are the possible explanations for why there are fewer vegetable varieties?*

- Ask students to look at the photo. *What is a seed bank? Why is it necessary?*

- Ask if students can name any varieties of fruits or vegetables. *How many varieties can you name?* (For example, apple varieties include Gala, Macintosh, etc.)

Building Vocabulary

🎧 track 3-26 **Exercise A. | Meaning from Context**

- Write this question on the board: *What is one advantage and one disadvantage of modern-day farming methods? How could seed banks save us in the future?*

- Play the audio while students read. Then discuss the answers to the questions.

Exercise B.

- Allow time for students to read the definitions and complete the exercise.

- Remind them to use the context to work out the meanings of the words in blue.

Answer Key

1. offset	5. advocate	9. monitor
2. devote	6. welfare	10. diminished
3. via	7. conventional	
4. modify	8. intense	

TIP Go over the answers by asking questions using each vocabulary word, emphasizing the new words as you do so. Then ask a follow-up question about each one to check comprehension. For example:

T: What is an *intense* need for food?
S: It is a very great need.
T: Why is the need for food so intense?
S: Because of the increase in population.

Using Vocabulary

Exercise A.

- Do the first item together. Remind students to use the correct form of each word.

- Ask students their opinions of this experiment. Ask: *Would you eat these apples?* Take a class vote on those who would and those who wouldn't eat these apples.

Answer Key

1. modified, via 2. conventional 3. advocate 4. devoted 5. monitoring 6. intense, diminish 7. welfare 8. offset

Critical Thinking Focus: Remaining Objective | Go over the information in the box. Ask students to give some examples of research questions or methods that are not objective.

Exercise B. | Brainstorming

- Refer students back to the text on page 184. Allow time for students to work in groups.

- Ask volunteers to come to the board and write their group's ideas in a T-chart. Then evaluate all the ideas by taking a class vote on each argument.

Answer Key *(Answers will vary. Some possible answers are below.)*

In favor of monoculture: better use of resources, less labor, increased food production

Against monoculture: number of food varieties decreases, more vulnerable to diseases and / or pests, more reliance on chemical pesticides

Student to Student: Expressing Opinions
Go over the information in the box. Refer students back to the topic of exercise **A** and ask students to use these expressions to talk about their opinions of monoculture, seed banks, and genetically-modified food.

IDEAS FOR... Multi-level Classes

Students who finish exercise **B** early can make a T-chart about genetically-modified food. This activity could be used as an introduction to the listening that follows about GM foods.

Developing Listening Skills

(pages 186-187)

45 mins

Before Listening

Brainstorming | Brainstorm ideas with the class to begin. Encourage students to think of ideas that will help people in countries where they don't have enough food or where they have serious diseases. Discuss the ideas as a class.

Listening: A PowerPoint Lecture

 Exercise A.
track 3-27

- Direct students' attention to the photo. Ask what the benefits could be of genetically modifying these salmon.

- Allow time for students to read the questions.

- Play the audio while students choose their answers. Check the answers as a class.

Answer Key	1. a. 3, b. 4, c. 1, d. 2
	2. b
	3. a

 Exercise B. | Note-Taking
track 3-27

- Refer students to the photos and ask them to describe what is happening in each one.

- Have students read through the notes before they listen. Play the audio again so that students can complete the outline.

- Ask volunteers to write the missing words on the board.

IDEAS FOR... Checking Comprehension

Ask students whether these statements are true or false:

1. *Animals cannot be genetically modified.* (false)
2. *GM crops could become difficult to control.* (true)
3. *Products in the U.S. are not labeled as containing GM foods.* (true)
4. *The U.S. government does not approve the use of GM food.* (false)
5. *GM foods could be used to solve the problem of world poverty.* (true)

Answer Key *(Notes may vary.)*

GM animals and plants grow **faster, bigger**, produce **pesticides**

Ex. of GM experiments:

- Rat genes into lettuce to produce **vitamin C**
- **Moth** genes into apple plants to help them resist diseases
- Modify salmon to make it grow **twice** as fast
- GM cattle and sheep produce **medicines** in their milk

GM foods could be key to advances in **agriculture and health**

Critics think GM foods are being **rushed to market**

Exs. of critics' fears:

- Weeds with modified genes called **superweeds**
- Harmful effects on **insects and animals**

U.S. has been eating GM foods since **the mid-1990s**

Exs: Pizza, **ice cream, salad dressing, baking powder**

Countries with GM foods: **Argentina, Canada, China,** etc.

Corps. offset risks through **testing**; Government monitors **the production and sale of GM foods**

Gene flow definition: **the movement of genes via flowers and seeds from one population of plants to another**

Mixing GM plants with **conventional** plants could have a long-term impact

GM crops resist insects, insects could **get used to such crops**

- Result: **pests that farmers would have no weapons against**

Golden rice contains beta-carotene to help with **vitamin A** deficiency

Critics don't like that **big companies** control GM technology

Benefits of GM foods:

- **increase** the amount of food produced
- offer crops that **resist disease**

After Listening

Critical Thinking | Encourage students to evaluate the information on the audio and add their own ideas.

Exploring Spoken English
(pages 188-190)

45 mins

Language Function: Confirming Understanding

Go over the information in the box. Practice saying the expressions with the correct intonation.

track 3-28

Exercise A.

- Play the audio. Pause after each item to allow students time to write the phrases.

- Play the audio again and ask students to repeat the expressions.

Answer Key

1. OK so far?
2. Are you following me?
3. Does that make sense?

IDEAS FOR... **Expansion**

Ask students to explain the following terms to their partner: *genetically-modified food, organic food, conventional farming, monoculture.*
Remind students to use expressions from the box for confirming understanding.

Exercise B. | Summarizing

- Ask students to work in pairs. Each student will choose one topic. The first passage is about melons. The second passage is about tomatoes.

- Instruct students to read their chosen passage individually. While they are reading, provide help with unfamiliar vocabulary. For example: Rabies *is a viral disease that infects the brain and causes death. It can be spread to humans who are bitten by an infected animal. Animals that can carry rabies include dogs, cats, foxes, raccoons, and bats.*

- Once students have finished reading, they should orally summarize their passage for their partner. Encourage students to ask each other questions if they don't understand.

Grammar: Causative Verbs

- Go over the information in the box.

- Ask students to give examples of things that their school made them do when they were young and things their school allowed them to do. For example:
  S1: Our school made us wear a school uniform.
  S2: Really? Our school allowed us to wear any clothes we liked.

IDEAS FOR... **Presenting Grammar**

Write some sentences with causative verbs on the board. Ask students to choose the correct verb with or without *to.*
1. GM foods will let farmers (grow / to grow) more food.
2. Governments should require companies (test / to test) GM foods more thoroughly.
3. They shouldn't allow companies (have / to have) control of the seeds.
4. Governments should make companies (label / to label) all their GM food.
(**Answer Key: 1.** grow **2.** to test **3.** to have **4.** label)

Exercise A.

- Have students look at the photo. Ask them to describe what this woman is doing.

- Refer students to the map. Ask them to describe the exact location of the Philippines. Ask: *What kind of crops do you think are grown there?* Encourage students to make inferences based on what they know about the weather and climate in this part of the world. (The main crops are sugarcane, rice, coconut, and corn.)

- Allow time for students to read the text and underline their answers.

- Check the answers by asking students to read the underlined words aloud.

Answer Key

In 1991, the eruption of the volcano Mount Pinatubo ruined large areas of Philippine farmland. The hard soil and insect pests <u>forced many farmers to give up</u> on the land. Then in 2003, the Philippine government <u>allowed farmers to plant</u> GM corn. Although there were some fears about the dangers of GM corn, results of safety tests <u>convinced the government to approve</u> it.

Global agriculture companies <u>helped farmers get started</u> and taught them to plant GM corn. Farmers used insect-resistant varieties that grow well in hard soil. Since then, the government <u>has encouraged farmers to plant</u> more crops. GM corn <u>has enabled the farmers to produce</u> more corn per acre (hectare) than ever before. In fact, GM corn <u>has allowed farmers to produce</u> three to four times as much corn per acre (hectare) as was possible before.

The success story of GM corn in the Philippines <u>has motivated farmers to try</u> other varieties of GM crops. Recently, Philippine farmers were winners of an international prize for outstanding agricultural projects. The prize is designed to <u>inspire farmers to reach</u> for excellence in agriculture.

IDEAS FOR... Checking Comprehension

Ask students to write three comprehension questions about the reading from exercise **A**. They can choose anyone in the class to answer their questions. Questions cannot be repeated.

Exercise B. | Discussion

- Read the first situation. Ask volunteers to read the examples in the speech bubbles aloud.

- Ask students to discuss the situations in pairs. Encourage students to come up with as many suggestions as possible.

TIP You can assign one situation to each pair. Then you can gather ideas and suggestions on the board using the target language.

 ## Speaking *(page 191)*

30-45 mins

Role-Playing a Debate

Exercise A. | Ask students to work in pairs. At this stage, they will gather ideas for their debate. First, they will choose a role, either for or against GM crops. Remind students to look back at their notes from the audio on page 187 for ideas.

Exercise B. | Role-Playing

- Ask two students to read the examples in the speech bubbles aloud.

- Encourage students to give reasons and examples for each of their arguments.

- Remind students to use language for expressing their opinions from page 185.

Viewing: Slow Food
(pages 192-193)

30 mins

Overview of the Video | This video is about the Slow Food movement, which started in Italy and now has over 100,000 members worldwide.

Before Viewing

Exercise A. | Prior Knowledge

- Ask students to look at the map and identify the exact location of Greve in Italy.

- Have students look at the photo and ask them to describe what kind of farming and landscape is shown.

- Ask students if they have been to Italy and what they know about the foods that are common in the area.

- Ask students to work in pairs to discuss the question and make a list of typical Italian foods.

Exercise B. | Predicting Content Ask students to brainstorm ideas about the Slow Food movement. If students have trouble coming up with ideas, ask: *Do you think it is in favor of food that is cooked slowly? Or eaten slowly? Or takes a long time to grow or prepare?*

While Viewing

4:06

Exercise A.

- Direct students' attention to the photo on page 193. Ask: *What do you know about the process of making cheese? How could this cheese be different from other types of cheese?*

- Allow time for students to read the questions.

- Play the video while students choose their answers.

Answer Key	1. a 2. b 3. b 4. c

Exercise B. | Allow time for students to read the sentences and pencil in their ideas before playing the video again. Ask volunteers to read their answers aloud.

Answer Key

1. challenge	**5.** nice atmosphere	**9.** product
2. specialness	**6.** very easy	**10.** noticed
3. Slow Cities	**7.** the time	**11.** same pizza
4. live here	**8.** more calmly	**12.** respected

TIP Play the video again and stop at any scenes that illustrate the main theme of the video. Ask students to describe how the scene relates to the topic of the Slow Food movement.

After Viewing

Critical Thinking | Ask students to work in pairs. Encourage students to make inferences based on information from the video. They should support their answers with evidence from the video.

> **IDEAS FOR... Expansion**
>
> - As a continuation of After Viewing question 2, have pairs of students join with another group and design an advertisement, poster, or brochure about the Slow Food movement. The purpose of the visual is to try to get new members in the Slow Food movement. Groups should use ideas from question 2 and make their visuals exciting and interesting. Have groups share their visuals with the class.
>
> - Ask students to research information about the Slow Food movement and the related Slow Cities movement. Have students make a list of four to six cities or areas that participate in the Slow Food or Slow Cities movements. Have students share the information with the class. Ask: *Have any of you visited one of these places?*

Building and Using Vocabulary *(pages 194-195)*

30 mins

WARM-UP

The Lesson B target vocabulary is presented in the context of problems affecting the world food supply. Discuss the possible causes of world hunger. Ask: *What should be done to help countries that don't have enough food?*

Building Vocabulary

track 3-29

Meaning from Context

- Allow time for students to read the sentences. Ask which words students are already familiar with and in what contexts they have heard them.

- Refer to the photo and ask students about the foods they eat daily. Ask: *How much of each food do you eat per day?*

- Allow time for students to read the text and choose their answers.

- Play the audio while students check their answers.

Answer Key

1. output	**5.** primarily	**9.** policy
2. apparent	**6.** scope	**10.** scenarios
3. presumed	**7.** coincide	
4. the norm	**8.** inclination	

IDEAS FOR... Expansion

Ask students to use the ideas in the text to gather arguments for and against the practice of vegetarianism (not eating meat). They can use a T-chart to organize their ideas. Students can role-play a conversation between someone who is in favor of the practice of vegetarianism and someone who is against it. Refer students to page 214 of the *Independent Student Handbook* for more information about using T-charts.

Using Vocabulary

Exercise A.

- Ask students what they know about modern versus traditional farming methods.

- Have students look at the photo and discuss differences in farming throughout the world.

- Advise students to read the text all the way through before selecting their answers.

TIP To make this exercise more challenging, have students cover the word bank and try to remember the words from the previous exercise.

Answer Key

1. output	**5.** apparent	**9.** scope
2. coincided	**6.** inclination	**10.** primarily
3. presume	**7.** scenarios	
4. the norm	**8.** policy / policies	

Exercise B. | Critical Thinking Encourage students to use examples from their own experience to discuss these questions.

IDEAS FOR... Multi-level Classes

For lower-level students, write some alternative discussion questions on the board. Students can choose a question appropriate to their own level. For example:

1. Richer countries have an obligation to help poorer ones with financial aid or food. Do you agree or disagree?

2. Technology should be made available free of charge to farmers so that they can improve their food supply. Do you agree or disagree?

3. Every country should produce enough food for its own population so that it does not depend on other countries. How can countries do this?

Developing Listening Skills

45 mins

(pages 196-197)

Before Listening

Understanding Visuals

- Refer students to the graphs. Ask them to describe each one. Write helpful language on the board for reference. For example:
  The first graph is a line graph.
  It shows / represents / illustrates . . .
  The number of . . . has increased / decreased.
  There has been a great / slight / dramatic increase / decrease / decline / growth in . . .

- Discuss the meaning of *projected* (estimated future data based on current data and trends).

- Have students work in pairs to discuss the questions.

- Ask volunteers to share their answers with the class.

Answer Key *(Answers may vary.)*

1. It will start to decrease.

2. 24%

3. 0.8%

Listening: An Informal Conversation

track 3-30

Exercise A. | Listening for Main Ideas   Allow time for students to read the questions. Play the audio. Go over the answers as a class.

Answer Key   1. c 2. b 3. c 4. a

track 3-30

Exercise B. | Note-Taking

- Ask students to read the outline. Allow time for students to pencil in any answers they can remember.

- Play the audio again while students write their answers.

- Check the answers by writing the missing words on the board.

Answer Key

Problem:

Rise in food prices over the past **5 to 10 years**, quicker than the norm

Most available land is already **being farmed**

Reasons for problem:

- Dev. countries have more **money** to spend and eat more **meat and dairy**

- Feeding farm animals requires **a lot of grain**

- Supply and Demand: If only a little food, but many want it: the price **goes up**

- Some gov. policies restrict **grain exports**

- Some experts predict that areas of planet **will become desert**

Solutions to problem: Increase **amount of food grown on land**

- Increase output w/better **water management** and fertilizer management; **using GM crops**

IDEAS FOR...   **Checking Comprehension**

Ask students to explain these statements from the audio.

There are quite a few problems that are coinciding all at once.

That's the law of supply and demand, right?

After Listening

Critical Thinking | Encourage students to synthesize all the information they have learned in this unit.

track 3-31

Pronunciation: Syllable Stress

Go over the information in the box. Say some of the words again in random order. Ask students to show if they are nouns or verbs by raising their right or left hand, respectively.

Collaboration | Ask students to work in pairs to write their sentences. Ask volunteers to read out their sentences.

Exploring Spoken English

(pages 198-199)

Language Function: Giving Recommendations

Go over the information in the box. Choose a problem. For example: *Transporting food across long distances is very expensive.* Ask students to suggest some solutions using the language in the box.

track 3-32

Exercise A.

■ Play the audio, pausing to allow students to write their answers.

■ Play the audio again and pause after each sentence for students to repeat with the appropriate intonation.

Answer Key

1. we ought to ask farmers to farm more land

2. Why don't they do something about it

3. if it were up to me

Exercise B. | Discussion

■ Have students look at the photo. Ask them whether they think preventing "ugly" food from being sold is good or bad. Ask students to brainstorm ideas on how this "ugly" food could be used.

■ Ask two volunteers to read the example sentences in the speech bubbles.

■ Organize students into groups of three or four to discuss the topics. Remind them to use expressions from the box.

■ Ask a spokesperson from each group to report to the class.

> **IDEAS FOR... Expansion**
>
> Ask each student to write a problem on a slip of paper. Collect the slips and redistribute them randomly. Students will walk around the classroom and tell each other their problems and make recommendations for their classmates' problems using the expressions from the box.

Grammar: Subjunctive Verbs in *That* Clauses

■ Go over the information in the box. Ask volunteers to read out the example sentences.

■ Ask students to suggest different ways to finish these sentences using the topics of world food supply and GM foods.

Exercise A. | Discussion

■ Have students form groups of three. Each person in the group can take one of the three situations and prepare a few sentences using the target language.

■ Have each person in turn present their ideas to the group. The other students can agree, disagree, or make additional recommendations.

Exercise B. | Self-Reflection

■ Allow time for students to list two or three ideas before talking to a partner.

■ You may want students to switch partners several times during this exercise so that they can get lots of different types of advice.

■ Ask each student to tell the class about one of their problems and the best recommendation they received.

> **IDEAS FOR... Multi-level Classes**
>
> Offer students a choice of topics for these problems. Lower-level students can talk about personal problems or job-related issues. Higher-level students may want to discuss topics related to the theme of the unit and recycle some of the vocabulary they have learned.

Engage: Creating a PowerPoint Presentation *(page 200)*

45 mins

Lesson Preparation Note | The presentation exercise in this Engage section requires students to do some research on the Internet or in the library. You may want to assign this research for homework or arrange to have Internet or library access available during the lesson.

WARM-UP

- Introduce the topic by talking about your favorite type of food. Bring in photos of or recipes for different types of food to show the class.

- Ask students to say what kind of food they like best and something about it. For example: *What kind of ingredients are used to make it? What does it taste like?*

Exercise A. | Ask students to work in pairs to choose a country.

> **TIP** One way to organize exercise A is to have students stand up and walk around the classroom until they find a partner who is interested in the same country as they are. Students who cannot find a partner will have to agree on a compromise.

Exercise B. | Researching

- As a class, brainstorm ideas for researching a particular food either on the Internet or in the library.

- Suggest ways of organizing notes such as using a chart with different categories (a grain, a dairy product, a type of meat or fish, and a fruit or vegetable).

Exercise C. | Creating Visuals

- Go over the steps involved in creating a PowerPoint or other slide presentation. If appropriate, have students in the class teach other students who are less familiar with this type of presentation.

- If students do not have computer technology available, modify this activity and instruct students to make a poster or other type of visual presentation. Similarly, students could plan out slides on sheets of blank paper.

- Tell students to study the example slide in the book. They should use this slide as a model and include similar information on their own slides.

- Go over the information in the Presentation Skills box.

- Remind students that they should prepare at least four slides: (1) a grain, (2) a dairy product, (3) a type of meat or fish, (4) a fruit or vegetable. All of the foods presented should be common in or originate from the country that they selected during exercise **A**.

Exercise D. | Presentation

- Make sure that each pair of students has at least four slides to show. Each student should present two of the slides.

- Pairs will take turns giving their presentations to the rest of the class.

- Encourage the rest of the class to ask questions and to give positive feedback at the end of each presentation.

Presentation Skills: Preparing Visuals for Display | Go over the information in the box. Advise students to evaluate their visual displays while keeping these questions in mind.

IDEAS FOR... Expansion

- Ask each student to write a recipe for one of their favorite dishes. They should list the ingredients and steps needed to prepare the food. Compile a booklet of the recipes for the whole class.

- Have students write a descriptive paragraph about their favorite food and say how it is produced and cooked. It can be displayed (with a visual) on the classroom wall or on the class Web site.

CD 1

Unit 1: Urban Challenges
Lesson A

Building Vocabulary

Track 2   A. Meaning from Context   Page 4

Finding affordable land for housing is a challenge in many of the world's largest cities. Some residents of Tokyo, Japan, have found a solution to this problem. They are building homes on pieces of land as small as 344 square feet (32 square meters). These "micro-homes" allow people to live close to central Tokyo and cost much less than other homes in the city. Many micro-homes have several floors and big windows that maximize sunlight.

Many cities have problems with air pollution and smog. What can big cities do to regulate the amount of air pollution and smog generated by cars and factories? An Italian company has come up with an innovative tool to reduce pollution: smog-eating cement. The cement contains a substance that converts pollution into harmless chemicals. The harmless chemicals wash off roadways when it rains. Smog-eating materials are also being used in roof tiles in Los Angeles, California, the smoggiest city in the United States.

Cities must find creative ways to build public parks, gardens, and outdoor areas when space is limited. In New York City, the High Line was an unattractive black steel structure that once supported railroad tracks. Today, the High Line has been restored as an elevated urban park. The park was financed by donations, and now it is one of the most inviting public spaces in the city. Visitors can walk through the gardens, relax on the sundeck, and attend public art exhibits and special events.

Developing Listening Skills

Listening: A Lecture

Track 3   A.   Page 6

OK, everyone, what I want to do today is continue our discussion about cities and the challenges they face, and, uh, I'd like to focus on the city of Venice, in Italy, which is an extraordinary example. So, to begin with, let's review a few of the points we've discussed so far. Remember that, for centuries, the city has been struggling with the problem of flooding. As you know, the regular floodwaters—called the *acqua alta*—are a big problem in the city. You may also recall that the government has started the innovative M.O.S.E. project to build water barriers and stop flooding from the ocean. Now, flooding is an important issue, but many Venetians say that the city has more serious problems than the *acqua alta* or the M.O.S.E. project. And most of these problems have to do with tourism.

Of course, tourism has both a positive and a negative side—tourism is extremely profitable. But the problem in Venice is too many tourists.

Track 4   Pages 6–7

OK, everyone, what I want to do today is continue our discussion about cities and the challenges they face, and, uh, I'd like to focus on the city of Venice, in Italy, which is an extraordinary example. So, to begin with, let's review a few of the points we've discussed so far. Remember that, for centuries, the city has been struggling with the problem of flooding. As you know, the regular floodwaters—called the *acqua alta*—are a big problem in the city. You may also recall that the government has started the innovative M.O.S.E. project to build water barriers and stop flooding from the ocean. Now, flooding is an important issue, but many Venetians say that the city has more serious problems than the *acqua alta* or the M.O.S.E. project. And most of these problems have to do with tourism.

Of course, tourism has both a positive and a negative side—tourism is extremely profitable. But the problem in Venice is too many tourists.

For example, in 2007 the number of Venetian residents was 60,000. And what do you think the number of visitors to Venice was in that year? Twenty-one million! Recently, on a *single* holiday weekend in May, 80,000 tourists visited the city. Public parking lots filled up and were closed. And tourists walked through the streets eating and drinking and leaving a lot of trash behind.

The result is that Venice's city services just can't handle so many people. The city has to pay more and more money for garbage collection to clean up all of the trash. In addition, public transportation on the famous boats and gondolas is so crowded that Venetian residents can barely find room to get on.

Along with trash and crowded transportation, city residents also have to deal with higher prices for food and for housing. Food prices continue to rise around the city. Some cafés charge as much as 13 U.S. dollars for a soft drink! In the Rialto Market—an area with many shops and stores—some of the grocery stores have been replaced by souvenir shops, which means that Venetians have fewer places to buy their groceries. In popular tourist areas, rent has almost tripled, and many small local businesses—for example, toy stores and hardware stores—can't afford to pay.

Let me add that there is a serious housing problem in Venice. At one time, there were regulations making it illegal to convert residential buildings into hotels. But a law in 1999 removed those regulations, and the housing problem got even worse. Since then, the number of hotels and guesthouses has increased by 600 percent, and the number of houses that are available for local residents has gone down.

These days, housing is only affordable for the very rich or for people who already own houses because they have been passed down by family. Young Venetians simply can't afford to buy any property in the city. This has forced a huge number of Venetian residents to move out of the city. Thirty years ago, the population of Venice was around 120,000. Now it's less than 60,000.

So, why does Venice continue to encourage tourism when it causes so many problems? Mainly, it's because tourism in Venice generates more than two billion U.S. dollars a year in revenue—and many think that the amount is much higher.

Also, there's a lot of financial pressure on Venice. The cleaning of canals . . . restoration of old structures . . . and the M.O.S.E. project are all very expensive. Tourism brings in money to help the city solve these problems.

Another point I want to make is that many people in Venice have jobs related to tourism. As more tourists come to the city, hotels, restaurants, and museums need to hire more workers. In fact, the city of Venice has a lower unemployment rate than the rest of Italy, and it's likely a result of the tourism industry.

Some people think that Venice is to blame for its own problems—that these problems are the result of greed for tourists' money. There's a lot of talk about limiting tourists, taxing tourists, and even asking tourists to avoid the busy seasons of Easter and Carnival. However, as you can see, maximizing the number of tourists in Venice is also necessary. So, there seem to be no simple solutions to Venice's tourism problem.

Exploring Spoken English

Track 5   A.   Page 8

1. OK, everyone, what I want to do today is continue our discussion about cities and the challenges they face . . .
2. So, to begin with, let's review a few of the points we've discussed so far.
3. Let me add that there is a serious housing problem in Venice.
4. Another point I want to make is that many people in Venice have jobs related to tourism.

Lesson B

Building Vocabulary

Track 6   B.   Page 14

Singapore is one of Asia's most interesting countries. It is surprising that such a small nation has such a powerful economy. Many people believe that Singapore's economic success is because of the leadership of Lee Kuan Yew, Singapore's first prime minister. His ideas have dominated the politics of Singapore for decades.

Singapore's model of success is unlike that of any other country. The model is a unique combination of two ideas: the encouragement of business and the enforcement of strict laws. To follow this model, the people of Singapore have learned to live and work together in an orderly way. There are laws that encourage cooperation between ethnic groups, and like all laws in Singapore, they are strictly enforced.

Spitting, selling chewing gum, and littering are all prohibited by law. While these laws may surprise some visitors, many Singaporeans have internalized them, and for the most part, they follow the rules and laws without thinking about them.

Most Singaporeans believe that strict laws are compatible with an orderly and secure society. They are willing to conform to rules and laws if it will make life in Singapore more pleasant. Some Singaporeans and some people from other countries, however, may feel that the benefits of these laws are debatable.

Developing Listening Skills

Listening: A Conversation between Classmates

Track 7   Page 16

M: Hi, Linda. I've been looking for you. I wanted to return your notes from the lecture on Singapore. Thanks for letting me borrow them.

F: No problem. Sorry that you missed class. Are you feeling better?

M: Yes, a lot better, thanks. Do you have time to answer a few questions for me? There were a few things in your notes that I didn't understand.

F: Sure.

M: OK. So first, you wrote here "Singapura—lion." What did you mean by that?

F: Oh, that's an easy one. *Singapura* is the original name for Singapore. It means "lion city." And the symbol of the country is the Merlion—it's a unique creature with the head of a lion and the body of a fish. The head of the lion relates to the name *Singapura.* And the body of the fish is because Singapore started off as a fishing village.

M: Interesting. Do you remember when modern Singapore was founded? I couldn't really read your handwriting here.

F: Um, I think it was 18 something . . . maybe 1819? So, you know, it's still a young country.

M: OK. I don't really understand the section of your notes about Singapore's challenges. Could you explain that a bit more?

F: Sure. For one thing, Singapore doesn't really have much land, oil, wood, or other natural resources. Oh, and another thing . . . um, there's also a mix of people from different ethnic groups and with different religions and languages. They're all trying to conform to the laws and live together in a small space.

M: I didn't know that.

F: It's also a really small country—about 270 square miles, which is the size of the state of Hawaii.

M: Uh-huh.

F: And it's 100 percent urbanized—all the people live in built-up areas. You probably read in my notes that Singapore has a very powerful economy for such a small country.

M: Yes, I remember that part. Your notes said that Singapore was ranked second in the world for having an innovative economy. So, its economy is compatible with the economy of many larger countries.

F: It definitely is. And a lot of people think that Singapore couldn't have achieved that kind of success without Lee Kwan Yew.

M: He was the first prime minister, right?

F: Right. He was prime minister for, uh, 30 years, or something. And he stayed active in politics until he retired. It was recently, maybe 2011? So, his ideas dominated Singapore politics for over 50 years.

M: You know, the Singaporeans I've met all work very hard. They seem to want to be number one in everything.

F: I think you're right. It's probably got to do with the spirit of *kiasu.*

M: *Kiasu?*

F: Yes, it means "afraid to lose." It's an idea that some people have internalized, and it makes them work hard to be the best. For example, Singapore has one of the world's busiest shipping ports, and it has one of the world's best health care systems.

M: That's impressive. What about the laws in Singapore? What did you write about chewing gum?

F: Well, you can't sell chewing gum in Singapore. It's illegal, and the police enforce that law. Spitting on the street can also get you a huge fine. And then there's a fine for forgetting to flush the toilet in a public place.

M: I think that the laws seem way too strict, don't you?

F: Actually, no. I don't think so. Those laws make Singapore one of the cleanest and safest places to live in the world. In my opinion, I'd rather have strict laws and safe streets than lenient laws and more crime.

M: Hmmm. I'm not so sure about that. I think it's a debatable point. But I agree that Singapore is an interesting place.

F: Definitely.
M: OK, I think you've answered all my questions.
F: Good.
M: Thanks again for your notes. See you next class.
F: Yes, see you then.

Pronunciation

Pronouncing the letter *t*

Track 8   Page 17

that again	it is	what are
not now	what really	that language
what you	that you	at your

Track 9   B.   Page 17

1. at you
2. upset about
3. hit us
4. what now
5. thought your
6. not yet
7. eight o'clock
8. not really

Exploring Spoken English

Track 10   A.   Page 18

1. **M:** You know, the Singaporeans I've met all work very hard. They seem to want to be number one in everything.
   F: I think you're right.
2. **M:** I think that the laws seem way too strict, don't you?
   F: Actually, no. I don't think so.
3. **F:** In my opinion, I'd rather have strict laws and safe streets than lenient laws and more crime.
   M: Hmmm. I'm not so sure about that. I think it's a debatable point. But I agree that Singapore is an interesting place.

Unit 2: Protecting Our Planet
Lesson A

Building Vocabulary

Track 11   A. Meaning from Context   Page 24

Save the Whales!

A: Of the 70 species of whales and dolphins, nearly all have been affected by human activities.
B: Does that mean that all whales are endangered?
A: Not all, but many. Most species of baleen whales, such as blue and humpback whales, have been significantly reduced. Their status today is the result of commercial whaling in the 19th and 20th centuries, when whales were exploited for meat and oil. Of the 11 baleen species, nine are currently endangered. We have evidence that many toothed whales are also in danger of dying. Threats to whales include hunting, habitat destruction, and pollution.
B: What kinds of conservation efforts are taking place?
A: Many ongoing conservation strategies are helping whale populations. For example, the International Whaling Commission (IWC) ordered a stop to commercial whaling.

Unfortunately, a number of countries have chosen to violate the rule and continue to kill whales.
B: Can whale populations recover?
A: Although it may be too late for some species, there are some indications that conservation efforts are working. For example, the California gray whale, which was near extinction, has made an amazing recovery. Gray whales were removed from the Endangered Species List.
B: How can I help save the whales?
A: You can help by learning about whales and their habitats. Donate your time to conservation organizations, and alter your behavior so that you create as little waste as possible. If we all participate in these efforts, we can help protect these magnificent animals.

Developing Listening Skills

Listening: A Guided Tour

Track 12   B.   Page 26

Tour Guide: OK, everyone, here's our next exhibit. Do you see the body of the little bird in that bottle? That is a dusky seaside sparrow. It was an old male that died on June 16, 1987. It's kind of sad because he was the very last dusky seaside sparrow in the world. They're now extinct. . . . Yes, you have a question?

Male: Do you know why they became extinct?

Tour Guide: Basically, they lost their habitat. See, the dusky seaside sparrow lived only in one place—on Merritt Island in Florida. The island had a lot of mosquitoes and wetlands. The people on Merritt Island used chemicals to kill the mosquitoes. Those chemicals were also very harmful to the sparrows, and many died. In addition, the people on Merritt Island tried to control and exploit the wetlands. As they altered them, the wetlands were no longer a good habitat for the sparrows. The birds died one by one until there weren't any left.

Track 13   Page 27

Tour Guide: OK, everyone, here's our next exhibit. Do you see the body of the little bird in that bottle? That is a dusky seaside sparrow. It was an old male that died on June 16, 1987. It's kind of sad because he was the very last dusky seaside sparrow in the world. They're now extinct. . . . Yes, you have a question?
Male: Do you know why they became extinct?
Tour Guide: Basically, they lost their habitat. See, the dusky seaside sparrow lived only in one place—on Merritt Island in Florida. The island had a lot of mosquitoes and wetlands. The people on Merritt Island used chemicals to kill the mosquitoes. Those chemicals were also very harmful to the sparrows, and many died. In addition, the people on Merritt Island tried to control and exploit the wetlands. As they altered them, the wetlands were no longer a good habitat for the sparrows. The birds died one by one until there weren't any left.
Female: So, if people were to blame, can't we make sure something like that never happens again?
Tour Guide: We're trying. The situation with the dusky seaside sparrow makes one thing very clear. We need to protect endangered animals. However, it's a better strategy to protect the animals and their habitats, too. After all, if an animal's habitat is destroyed, the animal will likely become extinct.

That's why the Endangered Species Act, which was passed in the United States in 1973, protects both endangered animals and their habitats. For example, the steelhead trout lives in rivers and streams on the west coast of the United States—the Columbia River in Washington state for instance. Recently, both the fish and the river came under the protection of the Endangered Species Act.

Male: But how can we protect large areas such as rivers and forests? No one—not even the government—can afford to buy or control all the land that endangered species live on.

Tour Guide: Good point. In fact, that's what makes the Endangered Species Act difficult to fully enforce. There's an ongoing conflict between some landowners and the government. Take the case of the gray wolf, for instance. At one time, the wolves were common all over North America, but by the 1930s they were nearly all killed. Then in 1973, the wolves came under the protection of the Endangered Species Act, along with huge areas of lands—in Wyoming and Idaho, for example. This angered ranchers. They think they should have the right to shoot wolves that threaten their sheep and cows.

So, landowners may understand the need for the protection of endangered species, but it's understandable that they might also feel that the Endangered Species Act violates their rights. Yes?

Female: Is the law working? I mean, what is the status of endangered species today in the United States?

Tour Guide: Unfortunately, the situation of threatened and endangered animals is *worse* now than in 1973, even with the Endangered Species Act in place. Reports on topics such as habitat loss, deforestation, and overfishing show that the situation for many species is far worse now than it was in 1973.

Let me be more specific . . . right now over 1300 species in the United States are listed as endangered or threatened. And, it's important to keep in mind that not many species are ever taken off the list. Since 1973, in fact, only around 39 species have been removed from the Endangered Species list. But that number doesn't indicate the complete story. What's significant about that number is that only 14 species were removed because they had actually recovered. Nine species became extinct, and the others were removed from the list after scientists found evidence that listing the species had been a mistake in the first place. Meanwhile, another 300 species may soon be added to the list, including a plant, the Las Vegas buckwheat, and an insect, the Miami blue butterfly.

So, you see, even with the Endangered Species Act in place, we're not making as much progress as we would like.

Any more questions? OK, let's move on to the next exhibit. This way, please.

Exploring Spoken English

Track 14   A.   Page 28

1. That's why the Endangered Species Act, which was passed in the United States in 1973, protects both endangered animals and their habitats. For example, the steelhead trout lives in rivers and streams on the west coast of the United States . . .
2. There's an ongoing conflict between some landowners and the government. Take the case of the gray wolf, for instance.
3. Reports on topics such as habitat loss, deforestation, and overfishing show that the situation for many species is far worse now than it was in 1973.
4. Meanwhile, another 300 species may soon be added to the list, including a plant, the Las Vegas buckwheat, and an insect, the Miami blue butterfly.

Lesson B
Building Vocabulary

Track 15   A. Meaning from Context   Page 34

Q: What does a fish biologist do?

A: Well, lots of things. I teach at a university and research ways to maintain fish populations. I spend a lot of time trying to raise funds for research and contacting authorities to get permission for the research I want to do. And I get to travel around the world and educate people about sustainable fishing.

Q: What's the focus of your research?

A: My interest is to protect large freshwater fish and their habitats. Forty percent of the freshwater fish in North America are in danger of extinction. That's 700 endangered species. And that's just in North America! Each year, when I join other biologists for our annual meeting, someone reports on the extinction of another species. That's hard to hear.

Q: Don't you get discouraged?

A: On the contrary, it just makes me want to work harder. I've always loved water, and I've always loved fish. I'm inspired to do what I can to help them survive.

Q: If you could tell people to do one thing to help save freshwater fish, what would it be?

A: Get involved! Contribute as much time as you can. Volunteer to help clean up a river, or write letters to politicians to make them aware of the issues. Above all, don't ignore the problem because things are not going to get better without our help.

Developing Listening Skills
Listening: A Student Debate

Track 16   Page 36

Professor: OK, settle down, everyone. As you know, today we're going to hear our first student debate. Today's topic is on the pros and cons of legalized hunting. First, Yumi will present arguments in support of hunting. Raoul will respond to her points and present his arguments against hunting. Speakers, are you ready?

Raoul: Yes. / **Yumi:** Ready.

Professor: Yumi, please begin.

Yumi: Thank you. Well, the main argument I want to make today is that hunting contributes to wildlife conservation in a few important ways. First, uh, contrary to what you might think, hunting actually helps many species survive by controlling their populations. So, for example, without hunting, deer populations would be too large, and many animals would starve because there wouldn't be enough food to sustain them.

Raoul: That's a good argument, but I think you're ignoring an important point. Another reason deer populations could grow too large is because we have killed off wolves and mountain lions . . . um, and other animals that used to hunt deer. So, instead of allowing humans to hunt, we should allow populations of meat-eating animals to recover.

Yumi: OK, but don't forget that wolves and mountain lions don't just eat deer and elk. They also eat sheep . . . and cows, and that's, that's a problem for ranchers. So, this is not a simple issue.

Anyway, let me continue with my next point. The second way that hunting supports wildlife conservation is through the sale of stamps. Many hunters have to buy stamps before they can legally hunt birds—for instance, ducks and geese. Oh, and when I say stamps, I don't mean the type of stamps you use to mail a letter. The stamps I'm talking about are a kind of license to hunt. In the United

States, the government's Duck Stamp program raises more than 25 million dollars annually. And a lot of that money is used for protecting and maintaining bird habitats. Since 1934—that's when the first stamps were sold—these funds have been used to buy 2.1 million hectares of land for wildlife conservation. So, as you can see, hunters actually help wildlife conservation efforts.

Professor: Thank you, Yumi. Now let's hear from Raoul, who will present the other side of the issue.

Raoul: Thank you. Before I get started, I want to respond to Yumi's point about money that's raised through the Duck Stamp program. It seems to me that if hunters need a license to kill ducks and other wildlife, we could also make tourists pay when they visit and observe animals in their natural habitats. In fact, I think that's what the national parks do. I visited Yosemite National Park last May, and it cost me $20 per car to get in. We could raise those fees if necessary.

OK, so to get back on topic . . . my main argument against hunting is that it's cruel. Many animals that are shot don't die immediately. It must be really painful and, um, that's why hunting should be outlawed.

Yumi: I have to respond to that. Do you eat steak? What about the suffering of cows when they are killed for meat? Do you care about that? Most hunters are careful to cause as little suffering as possible.

Raoul: Maybe most hunters do, but not all. Some hunters leave wounded animals to die slowly and painfully as the hunters pose for photographs. And some, some kill large numbers of animals that they have no intention of eating.

In addition, there is a lot of irresponsible hunting that goes on. In rural Virginia—where I'm from—some of my neighbors drive the roads at night, using illegal lights to find and shoot deer. They also shoot deer out of season, and that's illegal. And in Shenandoah National Park in Virginia, authorities recently caught a group of hunters who were shooting black bears and selling their body parts for medicines.

Yumi: You're right that these kinds of violations occur. However, they are rare. That's why you read about them in the newspapers when they happen. Instead of focusing on the small number of irresponsible hunters, we need to think about the 98 percent of hunters who follow the law and kill only what they can eat. Hunters make it possible for the rest of us to enjoy seeing wild animals in their natural habitat.

Professor: I'm afraid that's all the time we have. Thanks to both Yumi and Raoul for contributing their arguments to our debate. Now, let's take a vote. Which side of the issue do you find more convincing? After listening to our speakers, are you in favor of hunting or against it?

Pronunciation

Pronouncing -s endings

Track 17   Page 37

ducks, hunts, photographs
bears, bees, mangroves
grasses, buzzes, fishes, catches

ducks in danger
hunts after dark
bears and deer
dollars annually

Track 18   B.   Page 37

1. government's
2. hunters
3. crashes
4. whales
5. elks
6. boys
7. stamps
8. passes

Track 19   C.   Page 37

government's actions	crashes into
elks' antlers	stamps in use
hunters' activities	whales ahead
species of birds	passes out

Exploring Spoken English

Track 20   A.   Page 38

1. **Yumi:** Without hunting, deer populations would be too large, and many animals would starve because there wouldn't be enough food to sustain them.
   Raoul: That's a good argument, but I think you're ignoring an important point.
2. **Raoul:** So, instead of allowing humans to hunt, we should allow populations of meat-eating animals to recover.
   Yumi: OK, but don't forget that wolves and mountain lions don't just eat deer and elk.
3. **Raoul:** And in Shenandoah National Park in Virginia, authorities recently caught a group of hunters who were shooting black bears and selling their body parts for medicines.
   Yumi: You are right that these kinds of violations occur. However, they are rare.

Unit 3: Beauty and Appearance
Lesson A

Building Vocabulary

Track 21   A. Meaning from Context   Page 44

In the world of high-fashion models, you don't see the variations in body type that you find with random people on the street. In fact, the classic runway model is skinny, or thin. Many people are disturbed by extremely thin models in fashion shows and magazines. Some models have a height-to-weight ratio that is unhealthy. For example, a model with an unhealthy height-to-weight ratio might be around five feet six inches tall (173 centimeters tall) but weigh only 108 pounds (49 kilograms).

The modeling business is slowly evolving, and the type of model that designers prefer is changing. In the past, fashion shows consistently featured extremely skinny models. Now, healthy-looking models are also appearing on runways. In some countries—Australia, for example—the government has even asked fashion designers and magazines to stop hiring extremely thin models for fashion shows and photo shoots. Now when designers think about presenting their clothes in a fashion show, they often envision their clothes on people with different body types. As a result, people's perception of fashion models and their opinion of what constitutes beauty are starting to change.

Developing Listening Skills

Listening: A News Report

Track 22   Pages 46–47

Announcer:

What is beauty? An often-quoted expression is "beauty is only skin deep." In other words, someone can be beautiful on the outside, but be mean or unpleasant on the inside. Another famous saying is "beauty is in the eye of the beholder." That is to say, each person's idea of beauty is different. But is it true that each person perceives beauty differently? Or, does our social and cultural background influence our ideas about beauty? We turn to reporter Gwen Silva for the answer to this question.

Reporter:

It's said that beauty lies in the eye of the beholder, yet the opposite seems to be true. People within a culture usually have similar ideas about beauty. Numerous studies on beauty have had surprising results. These studies have shown that most people believe that average faces are the most beautiful faces.

It was Judith Langlois, a professor of psychology at the University of Texas, who showed that most people think average-looking faces are beautiful. In addition, the research shows that a beautiful face is a symmetrical face. To put it another way, if both sides of the face are exactly the same, we consider a person beautiful. Extreme variations in symmetry are usually not considered beautiful, Langlois says, and may even be disturbing to observers.

The latest research on facial beauty was completed by psychologists Pamela M. Pallett, Stephen Link, and Kang Lee. These researchers were interested in finding out if there was a relationship between the parts of the face that people considered to be most beautiful.

So, in four separate experiments the researchers asked university students to compare images of twelve faces. Each face was actually the same person—but there were different distances between the eyes and the mouth.

After the experiments, the researchers discovered a "golden ratio"—the ideal distance between the eyes, the mouth, and the edge of the face. Faces were judged most beautiful when the distance between the eyes and the mouth was 36 percent of the length of the face. Not surprisingly, these measurements are exactly those of an "average" face.

Scientists have also studied the role of beauty in the attraction between the sexes. In studies by psychologists Victor Johnston and David Perrett, men consistently preferred women with large eyes, full lips, and a small nose and chin. Think of classic beauties such as Elizabeth Taylor and Audrey Hepburn or, nowadays, Angelina Jolie or Halle Berry. This preference for big eyes and full lips is not random. According to anthropologist Don Symons, the brain tells men that full lips and big eyes equal health and the ability to produce healthy babies. It's an instinct that has evolved over a hundred thousand years, Symons believes.

However, not everyone agrees. Anthropologists do not agree that there is one standard idea of beauty. Around the world, different cultures have different ideas about what constitutes beauty. For example, the Mayan people of Central America considered crossed eyes beautiful. A number of African tribes think scars make both men and women more beautiful. Among the Maori people of Australia, a woman is considered most beautiful when her lips are tattooed blue.

It does appear, therefore, that the old saying is wrong: Beauty does not lie in the eye of the beholder . . . well, at least not entirely. People from the same culture usually envision beauty in the same way, but there are many variations—and many different types of beauty—around the world. This has been Gwen Silva, reporting.

Exploring Spoken English

Track 23   A.   Page 48

1. An often-quoted expression is "beauty is only skin deep." In other words, someone can be beautiful on the outside, but be mean or unpleasant on the inside.
2. Another famous saying is "beauty is in the eye of the beholder." That is to say, each person's idea of beauty is different.
3. In addition, the research shows that a beautiful face is a symmetrical face. To put it another way, if both sides of the face are exactly the same, we consider a person beautiful.

Lesson B

Building Vocabulary

Track 24   A. Using a Dictionary   Page 54

1. Joanne tried to convince Steven to enter his design in the fashion show.
2. Eco-fashion is an alternative type of fashion that uses recycled materials.
3. The artist is going to exhibit her latest work at a museum in Barcelona.
4. The workers in that textile factory are treated fairly and paid well.
5. To sew the dress, insert the needle into the fabric and make small stitches.
6. You can derive a light, smooth fabric called rayon from plant cells.
7. The architect will integrate traditional and modern elements in the building he is designing.
8. My new job as a nurse pays considerably more than my old job as an office worker.
9. They will transport the trees to the park by truck.
10. The fashion show will be sometime in May, but the exact date is not yet definite.

Developing Listening Skills

Listening: An Informal Conversation

Track 25   Pages 56–57

Sandra: I'm so hungry. I hope the food comes soon.
David: Me, too.
Ana: I'm not so hungry yet, so I don't mind waiting. Hey—by the way—I forgot to ask you about the fashion show? Dad, did you like it?
David: Actually, yes. I'm really glad your mother convinced me to go. It was really interesting.
Ana: And did you like it too, Mom?
Sandra: I did. It certainly wasn't a boring fashion show. The clothes were so imaginative, weren't they?
David: Yes.
Sandra: That antigravity jacket was like a piece of science fiction.
Ana: Antigravity jacket? What exactly is an antigravity jacket?
David: I guess you could say it's a balloon.
Sandra: Right . . . well, it's part balloon, but it's also part jacket. When the wearer takes it off, it just floats in mid-air like a balloon.
Ana: That sounds cool!
Sandra: Oh, it was. The designer, Alex Soza, said he gets his ideas from daydreams, and the antigravity jacket was just one of his daydreams.

David: That jacket was interesting, I guess. But what amazed me was the vest made of Kevlar.

Ana: Sorry, what does Kevlar mean?

David: Well, Kevlar is a man-made fiber and they use it to make a cloth which is stronger than steel. You've probably heard of it before. Police officers wear Kevlar—or bullet-proof vests—sometimes to make sure they don't get hurt if they are shot.

Ana: Oh, that's right. I know what you're talking about now.

Sandra: Kevlar is used in ropes, too—for astronauts in space.

David: A model dressed as a police officer was walking a police dog, and the dog was wearing a Kevlar vest.

Sandra: Oh, yeah. That dog was cute, wasn't he?

Ana: It's amazing that Kevlar can actually stop bullets! It must be very strong.

David: Oh, yes, it is. But it was developed back in the 1960s. These days they're working on fibers that are considerably stronger.

Ana: Really? Like what, for example?

Sandra: Well, they said at the fashion show that spider silk is a natural fiber that is five times as strong as steel. And textile manufacturers would love to get a lot of spider silk at once, but it's difficult to raise large groups of spiders together.

Ana: Why?

David: Umm, because spiders sometimes eat each other.

Ana: Eww!

Sandra: Instead, some scientists have found an interesting alternative. They call it BioStrong, don't they?

David: Actually, no, I think it's called BioSteel.

Sandra: Oh, that's right. Scientists make BioSteel by inserting the spider-silk gene into goats. So, now the goats produce spider-silk protein in their milk, and scientists have derived a super-strong fiber from the goat milk.

Ana: That's neat. What do they use it for?

Sandra: They said that instead of using rockets to transport things into space, they envision that BioSteel will help pull things up to space and down again without having to use rockets.

Ana: That's really amazing.

David: So, what did you do this weekend, Ana?

Ana: Well, my friend was exhibiting some of her designs at an art gallery downtown, so I went there. She designs wearable electronics.

Sandra: What do you mean by wearable electronics?

Ana: Well, wearable electronics integrate clothes and electronics. She makes some really useful pieces—for example, a jacket with a cell phone right in the collar. My favorite item though was the GPS sneakers, um, sneakers with a global positioning system in them . . . to allow parents to track lost children or rescue teams to track lost hikers.

David: How innovative! And it sounds really useful, too.

Ana: Oh, yes, definitely. Now, where's our food? I'm starving.

Pronunciation

Pronouncing / ŋ / and / ŋk /

Track 26   Page 57

/ŋ/   song, walking, ring
/ŋk/ uncle, ankle

Exploring Spoken English

Track 27   A.   Page 58

1. **Sandra:** That antigravity jacket was like a piece of science fiction.
   Ana: Antigravity jacket? What exactly is an antigravity jacket?

2. **David:** That jacket was interesting, I guess. But what amazed me was the vest made of Kevlar.
   Ana: Sorry, what does Kevlar mean?

3. **Ana:** Well, my friend was exhibiting some of her designs at an art gallery downtown, so I went there. She designs wearable electronics.
   Sandra: What do you mean by wearable electronics?

 CD 2

Unit 4: Energy Issues
Lesson A
Building Vocabulary

Track 2   A. Meaning from Context   Page 64

On April 20, 2010, one of the worst oil spills in history began in the Gulf of Mexico. The spill occurred at an oil rig, called the Deepwater Horizon, which is owned by the BP company. A buildup of pressure caused natural gas to shoot up suddenly from the ocean floor. The gas triggered a terrible explosion and a fire on the oil rig. After the explosion, the crew abandoned the platform and escaped in lifeboats. Unfortunately, 11 workers were never found.

For weeks, no one was sure how much oil was being released into the Gulf of Mexico. Gradually, information about the damage from the oil spill emerged. It was discovered that between 50,000 to 60,000 barrels of oil a day were flowing into the Gulf. Experts from BP and other organizations tried to stop the spill, but it continued for nearly three months. By the time the leak was stopped, the beautiful blue waters of the Gulf had been contaminated with nearly 5 million barrels of oil.

The disaster did serious harm to the fishing and tourism industries in the southern United States. Pictures of birds that had been exposed to the thick oil appeared daily in the news. The American public reacted angrily, and the spill created a huge controversy. Some people even wanted to stop oil companies from drilling in the Gulf of Mexico. BP set aside 20 billion dollars to compensate fishermen, hotel owners, and store owners whose businesses were impacted by the spill.

Developing Listening Skills
Listening: A Guest Speaker

Track 3   A.   Page 66

Professor: OK, everyone, can I have your attention please? Today we're going to continue to talk about energy issues. And, as promised, we have a guest speaker. Please welcome Dr. Alexandra Campbell, who is an expert on nuclear energy. She will be talking about the Chernobyl nuclear accident and nuclear energy in today's world. Feel free to ask her questions, just as you would ask me. Doctor?

Dr. Campbell: Thank you, professor, and hello, everyone. Well, first let me give you some background information. In the 1970s and 1980s, the former Soviet Union was developing nuclear energy technology. By 1986, it had 25 working nuclear power plants, but many of them had safety problems.

On April 26, 1986—just before 1:30 in the morning—the Chernobyl Nuclear Power Plant's number four reactor exploded. It appears that some mistakes were made during a safety test. The temperature of the nuclear reactor went up too high, and the water that cooled the reactor down turned into steam, which made the problem worse. The reactor—which was old-fashioned and unsafe—exploded. The explosion destroyed the building and started a terrible fire. I want to emphasize that Chernobyl had no containment structure. This building would have limited the fire and contained the radioactivity. Two power plant workers were killed in the explosion.

Track 4   Page 66

Professor: OK, everyone, can I have your attention please? Today we're going to continue to talk about energy issues. And, as promised, we have a guest speaker. Please welcome Dr. Alexandra Campbell, who is an expert on nuclear energy. She will be talking about the Chernobyl nuclear accident and nuclear energy in today's world. Feel free to ask her questions, just as you would ask me. Doctor?

Dr. Campbell: Thank you, professor, and hello, everyone. Well, first let me give you some background information. In the 1970s and 1980s, the former Soviet Union was developing nuclear energy technology. By 1986, it had 25 working nuclear power plants, but many of them had safety problems.

On April 26, 1986—just before 1:30 in the morning—the Chernobyl Nuclear Power Plant's number four reactor exploded. It appears that some mistakes were made during a safety test. The temperature of the nuclear reactor went up too high, and the water that cooled the reactor down turned into steam, which made the problem worse. The reactor—which was old-fashioned and unsafe—exploded. The explosion destroyed the building and started a terrible fire. I want to emphasize that Chernobyl had no containment structure. This building would have limited the fire and contained the radioactivity. Two power plant workers were killed in the explosion.

Female Student 1: Excuse me, Doctor? Was there a city anywhere near the power plant?

Dr. Campbell: Um, yes, there was, and it's very sad, really. The closest city was called Pripyat. It was a beautiful city, and the residents loved living there, of course. At first, when the reactor exploded, people were told to stay indoors and keep their windows closed. Other residents didn't really know how to react to the explosion. Some children still went to school that day. The children were told to go straight home after school and not play outside, but some children stayed outside anyway. They were exposed to a lot of radiation. City workers emerged and gave out medicine to protect people against some of the radiation. Then 1000 buses arrived to take people away from the town. And so, by 5 P.M., Pripyat was empty. Any more questions right now?

OK, great. Let me get back to the events of the accident. Soon after the explosion, 22 more workers and six firefighters died from the radiation that was released during the accident. The fire at the power plant burned for 10 days. And the smoke from the fire—well, it was full of radioactive materials, which spread quickly and contaminated tens of thousands of square miles of land in what is now northern Ukraine, southern Belarus, and parts of Russia. It was the worst nuclear accident the world has ever seen. As a direct result of the Chernobyl disaster, 300,000 people were forced to leave their homes, and the radiation triggered thyroid cancer in thousands of young people. Over the years, the economic losses—I mean the health and cleanup costs, compensation to the victims, lost work—have cost hundreds of billions of dollars. Yes, you have a question?

Male Student: Is the Chernobyl power plant still radioactive?

Dr. Campbell: Yes, that's a good question. The power plant is still extremely radioactive. There has been some controversy about how long it has taken to make this area safe again. Right now, there is a plan to build a huge concrete shell over the entire power plant that will finally seal it off.

Male Student: I have another question. How exactly did the radioactivity hurt the people who were nearby?

Dr. Campbell: Well, children were drinking milk—for example—that contained a radioactive substance. Cows had eaten contaminated grass, and it got into the milk. The substance affected the thyroid glands of children and caused cancer in many of them. Thyroid cancer can be cured, but it's important to remember that survivors must spend a lifetime taking medication. By the time the last victim dies, Chernobyl will have taken nearly 4000 lives—that's according to the International Atomic Energy Agency.

Female Student 2: Will the radioactivity ever disappear?

Dr. Campbell: Well, that depends on the radioactive material. Right now, many areas are still contaminated with a material called cesium 137. Cesium 137 has a half-life of about 30 years. That means if you start with two kilograms of cesium 137, one kilogram will have disappeared after 30 years.

Female Student 1: Are there any people living near Chernobyl now?

Dr. Campbell: This is very interesting, actually. Right after the accident, the government created an exclusion zone around the plant. Everybody had to leave, and the land was abandoned. But believe it or not, about 400 people, mainly the elderly, live in this area today. Many of them just couldn't get used to living in another place, and so they came back. Let me stress, however, that it will be decades before large numbers of people are allowed to come back and live in the exclusion zone.

Also, an amazing thing has happened. Wildlife has been coming back to the area of the exclusion zone. Wild horses, for example, live in the Chernobyl exclusion zone. What's really interesting about these particular horses, though, is that they are extinct in the wild. They can only be found in a few nature reserves and in the Chernobyl exclusion zone. You can also see deer, wolves, eagles, and even bears there, just to mention a few more examples.

OK, so now let's move on to another topic.

Exploring Spoken English

Track 5   A.   Page 68

1. I want to emphasize that Chernobyl had no containment structure. This building would have limited the fire and contained the radioactivity.
2. Thyroid cancer can be cured, but it's important to remember that survivors must spend a lifetime taking medication.
3. Let me stress, however, that it will be decades before large numbers of people are allowed to come back and live in the exclusion zone.

Lesson B
Building Vocabulary

Track 6   A. Meaning from Context   Page 74

When oil was inexpensive and abundant, people learned to depend on it for heat and fuel. More recently, oil has been more difficult to find, as it is hidden deep beneath the earth under many layers of solid rock. There have even been oil shortages, and we have had to wait in long lines and pay high prices for gasoline. A serious disadvantage of oil, coal, and similar fuels is the pollution they create around our cities.

Today, researchers are focusing on energy sources beyond oil. Countries and companies are pursuing alternative energy. They are looking for energy sources that are renewable and can never be used up. These alternative energies follow the principle that energy production should be sustainable, not temporary. People are showing a lot of enthusiasm for new energy technologies such as wind and hydroelectric power. Government incentives in the form of money or tax breaks have helped convince some companies to develop alternative energy technologies. Experts think that in the future the world will utilize alternative energy for a larger percentage of its total energy needs.

Developing Listening Skills
Listening: A Study Group Discussion

Track 7   Page 76

Jim: I'm glad you could all make it to tonight's study group. It's amazing, but in just two weeks we will have been meeting for three months. So anyway, I figured tonight we could rehearse for our group presentation on renewable energy. Is everyone ready to get started?

Tina/Michael/Anna: Sure. / Yeah. / Uh-huh.

Jim: OK, so we decided that I would speak first and review some facts about traditional energy sources, uh, fossil fuels. So, here I go . . . I'll start by talking about oil, which is no longer cheap—which you know if you've put gas in your car lately. By 2020, we will have been drilling oil wells for over 160 years. But the wells are getting deeper and more expensive to drill. And then there's natural gas, which is cleaner than oil but hard to transport and—and prone to shortages. Finally, coal. Well, it's true that we're not going to run out of coal anytime soon . . . but it causes air pollution and possibly contributes to the greenhouse effect, you know, climate change. In conclusion, I'll emphasize that these facts show why we need to pursue alternative sources of energy.

Track 8   Page 76

Jim: And now, I'll turn it over to Tina, who's going to talk about solar energy.

Tina: OK, good. Thanks, Jim. As we know from class, solar energy utilizes the power of the sun to produce electricity. To begin, you need a solar cell. Solar cells are made of several thin layers of special materials. When the sun hits this material, it causes electrons to start moving around, and that creates an electric current. It's a very simple principle.

So, in this process there's no fire and no pollution. Also, solar energy is free, and it's 100 percent renewable. The problem is that the cells are costly, and that makes solar energy a lot more expensive than other forms of energy. Another problem is that clouds and darkness can shut off the energy supply, and today's battery technology isn't good enough to store enough power. Still, like most electronic things, solar power has been getting cheaper and battery technology is getting better all the time, so the future looks promising. That's it for me. Who's next? Michael?

Michael: Yes, my turn. OK, I'm going to talk about wind power. So, today most wind power comes from turbines. They can be as tall as a 20-story building, and they have three long blades. They look like giant airplane propellers on sticks. Maybe you've seen them around. Anyway, the wind spins the blades, which turn a shaft. The shaft is connected to a generator that produces electricity. The biggest wind turbines generate enough electricity to supply about 600 modern homes. Wind farms have tens and sometimes hundreds of these turbines lined up together in particularly windy spots. But even one small turbine in your backyard can produce enough electricity for a single home or for a small business. Wind is a clean source of renewable energy that produces no emissions, so there's no air or water pollution. And since wind is free, wind energy costs almost nothing once a turbine is raised. Turbines are getting cheaper, and many governments offer financial incentives for wind-energy development.

On the downside, some people disapprove of wind turbines because they're ugly. They also complain about the noise the machines make, although most people think it's fine to put up wind turbines on farmlands. But there are other challenges, too. When the wind stops blowing, the turbines don't produce any energy, so power plants that run on coal or oil need to be standing by. Also, like for solar power, we don't know yet how to store wind energy produced by turbines. That's all I have.

Jim: Good job. And finally, Anna is going to present information on hydroelectric power. Take it away, Anna.

Anna: All right. Uh, when most people think of alternative energy, they probably think about solar or wind power, but hydroelectricity is actually the number-one renewable energy source in the world today. So—for those of you who don't know—hydroelectricity is when electricity is generated by falling or flowing water.

The most common way of producing hydroelectricity is by building dams. I'm sure you've seen pictures of dams—the High Aswan Dam in Egypt and the Pati Dam in Argentina, for example. These are big dams, but hydroelectricity can also be produced by paddle wheels or ocean waves—any kind of moving water.

There are several reasons why hydroelectric energy is an excellent way to produce power. First of all, water is an abundant resource in many places. And once a hydroelectric dam is built, it doesn't need much maintenance. And, of course, it doesn't need fossil fuels to operate, so there's no pollution.

Hydroelectric power is very cheap, so there's always a lot of enthusiasm when plans to build a new dam are announced. On the other hand, a big disadvantage of hydroelectricity is the terrible damage it does to the environment. A lot of people think it's wrong to destroy animal habitats this way. They also believe it's not right that people are forced to leave their homes. So the decision to build a hydroelectric power plant can create a lot of controversy. OK, that was my part.

Jim: Thanks, Anna. That was awesome, guys. I think we're ready for the presentation. Let's meet again just before class tomorrow, so we can set everything up. OK?

Tina: Sounds good.

Anna: Great.

Michael: See you then.

Pronunciation
Stressing Two-Word Compounds

Track 9   Page 77

book review   footprint   greenhouse   living room   moving van

The peas were grown in a **green**house.
I saw you standing in front of a **green house**.

1. I met an English teacher.
2. I had a glass of orange juice.
3. The police spotted a moving van.
4. Where should I put this hot plate?
5. That's a beautiful yellow jacket.

Exploring Spoken English

Track 11   A.   Page 78

1. On the downside, some people disapprove of wind turbines because they're ugly. They also complain about the noise the machines make, although most people think it's fine to put up wind turbines on farmlands.
2. A lot of people think it's wrong to destroy animal habitats this way. They also believe it's not right that people are forced to leave their homes.

Unit 5: Migration
Lesson A

Building Vocabulary

Track 12   A. Meaning from Context   Page 84

The first migrations in human history were probably voluntary. People chose to leave their birthplace in search of food, water, or living space. Other migrations have been involuntary, which means that people were forced to travel. Between the 16th and 19th centuries, for instance, European slave traders kidnapped an immense number of African natives and transported them against their will to the Americas. There, the Africans encountered a world unlike anything they had ever seen in their native lands. They were forced to work in terrible conditions, and many died young.

The practice of slavery declined in the 18th and 19th centuries. Subsequently, it was made illegal, and the descendants of those early African slaves became free. Africans were absorbed into the cultures of the Americas, and today they are described, for example, as African Americans, Afro-Caribbeans, or Afro-Latin Americans.

In recent years, DNA researchers believe that they have linked the DNA of all humans on our planet with the DNA of African natives. Scientists assume that the entire world was populated as a result of a migration that began in Africa around 70,000 years ago. The implications of this idea would have shocked the European slave traders. They probably would have found it incredible to think that the people all over the world were, in a sense, related to one another.

Developing Listening Skills

Listening: A Radio Show

Track 13   Pages 86–87

Interviewer: Good afternoon, everyone, and welcome to Science Radio! Our program brings you notable members of the scientific community speaking on questions of interest to us all. I'm your host, Matthew Phelps. My guest today is Dr. Howard Corke, a scientist, who will be explaining the implications of some recent genetic discoveries. Dr. Corke, welcome.
Dr. Corke: Thank you, Matthew.

Interviewer: So, Dr. Corke, what exactly is DNA, and how can it teach us about human history?
Dr. Corke: Well, DNA is the genetic material that contains all the information about the structures and functions of our bodies. DNA is passed from parents to children, from generation to generation. Every once in a while, a baby is born with a slight difference in its DNA. This difference, called a mutation, is then passed down to all of that person's descendants, even 50,000 years in the future.
Interviewer: Imagine that!
Dr. Corke: Yes, and when we analyze the DNA of people all over the world, we believe we can understand how people are related to each other. Scientists now think that all humans are related to one woman who lived roughly 150,000 years ago in East Africa. If they're right, all people are linked to that one woman by their mothers.
Interviewer: That's really quite surprising. When do scientists think humans left Africa and spread out over the world?
Dr. Corke: Well, the theory is that 50,000 to 70,000 years ago, a group of humans—a group that might have been as small as just a thousand people—left Africa. From there, this group of people and their descendants migrated all over the world.
Interviewer: Just a thousand people? Where did they go once they left Africa?
Dr. Corke: Well, scientists think they migrated from Africa to the Middle East. Then they broke into two groups. One group settled temporarily in the Middle East, while the second group followed the coast around the Arabian Peninsula, India, and beyond. By about 50,000 years ago, some of these humans had reached Australia.
Interviewer: What about the other group, the group that settled temporarily in the Middle East? What happened to them?
Dr. Corke: Well . . . we think they broke into two groups as well and migrated in two different directions. One group reached Central Asia about 30,000 years ago. The other group went the other way and ended up in southern Europe.
Interviewer: Were there already humans living in Europe or Central Asia at that time?
Dr. Corke: Yes, scientists believe there were. They think that modern humans entering Europe encountered Neanderthals, a less advanced human group. Modern humans entering Central Asia could have run into Neanderthals as well, but in smaller numbers, because Neanderthal populations were smaller in Asia than in Europe.
Interviewer: What happened to the Neanderthals?
Dr. Corke: Scientists assume that the number of Neanderthals declined as they were pushed into smaller areas and finally disappeared. We don't think they were absorbed into the modern human family. If they had been absorbed, DNA analysis would tell us that, you see. The evidence would be there in the DNA of Europeans today.
Interviewer: That's incredible! DNA certainly does tell us a lot. Have DNA researchers been able to understand how humans first came to the Americas?
Dr. Corke: Well, the DNA of some living Native Americans links them to Asia, and more particularly to the people who live in southern Siberia. We think people from southern Siberia crossed over to North America perhaps 15,000 or maybe 20,000 years ago.
Interviewer: I see. And how did they cross the ocean? Did they have large boats?
Dr. Corke: Actually, they probably came across on a land bridge that no longer exists today. Subsequently, as their population grew, they spread across the immense area of North and South America in just a few thousand years.
Interviewer: Fascinating. Thank you so much for your time, Dr. Corke. I hope you'll come back and talk to us again soon. Coming up next, a scientific discovery that may change the way you think about lettuce. First, a word from our sponsors . . .

Exploring Spoken English

Language Function: Expressing Surprise

Track 14   A.   Page 88

No kidding.
That's really surprising.
I'm really surprised to hear that.
I find that quite surprising.
Wow!
That's amazing!
That's astonishing!
That's incredible!
Imagine that!

Track 15   B.   Page 88

1. **Dr. Corke:** This difference, called a mutation, is then passed down to all of that person's descendants, even 50,000 years in the future.
   Interviewer: Imagine that!
2. **Dr. Corke:** If they're right, all people are linked to that one woman by their mothers.
   Interviewer: That's really quite surprising.
3. **Dr. Corke:** We don't think they were absorbed into the modern human family. If they had been absorbed, DNA analysis would tell us that, you see. The evidence would be there in the DNA of Europeans today.
   Interviewer: That's incredible! DNA certainly does tell us a lot.

Lesson B

Building Vocabulary

Track 16   A. Meaning from Context   Page 94

Interviewer: I'm talking with Maxine Felton, a butterfly expert. For more than 20 years, she has dedicated herself to the study of butterflies. What kinds of butterflies do you study, Maxine?
Maxine: I study the monarch butterfly. It is an orange, black, and white butterfly that's approximately 10 centimeters across.
Interviewer: What is special about the monarch butterfly?
Maxine: Well, it is the only butterfly that migrates north to south with the seasons, the same way that many birds do.
Interviewer: How interesting! And how do you follow the monarch butterfly migration?
Maxine: Well, I glue little numbered labels on their wings. The labels help me follow their migration patterns. The labels are small, so they don't interfere with flying. Nighttime is the best time to glue on the labels because monarchs stay on the ground at night. Their flying is restricted to the daylight hours.
Interviewer: And where do the monarchs go in the winter?
Maxine: Many go to the Mexican Monarch Butterfly Reserve. When the butterflies arrive there, they cover the trees in overwhelming numbers.
Interviewer: That must be a beautiful sight! It sounds like there are plenty of monarchs.
Maxine: Well, actually, there are fewer than there once were. There are various threats to monarchs. For example, in the Butterfly Reserve some illegal logging still takes place. In many places, plants such as corn and wheat have displaced many of the milkweed plants that monarchs need for food.
Interviewer: I see. Is there any good news for monarch butterflies?
Maxine: Yes, there is. Many new conservation agencies and areas have been established to protect monarchs. Recently, the World

Wildlife Fund, the Mexican government, and Mexican billionaire Carlos Slim invested 100 million dollars in a fund to protect wildlife in Mexico. Part of the money will go to ensure the continued protection of monarch butterflies in Mexico.

Developing Listening Skills

Listening: A Conversation between Friends

Track 17   Page 96

Sandy: Hi, Larry! Welcome back! How was your trip to Tanzania?
Larry: Oh, it was incredible, Sandy. I was actually in both Tanzania and Kenya and saw the wildebeest migration. I saw them crossing the Mara River. I mean, what a sight. They just kept coming and coming. The numbers were overwhelming!
Sandy: I saw a program about that on TV once. The area you're talking about, it's in the-the Serengeti National Park, isn't it?
Larry: Partly, but the migration isn't restricted to the Serengeti. There are hundreds of thousands of wildebeest, I think—and other animals too—and they migrate around the Serengeti and other parts of Tanzania and Kenya. Altogether the area is called the Serengeti Mara Ecosystem. It's over 100,000 square kilometers big.
Sandy: Wow! So much land dedicated to wildlife.
Larry: Yeah, well, unfortunately, it's not as much as it used to be. Our guide said that the ecosystem had shrunk to half of its former size because of the growing human population. It would be ideal if there were enough land for people and for animals, but there isn't.
Sandy: What do you mean? Isn't it a national park? I mean, doesn't that mean that the animals are protected and that humans are restricted from hurting them?
Larry: Well, yeah, but it's a tricky situation. So, the Serengeti National Park was established in 1950, and some local hunters—called the Ikoma people—were forced to move outside the park so that they wouldn't interfere with the animals.
Sandy: Oh, wow, that must have been incredibly difficult for them.
Larry: Yeah, I'm sure it was. So nowadays, this group of approximately 3000 people lives in a village called Robanda just outside the western gates of the Serengeti National Park. They make a living by selling stuff to the tourists who come to the park. But some people believe they're also hunting, eating, and selling wild animal meat, which is illegal.
Sandy: Why would they do that?
Larry: Well, the meat of wild animals—they call it "bush meat" in Africa—feeds more than a million people in northern Tanzania alone.
Sandy: No kidding? I see what you mean when you say the situation is tricky. They probably never wanted to move out of the park, and I bet they feel that the Serengeti in some sense still belongs to them.
Larry: It gets even trickier. There's a very powerful eco-tourism group that runs safaris in the Serengeti. They've invested maybe . . . millions of dollars in Tanzania to protect the Serengeti Mara Ecosystem and to fight illegal hunting. So, they're dedicated to protecting wildlife . . . but at the same time they also want to protect their business. Anyway, they've offered to pay the villagers of Robanda to move again.
Sandy: The villagers can't have been happy about being asked to move again.
Larry: Of course not. They love their land, and they have deep roots there. They say the eco-tourism company is their enemy. But that's not exactly true.
Sandy: Why not?

Larry: Because the eco-tourism company also tries to help the villagers. They build schools, drill new wells, um, and they provide job training so that villagers are less dependent on bush meat for survival.

Sandy: Hmm. I really hope that some compromise can be reached. I don't want the people of Robanda to be displaced again.

Larry: Me, too. But at least the animals there are doing all right.

Sandy: So, what kind of animals did you see?

Larry: Well, the wildebeest of course. And zebras, lions, elephants, black rhinos . . . you name it, I saw it.

Sandy: What a wonderful trip you had! I'm really jealous! It would be great to go on a trip like that. Can you show me some of your photos?

Larry: Sure, but give me some time to edit them, OK? I took more than 2000 pictures.

Pronunciation

Using Question Intonation

Track 18   Page 97

Do you have the time?
Can you show me the pictures you took?
How was your trip?
When did you get there?

Track 19   A.   Page 97

1. Have you ever tried bush meat? Would you like to?
2. Why do animals migrate? What about humans?
3. Is migrating dangerous for animals? What are the risks?
4. How many tourists visit Tanzania each year?
5. Do you enjoy photography?
6. Should the people of Robanda be forced to move?

Exploring Spoken English

Track 20   A.   Page 98

1. **Larry:** It would be ideal if there were enough land for people and for animals, but there isn't.
2. **Sandy:** Hmm. I really hope that some compromise can be reached.
3. **Sandy:** What a wonderful trip you had! I'm really jealous! It would be great to go on a trip like that.

Unit 6: Tradition and Progress
Lesson A

Building Vocabulary

Track 21   A. Meaning from Context   Page 104

Long ago, people lived as hunters and gatherers. Over time people learned how to grow plants and raise domestic animals. Once this happened, there was a transition to agriculture in many societies. However, even today there are groups who reject farming and continue to hunt animals and gather their own food.

The Hadza people are a group of hunter-gatherers who live in an isolated part of northern Tanzania. They have lived in the Great Rift Valley for a period of 10,000 years. The Hadza communicate in their own special language called Hadzane.

The Hadza are not part of the modern economic system of Tanzania. When they are hungry, they can hunt or gather what they need for free. Hadza [   ] make a little money by displaying their hunting skills [   ]s. It is an interesting contradiction that although the Hadza have very little, they share a lot. In fact, they share everything they have with others.

In the Great Rift Valley, modern farming has spread in recent years, and this development has had serious consequences for the Hadza. Their homeland is now only 25 percent of the size it was in the 1950s. Hunting is now more difficult for them, as there are fewer animals than before. The Hadza people anticipate that their way of life will disappear in the near future.

Developing Listening Skills

Listening: A Student Presentation

Track 22   A. Listening for Main Ideas   Page 106

Teacher: OK, class, let's get started with the first presentation. Sompel has prepared a short presentation about his home country of Bhutan. Go ahead, Sompel.

Sompel: Thanks. Um, hi, everybody! You know that my name is Sompel, but you may not know that I'm from Bhutan. Bhutan is a small country—high in the Himalaya Mountains—between India and China. In our language, Bhutan is known as *Druk Yul*, which in English is . . . land, land of the thunder dragon. The dragon is even displayed on our flag.

For many years, my country was isolated from the world, partly due to its geography—it is surrounded by high mountains—but also because of government policies. Our government had always been a, an absolute monarchy, I mean, a government headed by a king with unlimited power. Anyway, until very recently, Bhutan had no electricity, no cars or trucks, no telephones, and no postal service. You may be surprised to learn that in Bhutan people have only had television since 1999. It was the last country on Earth to get it.

You may be wondering: Why did Bhutan reject the modern world for so long?

Well . . . the government was trying to protect the people from negative influences such as high crime rates, youth violence, and pollution. But the king has admitted that the policy of isolation had many negative consequences. For example, the education system definitely fell behind. Some people never learned to read and write. Then, one of our kings began opening up Bhutan to the outside world, and our current king has continued the process. There are new roads, schools, and health clinics. The king doesn't want to open up the country all at once to the outside world and risk ruining it. He wants our country's development to be guided by . . .now let me think . . . oh, yes, Gross National Happiness.

Teacher: Sompel, sorry to interrupt . . . before you continue, could you define Gross National Happiness for the class, please?

Sompel: Um, sure. How should I put it? Well, you've probably heard of gross national product, which is a phrase that refers to the dollar value of all the goods and services produced by a country over a period of time. It's one way of measuring a country's success. But, Gross National Happiness is different. Actually, one of our kings invented the phrase *Gross National Happiness*. It's the approach the country takes to the domestic development of Bhutan—to help make sure that the people are always happy with their lives and with the country. There are four parts, um, four "pillars," to this approach: good government, sustainable development, environmental protection, and cultural preservation.

So, for good government, the king puts the needs of the country first. In fact, even though the people love him, he gave away most of his power to the people in 2006. That's when the country transitioned to democracy. The king still has an important role, but he no longer has absolute power. Real power belongs to the people and the officials that we elect.

Sustainable development means that we help our country grow without damaging the environment. And the pillar of environmental protection is closely related to sustainable development, too. Agriculture is very important in Bhutan, and we are trying to find new ways to farm without hurting the environment. Also, the government wants to keep 68 percent of the land covered in forests.

Cultural preservation—the last pillar—is a challenge though. Half of Bhutan's population is in their twenties or younger, and the government anticipates that some young people will get involved with gangs, crime, or drugs, for example. The government has banned television channels that they think are harmful. Even so, youth gangs are growing. Theft, which was not very common before, is also rising.

On the other hand, there is a positive side to all of the changes. In a mountainous country such as Bhutan, communication technologies—for instance, mobile phones and the Internet—allow people to communicate more easily than ever before. And it seems that the arts are really moving ahead. Twenty years ago, Bhutan had never produced a movie, but these days we produce over 20 a year. And some movies have even displayed the difficulties that Bhutan has had with the challenges of the modern world. These types of movies are important. They can help us explore the contradictions that have come with our changing culture.

Teacher: Sompel, how do you view Bhutan's future?

Sompel: Well, I'm hopeful about Bhutan's future. And I'm glad that the approach of Gross National Happiness is helping to make sure that we don't lose our beautiful environment and the best parts of our ancient culture.

Track 23   B. Completing an Idea Map   Page 107

Sompel: Um, sure. How should I put it? Well, you've probably heard of gross national product, which is a phrase that refers to the dollar value of all the goods and services produced by a country over a period of time. It's one way of measuring a country's success. But, Gross National Happiness is different. Actually, one of our kings invented the phrase *Gross National Happiness*. It's the approach the country takes to the domestic development of Bhutan—to help make sure that the people are always happy with their lives and with the country. There are four parts, um, four "pillars," to this approach: good government, sustainable development, environmental protection, and cultural preservation.

So, for good government, the king puts the needs of the country first. In fact, even though the people love him, he gave away most of his power to the people in 2006. That's when the country transitioned to democracy. The king still has an important role, but he no longer has absolute power. Real power belongs to the people and the officials that we elect.

Sustainable development means that we help our country grow without damaging the environment. And the pillar of environmental protection is closely related to sustainable development, too. Agriculture is very important in Bhutan, and we are trying to find new ways to farm without hurting the environment. Also, the government wants to keep 68 percent of the land covered in forests.

Cultural preservation—the last pillar—is a challenge though. Half of Bhutan's population is in their twenties or younger, and the government anticipates that some young people will get involved with gangs, crime, or drugs, for example. The government has banned television channels that they think are harmful. Even so, youth gangs are growing. Theft, which was not very common before, is also rising.

On the other hand, there is a positive side to all of the changes. In a mountainous country such as Bhutan, communication technologies—for instance, mobile phones and the Internet—allow people to communicate more easily than ever before. And it seems that the arts are really moving ahead. Twenty years ago Bhutan had never produced a movie, but these days we produce over 20 a year. And some movies have even displayed the difficulties that Bhutan has had with the challenges of the modern world. These types of movies are important. They can help us explore the contradictions that have come with our changing culture.

Exploring Spoken English

Track 24   A.   Page 108

1. He wants our country's development to be guided by . . . now let me think . . . oh, yes, Gross National Happiness.
2. There are four parts . . . um . . . four "pillars" to this approach: good government, sustainable development, environmental protection, and cultural preservation.

Lesson B
Building Vocabulary

Track 25   B.   Page 114

Saving the World's Languages

A: What is happening to the world's languages?

B: Well, most people don't know that a language dies every 14 days. When a language dies, no one can speak the language anymore. *National Geographic* helped found a project to save the world's most unique languages.

A: How many languages are dying?

B: Scientists think that over half of the languages spoken today may no longer exist in 2100. In Chile, for example, the Huilliche language may die soon. Only a small portion of people can speak the language and most of the speakers are over 70 years old.

A: Why does a language disappear?

B: There are many reasons. Governments sometimes create federal policies that tell citizens to speak only one language. Also, people may forget a language if they do not speak it often.

A: What made you undertake the task of trying to save these languages?

B: Language is the key to understanding how speakers think and communicate. Our objective is to help people keep their cultures alive. From my perspective as a scientist, I think our work is very important.

A: What do you do to help groups regain dying languages?

B: We enable people to study their language by giving them recording devices. We make dictionaries, and we highlight how people can teach their language to others. In the future, we can grant access to the recordings so people can learn the language and keep it alive.

Developing Listening Skills

Listening: A Study Group Discussion

Track 26   Pages 116-117

Jose: So, are you all ready to review for the test?
Matt, Amina: Yes. / Sure.
Jose: What should we review first?
Amina: I think we should start with the chapter on Native Americans. There is a lot of information in that chapter.
Lauren: Oh, definitely.
Jose: OK. So what do you think were the most important facts from that chapter?
Matt: Well, I found the whole chapter interesting. You know, when I was growing up, we didn't learn much about Native Americans in school.
Amina: Me, neither. I had no idea that there are more than 300 Native American reservations in the United States, did you?
Jose: No, I definitely didn't. And I wasn't aware that the reservations only make up two percent of the total land area of the United States. I thought it was a lot more.
Matt: Really?
Lauren: Well, just think, that's only a small portion of the land they used to have.
Jose: Yes. And it seems that the land is very important to them. It's a big part of their culture and traditions.
Amina: Right. Native Americans believe in living in harmony with the land, the plants, and the animals. They have a lot of knowledge about these things.
Jose: I think the chapter said that nature was part of their traditions and their religion, too.
Matt: Uh-huh. And then the federal government took away their land.
Amina: And they were forced to adopt American traditions and language. It must have been very hard for them.
Matt: What did Professor Hawkins say about the reservation lands? That most of them are west of the Mississippi River?
Lauren: Yeah, and he highlighted the fact that the land in a lot of reservations is really dry and not suitable for agriculture. For a long time, the people who lived there lived in bad economic conditions.
Jose: I didn't realize that. So, when did things begin to get better?
Amina: I think Professor Hawkins said it was around 1970 when the federal government—or the Supreme Court, maybe— granted Native Americans the right to run various businesses on their reservations.
Matt: Right, and the money from their businesses has enabled them to improve their lands and undertake other big projects. The chapter mentioned a good example—the Inter Tribal Sinkyone Wilderness area.
Amina: Where's that place again?
Lauren: Um, it's on the coast north of San Francisco, California.
Matt: Exactly. It was founded in 1997 by a group of Native Americans who want the land to be as wild as possible. There's very limited access to the area. There aren't even any roads going through it.
Amina: I wonder why.
Matt: Well, they want to save the land for traditional cultural uses. Our book said that from the perspective of the people who live there, the coast and the redwood forests are sacred. That's where they gather food and medicine and hold their religious ceremonies.
Lauren: There's another example I know about. A Native American group down in Florida—um, the Seminole people—

are using their money to restore part of the Big Cypress Swamp, a place that's sacred to their people. They're bringing back animals that used to live there, and they're removing plants that weren't there at the time of their ancestors.
Jose: That's neat! It's great that they're trying to protect and regain some of their old traditions.
Amina: Yes, that's an awesome objective. I hope they're successful.
Matt: Me, too. That seems like a good review of this chapter, right?
Lauren: Yes, that covers everything. Let's move on to the next topic.

Pronunciation

Track 27   Linking Consonants to Vowels   Page 117

turn off
deer and other animals

Track 28   A.   Page 117

1. on	click on
2. again	out again
3. opinion	an opinion
4. offer	an offer
5. improved	and improved
6. easy	isn't easy

Track 29   B.   Page 117

1. Click on the file to open it.
2. You should speak out again.
3. He doesn't have an opinion.
4. The car dealer made an offer.
5. This car is new and improved.
6. Land conservation isn't easy.

Exploring Spoken English

Track 30   A.   Page 118

1. **Amina:** I had no idea that there are more than 300 Native American reservations in the United States, did you?
   Jose: No, I definitely didn't. And I wasn't aware that the reservations only make up two percent of the total land area of the United States.
2. **Lauren:** For a long time, the people who lived there lived in bad economic conditions.
   Jose: I didn't realize that. So, when did things begin to get better?

 CD 3

Unit 7: Money in Our Lives
Lesson A

Building Vocabulary

Track 2   A. Meaning from Context   Page 124

Credit card debt is a major problem in the United States, as these statistics show:
- The average debt per household is reported to be about $15,799.
- Unpaid credit card bills in a recent year totaled around 69 billion dollars.

Kelly Jones got herself in debt by using 10 credit cards, but she recently ceased using them completely. To pay off her $15,000 debt, Jones works 64 hours a week at two jobs. She started a debt-management plan and hopes to pay off her bills in seven years. She will no longer purchase unnecessary items. "I have no idea what I bought. I have nothing to show for it," she says. Now, Jones warns young people not to repeat her errors and tells them about what can happen if they rely on credit cards too much.

A financial counselor sorts through thousands of pieces of cut-up credit cards. Obviously, these cards won't be used again. Counselors ask people who are in debt to cut up all of their credit cards. This is just one component of a process to help people pay their bills. Counselors display the cut-up cards to demonstrate that people are not alone. Cutting up credit cards shows the commitment that hundreds of people have made to control their spending. Each year millions of people seek help to get out of debt. Many of these people receive counseling and education to promote better money management.

Developing Listening Skills

Listening: A Radio Interview

Track 3   Pages 126–127

Dave Martin: Hello and welcome to *Money Matters*. I'm your host, Dave Martin. Tonight we're very lucky to have Dr. Regina Simons of the Simmons Institute here with us to talk about money and happiness. As usual, we'll be taking calls from you, the listeners. If you have a question for Dr. Simmons, please call in. Good evening, Dr. Simmons.

Dr. Simmons: Good evening, Dave. It's great to be here.

Dave Martin: The pleasure's ours. Dr. Simmons, let me start by asking you this question: What's the relationship between money and happiness?

Dr. Simmons: Well, Dave, a recent study by psychologist Elizabeth Dunn at the University of British Columbia seems to show that—for most of us—what makes us happy is giving money away, not spending it on ourselves. That's what Dunn said in a recent interview with *National Geographic*.

Dave Martin: Really? How did she discover that?

Dr. Simmons: Well, it was when Dr. Dunn started making more money—uh, when she got a job as a professor. She started to get interested in whether money could buy happiness or not. She wanted to use the extra money she was making in ways that would bring her happiness. As a scientist, she looked for studies and research on the subject of money and its relationship to happiness. To her surprise, very little information on the subject existed. So Dr. Dunn decided to do some scientific research to see if people might get more happiness from using their money to help other people, rather than themselves.

Dave Martin: Uh-huh. . . . And how did she research this topic?

Dr. Simmons: That's a good question. Let me give you an example. In one of her first studies, Dr. Dunn and her fellow researchers gave a group of people a small amount of money in the morning. They asked some of the people to spend it on other people, and some to spend it on themselves. At the end of the day, the researchers interviewed everyone. The researchers discovered that the people who spent the money on other people were happier than those who had spent it on themselves. Since then, Dr. Dunn has completed a lot of other research on money and happiness.

Dave Martin: Has she? Oh, excuse me, but I think we have our first caller. Hello, you're on the air.

Caller 1: Uh, hello, I wanted to know what are some of the mistakes people might make if they try to buy happiness with money.

Dave Martin: Thank you, caller. Dr. Simmons?

Dr. Simmons: Yes, well one very common error is to make a major purchase such as a big house that you can't really afford. Many people simply assume that owning an expensive item—a home or a car—will make them happy. But, you know, buying a home is a big financial commitment . . . and in fact people often go deep into debt to buy one. Actually, there are no statistics to prove that owning a home makes people happy.

Dave Martin: I see. Are there other studies relating money and happiness?

Dr. Simmons: Oh, sure. Another interesting study was recently done by researchers Leaf Van Boven and Tom Gilovich. They looked at the value of spending money on experiences. People can buy items such as cars, houses, clothes, and DVDs. But experiences are different from other items that people purchase. For example . . . vacations, concerts, or language lessons are experiences. So, anyway, these scientists used surveys to ask people how they felt about the items they bought compared to the experiences they bought. Well, the researchers discovered that money spent on experiences made people happier than money spent on items. The reason for this is probably because experiences are more meaningful to a person, and they contribute more to successful social relationships.

Dave Martin: Interesting! Oh, we have another caller on the line. Go ahead, caller.

Caller 2: Hello. My question is how much money do you need to be happy.

Dave Martin: How about that, Dr. Simmons? How much money *do* we need?

Dr. Simmons: Well, OK, obviously that's not an easy question to answer. People like to say that "the best things in life are free," which implies that money doesn't matter to happiness. And we all know that's not true. Money is definitely not the most important component of happiness, but at the same time, having no money can definitely affect happiness.

There was a very interesting study recently done by an economist, Angus Deaton, and a psychologist named Daniel Kahneman. They wanted to know whether more money means more happiness. They analyzed surveys written by thousands of people. Their research demonstrated some very interesting things about money. Once a person earns more than $75,000 a year, making more money ceases to significantly change one's level of happiness.

Dave Martin: So, in other words, after a person earns more than $75,000 a year, more money doesn't have a big effect on your everyday happiness.

Dr. Simmons: Exactly. The thing that's important to remember is this: It's not about how much money you have. When it comes to money, it's what you do with the money that can promote your happiness—especially if you use it to help others and to have your own enjoyable experiences.

Dave Martin: Thank you very much, Dr. Simmons. We're going to pause now for a short commercial break.

Exploring Spoken English

Track 4   A.   Page 128

1. **Dr. Simmons:** That's what Dunn said in a recent interview with *National Geographic*.
   Dave Martin: Really? How did she discover that?
2. **Dr. Simmons:** So Dr. Dunn decided to do some scientific research to see if people might get more happiness from using their money to help other people, rather than themselves.
   Dave Martin: Uh-huh. And how did she research this topic?

3. **Dr. Simmons:** Since then Dr. Dunn has completed a lot of other research on money and happiness.
   Dave Martin: Has she?
4. **Dr. Simmons:** Actually, there are no statistics to prove that owning a home makes people happy.
   Dave Martin: I see. Are there other studies relating money and happiness?

Lesson B

Building Vocabulary

Track 5   A. Meaning from Context   Page 134

Q: The world's financial crisis shows that the way individuals manage their money can affect the whole world. Still, many people are unsure of how the crisis began. I'm speaking with economist Ken Lonoff. Mr. Lonoff, where did the crisis begin?

A: It began in the United States. As you know, most people want to buy their own home, but very few people can pay in paper currency—cash, that is. Banks have to help these consumers by loaning them money to buy things. People need to meet certain criteria to get a loan. For example, they need to have a job and be able to pay their bills.

Q: So, how exactly did this crisis begin?

A: Well, in the years that preceded the crisis, the economy was good. Financial professionals made as many loans as they could and earned a fee for each one. They were happy to assist anyone who wanted a loan. Even people without jobs were capable of getting loans. A huge number of these loans were made.

Q: When did things start to go wrong?

A: Things started to go wrong in 2007, when many people could not pay back their loans. These loans were the foundation for many businesses in the United States and all over the world. Huge sums were lost, and many companies went out of business. Loans became very difficult to get, and as a result, economies of countries around the world were affected.

Developing Listening Skills

Listening: A Conversation between Friends

Track 6   Pages 136–137

James: This place is so crowded today. Do we really have to eat here, Tina? I only have half an hour for lunch. Can't we go to the place next door? It's cash-only and the line moves fast.

Tina: I'm really sorry, James, but I don't have any cash. I was planning to use my debit card for lunch, and there aren't any ATMs around here.

Donna: You know, I hardly ever go to the ATM anymore. I just get cash back at the supermarket. Besides, I pay for nearly everything with my debit card or some kind of stored-value card—especially on the subway or at the coffee shop.

James: Same here, Donna. Do you two ever use credit cards?

Tina: I have one, but it's only for emergencies. Even though credit cards are useful, I think they're dangerous. It's so easy to get into debt. It's like a trap for consumers.

Donna: I know it. Actually, all these electronic payment systems worry me a little. I mean, what if someone knows a lot about computers and figures out how to steal the money out of my bank account, or maybe gets my credit card number and uses it to buy stuff?

James: You worry too much. Bank accounts are safe, and credit card companies don't make you pay if someone steals

your card and uses it. But hold on tight to your stored-value cards. If you lose those, there's no way to get your money back.

Tina: By the way, here's a trivia question for you. Which came first—the credit card or the debit card?

James: I don't know.

Donna: I think debit cards probably came first.

Tina: Actually, credit cards preceded debit cards. The first credit cards came out in the 1950s, I think, and the first debit cards came out in the 1970s.

James: Really? That's interesting. I'll have to look that up online . . .

Donna: I'm thinking about taking out a loan to help me buy a car, so I don't have to take the subway anymore. Do you think it's a good idea?

Tina: Oh, I don't know. If you're capable of paying it back right away, then it might be OK.

James: That reminds me, I read about an interesting way of borrowing and lending money. It's called peer-to-peer lending. You might want to check it out, Donna.

Donna: How does it work?

James: It's simple. You go online and create a loan request, explaining why you need the money and how you plan to repay the loan. But it's not banks or finance professionals who assist you—it's individuals. A person will decide if you meet their criteria, and if you do, they will lend you the sum you request.

Tina: Does that really work?

James: It's worked for a lot of people. There's even a service that lends money to people in developing countries. The loans are usually pretty small, but even so, it's surprising how much a $50 loan can help someone. Sometimes it can buy a lot when it's exchanged for local currency.

Donna: Hmm, well I would only do it if the interest on the loan and the fees were very low.

James: Those vary a lot, depending on the Web site. You should do some research first.

Hey, you know what, we've been waiting for a while now. I'm hungry! Donna, Tina, let's go to the place across the street. I'll pay for lunch today.

Donna: Really? Thanks, James!

Tina: That's so nice of you. Next time, I'll pay for lunch instead, all right?

Pronunciation

Track 7   Vowel-To-Vowel Linking   Page 137

happy ending   happy /y/ ending

hardly ever
nearly everything
see it
the end

do over   do /w/ over

Do you ever
go online
do it
so easy

Track 8   A.   Page 137

1. be able
2. the value of
3. Do it again.
4. Say it in English.
5. nearly all
6. the answer
7. Who ate it?
8. want to understand

Exploring Spoken English

Track 9   A.   Page 138

1. **Tina:** By the way, here's a trivia question for you. Which came first—the credit card or the debit card?
2. **James:** That reminds me, I read about an interesting way of borrowing and lending money. It's called peer-to-peer lending.

Unit 8: Health and Fitness
Lesson A

Building Vocabulary

Track 10   A. Meaning from Context   Page 144

In the well-known song *Big Yellow Taxi*, the singer asks a farmer to "put away the DDT." DDT is a pesticide—a chemical compound used to kill insects. Many farmers throughout the world spray pesticides on their growing crops to keep bugs and other insects away. In the past, DDT was considered a safe pesticide. It was sprayed directly on children to kill insects and was even used to help make wallpaper for bedrooms. Since then, DDT has been assessed by scientists. After years of testing, scientists concluded that DDT was harmful to humans, birds, insects, and even some other kinds of animals. Farmers in many countries stopped using DDT after they learned it could be harmful. However, DDT was not eliminated from the environment. According to scientists, DDT persists in the environment for many years. Traces of the pesticide have been found in soil, animals, and in humans all over the world.

In the past several decades, more and more markets have been offering shoppers the option of fruits and vegetables grown without pesticides or other chemicals. There is a growing number of people who appreciate these organic fruits and vegetables. People who buy organic food fear that the constant consumption of food grown with pesticides could be dangerous to their health. They worry that, little by little, small amounts of dangerous chemicals will accumulate in their bodies until the amount is large enough to cause health problems. Scientists are still researching the effects of pesticides on humans, but it is clear that the amount of organic food available is growing. According to the Research Institute of Organic Agriculture, people around the world spent over $50 billion on organic products and food in 2010.

Developing Listening Skills

Listening: A Question-and-Answer Session

Track 11   Pages 146–147

Announcer: Everyone, I just want to thank Dr. Wallace again for being the first guest speaker in our *Healthline* series. We hope that this is the first of many seminars about healthy living in today's world.
Dr. Wallace: It was my pleasure to be here.
Announcer: So, now you've heard what Dr. Wallace has to say about pesticides and how they relate to our health and the environment. Let's open the floor up for questions. We would appreciate hearing from you.

I think we have our first question. Go ahead, sir.

Male Speaker #1: OK. Here's my question. Dr. Wallace, I heard that flame-retardants are now turning up in the human body. Is this true, and if so, how dangerous are those chemicals?
Dr. Wallace: All right. Well, flame-retardants—which are chemicals that make products difficult to burn—are added to just about any product that can burn, and they save hundreds of lives a year in the United States alone. Unfortunately, one family of flame-retardant compounds called PBDEs have been showing up in the blood of humans, but little is known about their impact on our health. In high amounts, they have caused health problems in laboratory animals. However, it looks as though the small amounts of PBDEs that normally accumulate in the human body aren't worth worrying about.
Announcer: Thank you, Doctor. We have another question. The woman in the third row. Go ahead.
Female Speaker #1: Hi, Dr. Wallace. I'm a mother of two young children, and I recently moved into a new apartment. I just found out that the walls are painted with lead paint. What should I do?
Dr. Wallace: Well, it's known that even very small amounts of lead can cause brain damage in children. If the paint is chipping or flaking, call your landlord. It's his or her responsibility to fix the problem. Another good option is to move, but if you can't, at least make sure that your children aren't exposed to paint chips or dust.
Announcer: That sounds like good advice. Let's take another question. OK, go ahead.
Male Speaker #2: Hello, Doctor. I eat a lot of seafood—especially swordfish and tuna. Is there any danger to me from mercury in those fish?
Dr. Wallace: Mercury is a very dangerous pollutant which persists for a long time in the environment. It needs to be taken seriously because mercury poisoning can permanently damage memory and our ability to learn. Coal-burning power plants are a major source of mercury. It gets into the water and into the bodies of the smallest animals first. These small animals are eaten by larger ones, which are then eaten by even larger ones, and so on up the food chain. Large fish at the top of the food chain, such as tuna and swordfish, accumulate high amounts of mercury—and pass it on to people who eat seafood. Now, it doesn't appear that traces of mercury in the blood are a serious problem, but I could be wrong. Eating too much of those fish could raise the amount of mercury in your body to a dangerous level, so I would advise you to eat them in moderation—meaning a reasonable amount.
Announcer: Well, it looks like we have time for one more question. The lady in the red shirt. Go ahead.
Female Speaker #2: Hello and thanks for taking my question. What I'm concerned about is my constant cell-phone use. Could it have a negative impact on my health?
Dr. Wallace: That's an interesting question and one I'm sure many are concerned about. One common concern is the danger of driving and using a cell phone at the same time. Cell phones take our attention off the road, and that can lead to accidents. The solution to that problem is simple: turn off your cell phone while driving, and don't ever text message while driving. Another concern has to do with radiation. For those of you who aren't familiar with this—radiation is energy that certain machines and some substances produce. Large amounts of radiation can be dangerous. Cell phones send information using radiation, so naturally we're exposed to that radiation when we use our phone. Cell-phone radiation has caused brain cancer in rats, but its danger to humans is difficult to assess. Some studies have indicated that cell phones are safe, but some other studies seem to link cell-phone radiation with brain cancer in humans, especially in people who have been using cell phones for a decade or longer.

I'm not altogether sure that you can eliminate radiation exposure from cell phones, but people who are concerned about it can reduce the risk by using a headset. This keeps the phone away from your head and exposes you to less radiation.

Announcer: I'm afraid that's all the time we have. Thanks very much, Dr. Wallace, for the information and advice. We'll see you all at next month's seminar about organic foods.

Exploring Spoken English

Track 12   A.   Page 148

1. In high amounts, they have caused health problems in laboratory animals. However, it looks as though the small amounts of PBDEs that normally accumulate in the human body aren't worth worrying about.
2. Large fish at the top of the food chain, such as tuna and swordfish, accumulate high amounts of mercury—and pass it on to people who eat seafood. Now, it doesn't appear that traces of mercury in the blood are a serious problem, but I could be wrong.
3. I'm not altogether sure that you can eliminate radiation exposure from cell phones, but people who are concerned about it can reduce the risk by using a headset.

Lesson B

Building Vocabulary

Track 13   A. Meaning from Context   Page 154

Yoga was initially practiced over 5000 years ago in India. In India, yoga is a tradition that is related to both religion and culture. Prior to the 19th century, yoga was not well understood and was rarely practiced in other parts of the world. The introduction of yoga to other countries is attributed to the Indian yoga master Swami Vivekananda, who toured Europe and the United States in the 1890s.

Many different versions of yoga are practiced, from traditional styles such as hatha and Sivananda yoga to modern versions such as chair yoga and laughter yoga. For fans of yoga, it is the ultimate workout because it involves not only the body but the mind as well. There are many health benefits associated with yoga. It helps you be more flexible, stronger, and it relieves stress. Yoga-style meditation called *yoga nidra* can be very relaxing. Some yoga teachers claim that just a half hour of yoga nidra is equivalent to two or three hours of sleep.

As yoga grows in popularity, more people are teaching yoga, and more yoga schools and centers are opening. Since the 1960s, the expansion of yoga has been remarkable, and today yoga is taught and practiced everywhere. It has become a truly global business with yoga retreats in the United States, Mexico, Thailand, New Zealand, France, Egypt, and many other countries. According to data in the *Yoga Journal*, 14.3 million people in the United States alone practiced yoga in 2010. Scientists and researchers are now completing the first World Yoga Survey to count how many people around the world practice yoga. It is estimated that more than 30 million people practice yoga around the world and that there are over 70,000 yoga teachers. In many places, there are no laws controlling the quality of schools and teachers. Some people are asking for legislation to make sure the quality of yoga education remains high.

Developing Listening Skills

Listening: A Conversation between Friends

Track 14   Pages 156–157

Jennifer: Hi, Stan. How are you? How was your day?
Stan: Hi, Jennifer. It was great. I spent today at Yosemite National Park. I was rock climbing.
Jennifer: That.must have been fun. How long have you been rock climbing?
Stan: Well, I started doing it for the exercise a few years ago. A half hour of rock climbing is equivalent to about an hour of jogging, and I was climbing for three hours today.
Jennifer: You must be exhausted.
Stan: Oh, yes, it's really challenging. And it's great strength training too . . . for just about every muscle in the body.
Jennifer: But isn't it a little dangerous?
Stan: Well, that really depends on which version of climbing you do. Indoor climbing takes place in a climbing gym. You can use safety ropes that catch you if you fall. The walls are pretty easy to climb—not too high—and the floor is usually pretty soft, so it doesn't hurt so much if you *do* fall.
Jennifer: It must be pretty safe, then, huh?
Stan: It is, and it's becoming really popular. Prior to 1980, there weren't any climbing gyms in the U.S. Since then there's been a big expansion, and today there are climbing gyms in all 50 states. And it's not just in this country. The expansion has been global, too. There are thousands of climbing gyms around the world.
Jennifer: I didn't know it was so popular!
Stan: Oh, definitely. But a step up in difficulty from indoor climbing is outdoor climbing on huge rocks, you know, boulders, that are maybe 16 feet high. You can use ropes for that, too, for extra safety. That version of rock climbing is known as bouldering. But . . . even more difficult than that is traditional rock climbing. In traditional rock climbing, pairs of people go very high up on a rock wall—usually on the side of a hill or mountain. They bring lots of equipment with them. They connect ropes to the rocks so that they don't fall off.
Jennifer: Wow, there's a lot of types of rock climbing. What kind do you do?
Stan: Well, I do a different type—free solo climbing. It's really the ultimate climbing experience.
Jennifer: What's free solo climbing?
Stan: It's rock climbing very high on rock walls alone and without any ropes. That's . . .
Jennifer: No ropes at all? Way up on the side of a rock wall? That must be terrifying!
Stan: Yeah, I suppose initially I *was* terrified. But now I really love doing it. I can't describe what a wonderful feeling I get from it. It's such a thrill.
Jennifer: But isn't it too dangerous?
Stan: Well, free solo climbing is only for experienced climbers. It's true that if you fall, you can get hurt really badly or even die. In fact, there was a climbing accident in Yosemite last year, and now some people are demanding legislation to ban free solo climbing in the park.
Jennifer: Are rock-climbing accidents very common?
Stan: Well, that's hard to say, but according to the data I've seen, there is one death every for every 300, um, every 320,000 climbs. And the *American Journal of Preventive Medicine* says over 40,000 patients were treated in U.S. emergency rooms for rock-climbing related injuries between 1990 and 2007.

Jennifer: That's scary. Doesn't that make you want to stop rock climbing?

Stan: Not really. I believe that most accidents can be attributed to climbers being overconfident or careless. I only go where the climbing isn't too difficult for me, and I always try to be extremely careful.

Jennifer: But what about bad luck? Something could go wrong. The rock you're holding on to could break, or your shoe could slip, or . . .

Stan: Yeah, I know. But you can't control everything in life. If you don't take any risks, you'll never have any fun! I'm looking forward to going again next weekend.

Pronunciation: Dropped Syllables

Track 15   Page 157

every   ev'ry
mystery   myst'ry

Track 16   Page 157

1. int'resting
2. veg'table
3. diff'rent
4. fav'rite
5. choc'late
6. asp'rin
7. hist'ry
8. ev'ning
9. gen'rally
10. bev'rage
11. cam'ra
12. rest'rant

Exploring Spoken English

Track 17   A.   Page 158

1. **Stan:** I spent today at Yosemite National Park. I was rock climbing.
   Jennifer: That must have been fun.
2. **Stan:** A half hour of rock climbing is equivalent to about an hour of jogging, and I was climbing for three hours today.
   Jennifer: You must be exhausted.
3. **Stan:** The walls are pretty easy to climb—not too high—and the floor is usually pretty soft, so it doesn't hurt so much if you do fall.
   Jennifer: It must be pretty safe, then, huh?

Grammar

Track 18   B.   Page 159

Tonya: Hi, Marc, how are you?

Marc: Tonya! What are you doing here? Isn't today your day off?

Tonya: I'm doing my grocery shopping, and I wanted to drop in on you to say hello. Are you feeling OK? I thought maybe you had a headache.

Marc: Yes, I do. Maybe I'm coming down with a cold or something.

Tonya: Really? Why don't you take some cold medicine? That usually gets rid of my colds right away.

Marc: No, I can't. I'm working, remember?

Tonya: Well, why don't you ask if you can take the afternoon off? Just come up with an excuse to tell the boss.

Marc: That's OK! I'm fine, really. I've got a lot to do and I have to get down to work. Thanks for coming to check on me.

Tonya: No problem. See you later!

Unit 9: Mind and Memory
Lesson A

Building Vocabulary

Track 19   B.   Page 164

Are animals capable of showing concern for members of another species? According to the philosophies of many great thinkers such as Aristotle and Descartes, the answer is *no*. Recently, however, there has been a shift in the way many scientists think about this subject. The question is difficult because it is so abstract. Let's look at one specific case.

A video filmed at a small pond in Africa shows an antelope trying to cross the pond. A crocodile grabbed the antelope and tried to pull it under the water. Just then, a hippo resting in an adjacent pond ran over and scared the crocodile away. The crocodile released the injured antelope. Then the hippo, trying to help, gently nuzzled the antelope.

How should we interpret the hippo's actions? It seems that the hippo's motive was to help the antelope, although the hippo didn't gain anything from it. The actions of the hippo correspond to what we in the human world would call altruism. This video raises the question of whether we humans underestimate an animal's capacity to help other animals. This case can also illustrate how complex animal society can be. We should remain flexible and open to the possibility that animals can be altruistic, too.

Developing Listening Skills

Listening: A TV Show

Track 20   Pages 166–167

Narrator: The French philosopher René Descartes, who lived in the first half of the 17th century, believed that animals were beings without minds. According to his philosophy, animals were simply biological machines, that is—machines that could live and breathe, but not think on their own. In recent years, however, we've seen a move away from this idea. Today many scientists believe humans have been underestimating animals. New studies show that animals have a variety of mental skills, such as a good memory, the ability to understand symbols, and an awareness of self. Some animals can even understand others' motives, imitate voices, and show creativity. How do scientists prove whether animals have the capacity to think intelligently? On today's program, *Amazing Science* interviewed three people who work with some of the world's most intelligent animals.

Diane Willberg is a scientist who has done important research involving birds and thinking. Most people think that birds are . . . well, bird-brained, which is to say not very smart. But do birds have higher mental skills?

Diane: Well, for one thing, I've found that crows are able to use tools, and they can actually make the tools themselves. For another, my research shows that parrots understand abstract concepts such as shapes and colors. Each of my parrots is very special. Perhaps the most intelligent one is named Alex. When I show him two green objects and say the two words "What same?" he answers "color." If I show him a basketball and a baseball and ask "What same?" he says "shape." I think this illustrates the ability to use the abstract concepts of shape and color.

Crows are also very intelligent animals, too. In my laboratory, we conduct an interesting experiment. In a bottle, just out of reach of the crow, we put a piece of meat. Beside the bottle we put a thin piece of metal about the length of a pen. The metal is flexible, and the crows first bend it to shape it into a kind of hook, which they then use to pull the meat from the bottle. It's really clear from research that these birds are learning . . . they're showing clear signs of intelligence, and they know how to figure things out.

Narrator: A wide range of animal studies confirms that animals can learn and change. This skill is best illustrated by dogs. Samantha Bean owns a Border collie named Betsy. Betsy can remember and recognize over 200 objects, and frequently performs on television. But how did the dog learn to do this?

Samantha: Well, in one room we have pictures of two hundred objects, and in an adjacent room we have the two hundred objects themselves. First, I show Betsy a picture, then she goes into the next room, chooses the corresponding object, and then brings it back to me. She can do this for all two hundred objects. Recognizing an object in a picture is clearly a type of abstract thinking.

Narrator: There's one animal—the dolphin—who has a brain that's even larger than a human brain. But does that mean that they are more intelligent than humans? Researcher Matthew Leonard explains.

Matthew: I don't think they're smarter than humans, but all of our dolphins are very intelligent. Along with humans, elephants, and apes, dolphins exhibit self-awareness. That is to say, when they look at themselves in a mirror, they see the image and can interpret that they are looking at themselves.

Narrator: Whether or not animals are intelligent is a question that scientists will study for years to come. But after hearing about the amazing things that animals can do, it's clear that we're only just beginning to learn about the animals on our planet. Coming up next on *Amazing Science* . . .

Exploring Spoken English

Track 21 A. Page 168

1. Well, for one thing, I've found that crows are able to use tools, and they can actually make the tools themselves. For another, my research shows that parrots understand abstract concepts such as shapes and colors.
2. First, I show Betsy a picture, then she goes into the next room, chooses the corresponding object, and then brings it back to me.

Lesson B

Building Vocabulary

Track 22 A. Meaning from Context Page 174

The amount of information that the human brain can hold is virtually limitless. Most people do not have an aptitude for remembering complex lists or numbers. Some people, however, use their memory much more than the average person. A person who is able to remember long lists of data such as names and numbers is called a *mnemonist*. This word is derived from the word *mnemonic*, which originated from an Ancient Greek word meaning "of memory."

Each year, mnemonists participate in the World Memory Championships. This championship is a series of games that test a person's memory. Contestants are expected to behave in an ethical way at all times: there must be no cheating, no help from others, and no use of drugs that enhance the memory. Some of the events include memorizing numbers, words, faces, or images. There is also a "Speed Cards" event in which individuals must memorize the exact order of 54 cards as quickly as possible. The world record is 21.90 seconds.

One of the most successful mnemonists in the world is a British man named Dominic O'Brien. He has won the World Memory Championship an unprecedented eight times. O'Brien uses his own memorization method. He uses information he already knows as a framework and adds new facts to this information. He says that practicing memorization techniques can result in a dramatic increase in almost everyone's memory.

Developing Listening Skills

Listening: A Conversation between Classmates

Track 23 Pages 176–177

Maria: I don't want to study any more. Do you want to go to the Student Center, Heather? I think they're showing a movie tonight.

Heather: Um, maybe later, Maria. I have to finish preparing for the memory contest.

Maria: What memory contest?

Heather: Well, we're having a memory contest in my psychology class.

Maria: Why?

Heather: Because we're learning about memory, and the professor thought it would be a good experiment. Have you ever heard of "superior autobiographical memory"?

Maria: Superior autobiographical memory? No, I don't think I have. What is it?

Heather: It's when a person has an incredible aptitude for remembering things about their own life. People with superior autobiographical memory can remember virtually everything that's ever happened to them.

Maria: Oh! I saw a TV show about that. You know about that show *Amazing Science,* don't you?

Heather: Yes.

Maria: So, on the show they asked people questions such as, "What were you doing on August 10th, 2005?" And these people were able to answer the questions exactly. They almost never got a question wrong. It was really fascinating.

Heather: Yeah. People like that have always been very rare, I think, but in class I learned that researchers at the University of California say they've found at least eight people who have superior autobiographical memory—including one TV star. It's really unprecedented.

Maria: How do they do it? I mean, how do they remember everything so clearly?

Heather: Well, the scientists found that some parts of these people's brains are bigger than normal, including the part called the hippo, um, the hippocampus.

Maria: I'm not sure I know what that is. What can you tell me about it?

Heather: Not much! I know it's part of the brain, and obviously it's really important for memory function. Oh, and I know the word originated from two ancient Greek words: *hippo* meaning "horse" and *campus* meaning "sea monster."

Maria: It means "sea horse monster"?

Heather: That's right! It was called that because it sort of looks like a sea horse. Anyway, one of the case studies I just read about was about this famous case in Connecticut in 1953. A doctor named William Scoville had a patient with epilepsy, which is a brain condition that affects some people. He—Scoville, I mean—removed most of the patient's hippocampus trying to cure the man's epilepsy.

Maria: What? That doesn't sound ethical to me.

Heather: Well, epilepsy is a serious condition, and I guess the doctor thought it was worth the risk. I mean, don't forget, it was 1953, and doctors didn't know then what they know now. So, anyway, after he removed most of the hippocampus, he found that the patient had lost his memory.

Maria: His *entire* memory?

Heather: Well, no. The man could still remember some things. And he was still able to have some happiness, and science gained a lot of understanding about the brain, thanks to him.

Maria: I see. Memory is so important. I have a really bad memory; I'd love to learn how to improve it.

Heather: Oh, there are lots of ways to enhance your ability to remember things. For example, do you know about the method of loci?

Maria: No, I don't think I've ever heard of it. What is it?

Heather: Well, it's also called the method of location. It's a good way to remember lists of words. First, in your mind, you need to picture a path that you know well, such as the way to school or to work, for example. The path is the framework that will hold the information.

Maria: OK.

Heather: Next, you look at a list of words and create an image for each word. For example, the image for philosophy could be a statue of a famous philosopher. An image for motive could be Sherlock Holmes, who's always looking for criminals' motives.

Maria: Right.

Heather: Then, in your mind, you put those images at places you'll remember along the path you chose. Later, at test time, or whenever, you can move along the path in your mind, and the images will remind you of the words.

Maria: I wonder if that really works. I have a history exam next week and I have to memorize a lot of information. I'm going to try to use the location method to study.

Heather: Good luck. I hope you see a dramatic improvement in your test grades.

Pronunciation

Track 24   Using Word Stress to Clarify Information   Page 177

Heather: So, anyway, after he removed most of the hippocampus, he found that the patient had lost his memory.

Maria: His *entire* memory?

Exploring Spoken English

Track 25   A.   Page 178

1. **Heather:** Well, we're having a memory contest in my psychology class.
   Maria: Why?
   Heather: Because we're learning about memory, and the professor thought it would be a good experiment. Have you ever heard of "superior autobiographical memory"?
2. **Maria:** Oh! I saw a TV show about that. You know about that show *Amazing Science,* don't you?
3. **Heather:** Well, the scientists found that some parts of these people's brains are bigger than normal, including the part called the hippo, um, the *hippocampus.*
   Maria: I'm not sure I know what that is. What can you tell me about it?

4. **Maria:** I see. Memory is so important. I have a really bad memory; I'd love to learn how to improve it.
   Heather: Oh, there are lots of ways to enhance your ability to remember things. For example, do you know about the method of loci?

Unit 10: Food Concerns
Lesson A

Building Vocabulary

Track 26   A. Meaning from Context   Page 184

The world population is now over 7 billion people. As a result, there is an intense need for additional food. Instead of using conventional farming methods, many large farms now only plant one crop such as corn, wheat, or rice. Farmers plant this crop over very large areas. This type of agriculture is known as monoculture. The benefit of monoculture is to maximize the harvest, but there are experts who say that the benefit is offset by its negative effects.

One serious problem of monoculture is the effect it has had on the number of vegetable varieties grown by farmers. The number of vegetable varieties has greatly diminished since 1903, and many crop species no longer exist. In the future, if one of the plants farmers rely on is destroyed via disease or climate change, this could cause major problems in the world's food supply. Therefore, some scientists are now trying to modify the genes of other vegetables to recreate the lost vegetable varieties.

It's important to monitor and save the vegetable varieties that remain. Many experts advocate setting up "seed banks" to collect and keep the seeds of plants that are no longer planted by farmers. Many farmers and scientists devote themselves to the important work of setting up these seed banks. Today there are about 1400 of them around the world. The vegetable seeds inside these seed banks could be extremely important to the welfare of the people on Earth.

Developing Listening Skills

Listening: A PowerPoint Lecture

Track 27   Pages 186–187

Lecturer: Let me just get my first slide up. Great. OK, everyone, today we're going to talk about genetically-modified foods— GM foods for short. These are foods with modified genes. Nowadays, scientists can modify the genes of any animal or plant to make them grow faster, grow bigger, or even produce their own pesticides. Genetic engineers can take a gene from virtually any animal or plant and insert it into virtually any other animal or plant. For example, they can put a rat gene into lettuce to make it produce vitamin C . . . or put moth genes into apple plants to help them resist diseases. Some GM plants produce chemicals that fight insects. This means that insects would not be able to destroy any crops. Scientists have modified the genes of Atlantic salmon to make them grow twice as fast. They've modified the genes of cattle and sheep so they produce medicines in their milk. Many scientists feel that GM foods could be the key to the next advances in agriculture and health . . . OK so far?

OK. Onto the next slide. On the other hand . . . there's another side to GM foods, too. Critics fear that these new foods are being rushed to market before their effects are fully understood. Scientists think that some weeds could pick up modified genes from other plants and become "superweeds." Superweeds could spread over wide areas of land and be very hard to kill. Scientists are also worried about possible harmful effects of GM plants on insects and animals. In North America and Europe, the value and impact of GM foods has become the subject of intense debate. . . . Are you following me? Yes, you have a question?

Student 1: Yes, um, are any of these GM foods in restaurants today?

Lecturer: Oh, sure. Most people don't even realize that they've been eating genetically-modified foods. In the United States, for instance, genetically-modified vegetables have been sold since the mid-1990s. More than 60 percent of all processed foods on U.S. supermarket shelves—including pizza, ice cream, salad dressing, and baking powder—contain ingredients from GM soybeans, corn, or canola. And the U.S. is certainly not alone. Argentina, Canada, China, South Africa, Australia, Germany, and Spain all plant plenty of genetically-modified vegetable crops. On the other hand, while scientists have created various GM animals, no GM animals have been approved for use as food yet. Any other questions?

Student 2: I have a question. Genetically modifying plants and animals sounds dangerous to me. Is it?

Lecturer: There are things to be concerned about, no question. But corporations try to offset risks by doing thorough testing— more than any other food we eat—that's according to one of the leading developers of GM products. Government agencies are also involved in monitoring the production and sale of GM foods. Some people want to require companies to label their GM products. However, in the U.S. at least, food companies don't have to specially label their GM products because government agencies haven't found GM foods to be significantly different from conventional foods. . . . Does that make sense?

OK, onto a new slide then. So far . . . there isn't any proof that GM foods hurt the environment. Some scientists are concerned, however, about what they call "gene flow." Gene flow is the movement of genes via flowers and seeds from one population of plants to another. Some scientists feel that mixing GM plants with conventional ones could have long-term impact on gene flow.

And there are other concerns, too. For example, advocates of GM crops point out a major benefit—GM crops have a resistance to insects. However, some critics fear that insects will gradually get used to such crops. The result could be super-pests that farmers would have no weapons against.

And finally . . . here's the last slide. While I've talked about the drawbacks to GM foods, I must mention that GM foods also have great potential to help feed the world. Let me give you an example. Golden rice is a recent food that has been genetically modified. White rice, which is an important food in many cultures, doesn't provide any beta-carotene, which allows our bodies to produce vitamin A. According to the World Health Organization, between 100 million and 140 million children in the world suffer from vitamin A deficiency.

The genes of golden rice plants have been modified so that they create beta-carotene. Skeptics say that golden rice alone won't greatly diminish vitamin A deficiency in the world, and it remains to be seen whether it will improve vitamin A levels. Still, it could prove very important to the welfare of millions of children.

It looks like class is almost over, but let me add one more thing. Some critics don't like the fact that big companies control genetic modification. These critics say the companies aren't devoting enough resources to developing seed technology for poor farmers. But, on the positive side, genetic modification can increase the amount of food we can produce, it offers crop varieties that resist pests and disease, and it provides ways to grow crops on land that would otherwise not support farming. And genetically-modified seeds are easy for farmers to use because the technology is built into them. Farmers just need

to plant them. With so many advantages, I think GM foods are only going to become more important in the future.

Exploring Spoken English

Track 28   A.   Page 188

1. Many scientists feel that GM foods could be the key to the next advances in agriculture and health. . . . OK so far?
2. In North America and Europe, the value and impact of GM foods has become the subject of intense debate. . . . Are you following me?
3. However, in the U.S. at least, food companies don't have to specially label their GM products because government agencies haven't found GM foods to be significantly different from conventional foods. . . . Does that make sense?

Lesson B
Building Vocabulary

Track 29   A.   Page 194

In the second half of the 20th century, there was a dramatic increase in the amount of food farmers were able to produce. Thanks to improved farming methods, agricultural output of corn, wheat, and rice increased around 50 percent. It seemed apparent that scientists could increase production of food as needed. People presumed that there would always be enough food to meet the world's needs.

Today, it seems that scientists might have been wrong. In recent years, shortages of important crops such as corn and rice have become the norm, and with these grains in short supply, their prices have been rising. The problem has been particularly serious for people who rely primarily on grain to fill their stomachs. The scope of the problem has been global, affecting consumers in Africa, Asia, Europe, and the Americas. There is not just one explanation for these shortages, but rather several reasons that coincide. One reason for the food shortage is that people are eating more meat and dairy products. Both meat and dairy products require large amounts of grain to produce. Another reason is the use of large quantities of grains to produce fuels instead of food. Water shortages and the growing world population have also contributed to the food problems.

There are probably no easy solutions to these problems. It seems very difficult to ask people to fight their natural inclinations to eat meat. A government policy that makes eating meat illegal would likely be very unpopular. However, some experts believe we have no choice but to take action. If we don't, the future many bring us unpleasant scenarios of too little food for the world's people.

Developing Listening Skills
Listening: An Informal Conversation

Track 30   Pages 196–197

Susan: Did you go grocery shopping today? Did you remember to pick up the rice?
Andy: Yes, I did go shopping, but I didn't get any rice. It was so expensive. I can't believe how much food prices have risen lately.
Susan: I know, and we'll probably see them go even higher.
Andy: What makes you think that?

Susan: I've been reading about it in this magazine. It seems that over the past five or 10 years, prices have been rising faster than the norm.

Andy: I've noticed that. Personally, I think we ought to ask farmers to farm more land.

Susan: Well, that presumes that there's more land to be farmed. I think most available land in the world is already being farmed, don't you? The scope of the problem is actually very large, I think, and there are quite a few problems that are coinciding all at once.

Andy: Like what?

Susan: Well, let me look back at this article. Hmm . . . yes, now I remember. . . . One big factor is the success of developing countries. Countries that are developing rapidly, such as India and China, have growing middle classes—people with extra money to spend. All around the world, the middle class has an inclination to eat more luxury foods such as meat and dairy products.

Andy: So? What does that have to do with the price of other foods?

Susan: Well, it says here that it takes about 3.2 kilograms of grain to get half a kilogram of meat. The grain is needed to feed the animals while they are being raised. So . . . I guess, with more people eating meat and dairy, there's less grain available. And if there's less grain, the price goes up.

Andy: That's the law of supply and demand, right? If there's a demand for something, but a low supply of it, it becomes more expensive.

Susan: Yes, I think that's right. . . . So, if people primarily eat grains such as rice and wheat for most of their daily calories, it'll be a problem. When grain prices go up, they will have very few other options.

Andy: Why don't they do something about it? The government, I mean, or the United Nations.

Susan: Well, governments have done some things. For example, some government policies don't allow grain to be exported. That way, more food stays in the country for their people.

Andy: That makes sense.

Susan: You know, I heard that some climate experts are predicting a scenario in which large areas in Africa and Asia will become deserts. That might be a problem, too—if the land is too dry to grow crops on.

Andy: Wow. Well, if it were up to me, I'd try to get the whole world to work together to stop that from happening.

Susan: Well, the experts say the only answer is to increase the amount of food grown on existing farms.

Andy: How can they do it, though?

Susan: Well, the U.S. Secretary of Agriculture recommended that each country make an effort to increase agricultural output. That means better water management, better fertilizer management, and using GM crops.

Andy: As far as I'm concerned, he's right. I mean, what's more important than food? They really should do it.

Susan: Yes, they should. Do you want to read the article after I'm finished, Andy?

Andy: No, thanks. I think you've already told me everything I need to know!

Pronunciation: Syllable Stress

Track 31   Page 197

conduct
con**duct**

conflict
con**flict**

extract
ex**tract**

project
pro**ject**

reject
re**ject**

Exploring Spoken English

Track 32   A.   Page 198

1. **Susan:** It seems that the over the past five or 10 years, food prices have been rising faster than the norm.
   Andy: I've noticed that. Personally, I think we ought to ask farmers to farm more land.
2. **Susan:** When grain prices go up, they'll have very few other options.
   Andy: Why don't they do something about it?
3. **Susan:** You know, I heard that some climate experts are predicting a scenario in which large areas in Africa and Asia will become deserts. That might be a problem, too—if the land is too dry to grow crops on.
   Andy: Wow. Well, if it were up to me, I'd try to get the whole world to work together to stop that from happening.

Unit 1: Tuareg Farmers

Narrator:
The Tuareg people have a proud tradition as nomads. But a long drought forced some to settle along the lake and try farming. Here, on the edge of Lake Gossi in Mali, they've made the Sahel bloom . . . and in turn attracted a group of giants. In the dry season, Omar Sowadou has come to expect these visitors.

Omar Sowadou, Farmer:
We are living here in this area, just beside the water. Of course, we use the water for our garden, and for our animals. But elephants, they come to drink water, of course, and they want to cool down their body, so all of us, we share the same water.

Narrator:
During the day, an uneasy peace settles over the lake. People fill their goatskins. The elephants drink. But when night falls, the truce will be broken.

Omar Sowadou:
After drinking they come straight away to the garden because they smell food—trees and crops. So we have to protect our garden.

Narrator:
It takes more than brush fences to keep out three tons of hungry elephant.

Omar Sowadou:
If an elephant spends just half an hour in a garden, he will eat at least 30 percent of it, and this is the big danger for farmers.

Narrator:
To lose a third of their crop is a catastrophe for any farmer, especially here. And this is not your average garden pest. As the sun sets the battle lines are drawn.

Omar Sowadou:
The farmer digs holes to keep the elephant away from the farm, to not damage the farm but it is not enough. They come all the time, spoil a lot of things, and you cannot even get to sleep during the night. It becomes like a nightmare.

Narrator:
Tonight, the nightmare appears—and the farmers are ready . . .

At first light, Omar finds he's had a near disaster.

Omar Sowadou:
I discovered that there were two elephants in the garden. I followed their footprints to the next garden. I found they had damaged a lot of crops and trees. I do remember since I was a kid we are doing the same . . . things every year, and for sure I will do it in the future, every year, and this is the daily fight among us and elephant. Every time we are facing the same problem with elephant, every year.

Narrator:
Throughout Africa, elephants and people do battle. For now, the elephants have headed south to search for fresh food. But in six months, they'll be back . . . and once again Omar Sowadou will not sleep.

Unit 2: Crocodiles of Sri Lanka

Narrator:
It's a problem all over the world. Increased human populations mean smaller habitats for our animal neighbors. Nowhere have human populations exploded as in India—and that has meant trouble for some animals. You might think that the mighty crocodile wouldn't be affected by human population growth—but you would be wrong.

Today the crocodile is on the run.

Rom Whitaker is a herpetologist. He studies amphibians and reptiles. Rom is determined to save the mugger crocodile from the growing pressure of India's human populations.

Rom Whitaker, Herpetologist:
Crocs live in wetlands. But most of India's swamps and riversides are now rice fields and farms. So crocs have lost virtually all of their habitat.

Narrator:
Rom founded the Madras Crocodile Bank in 1975 to breed and study native crocodiles. It is a reptile zoo—one of the largest in the world. There are thousands of crocs here including the largest captive population of mugger crocodiles in the world.

Rom Whitaker:
Another routine day at the crocodile bank size-sorting some of these bullies, getting them into another enclosure. You know, we have 3000 of these mugger crocodiles here, and nowhere to let them go. People moved into crocodile habitat here in India a long time ago. There's just nothing left.

Narrator:

The mugger once roamed the lowlands in large numbers from Iran to Myanmar. Today only a few thousand are scattered in the wild throughout the Indian subcontinent. Now the last hope for the mugger may lie to the south of India in the country of Sri Lanka.

Rom is headed back to Sri Lanka's Yala National Park after almost 30 years to see if the thriving mugger community he remembers is still there.

Rom Whitaker:

Really the only chance the mugger has in the wild is here, in Yala. If they die out here, they're probably gone for good. To the casual observer, this may not look much like croc country. But hidden in this dry forest are many lakes and ponds created by an ancient people to irrigate their crops. The people are long gone, but the pools remain. That's how the world's largest population of wild muggers has been able to survive.

Hey, a baby croc. Yeah, there you go. There you go. Ah, he's gorgeous. Look at those colors. For years I've wanted to come back to Yala to see how the mugger is doing. It's not a well-studied species, so the only way is to see for myself. Finding healthy young ones is a very good omen. But it's only a start. I won't really know how things are until I see how the full-grown mugger are doing.

Narrator:

From this part of Yala National Park, the modern world is not even visible.

Rom Whitaker:

This is a time of plenty. There's enough to eat and drink, and the waters are high. The key to everything here is the water—plants, trees, animals. They all depend on it, and life changes dramatically when it dries up.

Narrator:

The mugger does not make a habit of dining on humans, but any animal coming close to the water to drink better stay on guard. A certain edginess is understandable when 13 feet of reptile could be hidden just beneath the surface of the water. Using its powerful tail, the mugger can reach startling speeds underwater. But its most deadly skill may be patience.

Rom Whitaker:

Nighttime is the best time to census crocodiles. Their eye shine gives them away. They can't help it. The reflective tapetum in their eye reflects the light back. It's really bright . . . watch. Man, this place is absolutely teeming with crocodiles. I just counted 140 crocodiles probably, give or take 20 or 30.

Muggers can be solitary, but there are times of the year when they come together. One such time is for a ritual that can get quite bloody. Contrary to popular legend . . . muggers are for the most part pretty laid-back, sociable animals. In fact, they spend much of their time just basking in the sun. But when mating season approaches, they are also intensely territorial, and any spot with deep water is worth fighting for.

Narrator:

The battles are part of a fierce struggle for dominance. The winner gets the prize—his pick of the females. The combat can be very brutal and sometimes fatal. In the final stage of the dominance fight, this big male flaunts his position by raising his head and tail out of the water. One young male issues a challenge. The big male boldly responds, and the younger croc decides to retreat.

Rom Whitaker:

It's amazing to watch this ritual unfold. These crocs could kill each other—and sometimes do—but in this test of strength, the losers usually live to fight another day.

Narrator:

Finally, the last rival is chased out of the pond.

Rom Whitaker:

This battle is over; the big male has the pond to himself now. And the stage is set for what's really important—courtship.

Narrator:

The victor has won the right to mate with the local female of his choice.

Rom Whitaker:

The male is all set to mate, but nothing is going to happen until she's good and ready.

Narrator:

It is said that in the natural world, the only real constant is change. But muggers have been acting out this ritual for more than 100 million years—since they shared the world with the Tyrannosaurus Rex. If the muggers can continue to live and produce healthy babies in Yala National Park, they can hopefully survive.

Unit 3: Skin Mask

Mike, Special Effect Artist:

Hi, Cassandra. I'm Mike, and this is Rick.

Narrator:

In a London special-effects studio, a brave model waits to have her face preserved as a life-like mask . . .

Mike:
This is silicone material.

Narrator:
Silicone is an often rubber-like material that includes silicon and other chemical elements.

Mike:
I hope this is going to do it.

Narrator:
First, a cap is placed over Cassandra's hair. Next, a thin layer of Vaseline over her eyebrows and lashes to keep them from sticking to the mask. Then a crucial step in the process—the gooey stuff. Artists paint her face in quick-drying silicone, starting with the eyes, nose, and mouth. She has to sit motionless for about an hour as the artists brush the icy cold silicone onto her face. It takes about three or four minutes for the silicone to dry.

Then the model's face is wrapped in plaster bandages . . . rather like a living mummy.

Mike:
Nice and solid.

Narrator:
The hardened material comes off, followed by the newly created mold, which conforms to the shape of the model's face.

Cassandra, Model:
Who said modeling was easy?

Narrator:
At a workshop, the artists create a series of positive and negative masks. A master mold is then prepared. The artists mix a soft silicone with a combination of chemicals, creating a natural color that's similar to human skin.

The mixture is then injected into the master mold. When it's dry, a face is created. A touch of makeup helps bring the skin to life. Eyebrows and lashes are carefully added. It can take up to three hours to do one eyebrow. The completed mask has all the aspects of real human skin.

It has more than just the look. It has the feel—a record of one person's face, preserved in a moment in time.

Unit 4: Solar Power

Narrator:
The most powerful source of energy on the planet is actually out in space. It's our sun.

More energy falls as sunlight on the United States in a single day than it uses in a year.

But it's been difficult to turn that sunlight into electricity.

Many people already use some solar energy. But the world's need for power is great . . . and for solar power to be an alternative to other energy sources, it has to be both affordable and reliable.

One good role model for solar power is in the state of California. Sacramento, the state capital, is one of the United States's leaders in solar power. Many new homes have solar cells, and solar panels shade parking lots and city buildings. But most importantly, Sacramento has shown that buying a lot of solar panels at once can dramatically reduce the price per unit . . . and that people can actually save money using solar power . . . or make money.

California, along with many other states, has started "net metering." It lets citizens sell their extra solar power back to the utility company for exactly the price they would be paying for it. If they use less power than they produce, the utility company sends them a check.

In California's Mojave Desert, there's a solar generating plant that makes all other solar plants seem small by comparison. The Kramer Solar Junction power facility, covering more than 1,000 acres (or 400 hectares) of land. It creates more energy from solar power than every other solar panel in America combined, 150 megawatts in all.

David Rib, Vice President, Kramer Solar Junction:
Which at that full capacity is enough power for the residential needs of about half a million people.

Narrator:
Unlike photovoltaic systems, which capture the energy in the sunlight directly, these mirrors reflect the light onto a tube filled with synthetic oil. The 700-degree oil then goes into a boiler that runs an electric turbine. Each segment also has a back-up natural gas generator; so, during all types of weather, they can always supply the power Los Angeles expects, while creating very little pollution or smog.

So long as the sun rises, solar power will continue to be a reliable solution to the world's energy needs.

Unit 5: Wildebeest Migration

Narrator:
Each year the Serengeti Plains in Tanzania are home to one of the greatest animal migrations on Earth. Some 2 million animals begin a round trip that will take them almost 2000 miles. Fossil evidence suggests that modern wildebeest grazed these plains more than a million years ago.

At the beginning of each year, the wildebeest gather on the outer edge of the Serengeti—all giving birth in the same month. Rapidly their numbers swell. The calves can run as fast as their mothers within two days of being born.

No one knows what triggers the migration. There is no clear signal—it just takes one or two to sniff the air and decide the time is right to leave.

The migrating animals' journey is a long and difficult one. Even without the attention of predators, around 200,000 of the weakest wildebeest and zebras will die from starvation, disease, or exhaustion during the migration. Every day fresh carcasses are left behind. The migrating animals rest at the streams and regroup.

A single cat finds it tricky to bring down a full-grown wildebeest . . . but if it can separate a wildebeest calf off from its mother, then it has a chance of a meal.

In Kenya's Maasai Mara, the migrating herds arrive. Rains have created a huge area of watered grazing. Here the wildebeest will stay until the smell of November's short rains tell them it's time to regroup and head southwards, back towards the Serengeti.

Unit 6: Farm Restoration

Narrator:
Dale Aden has been farming most of his life. Just like his father and his father's father.

Dale Aden, Farmer / Conservationist:
I'm a third-generation farmer on this land.

Narrator:
His land is in Okabena, Minnesota. Aden's farm is right along the Okabena Creek, where for many years, Aden watched helplessly as the creek flooded its banks and soaked his crops.

Dale Aden:
In wet years, this crop all drowns out and when you lose a crop it . . . basically, it takes about five years to pay for that one year that we had a loss.

Narrator:
After the losses took their toll, Aden had an epiphany. Why not stop farming the marginal land and set it aside for wildlife?

Dale Aden:
I thought as a legacy I would do this—put it to where it should be—better than what we found it.

Narrator:
Aden heard about a conservation program called Reinvest in Minnesota—or RIM—that would pay him to return some of his farmland to its natural state. The RIM program encourages farmers to keep farming their productive land, but sell the marginal land that's susceptible to soil and water erosion.

Aden planted trees and shrubs. And a friend is planting prairie grass that will soon provide cover for animals.

Dale Aden:
Good to see her. She's sticking her head out over there.

Narrator:
Aden also made dozens of birdhouses like this one for a pair of tree swallows that will soon get a lot more crowded when these eggs hatch.

Dale Aden:
They can either be five, six, or seven.

Narrator:
Aden broke drainage tiles and let his farmland return to wetland.

Dale Aden:
Up until about three years ago, this was farmed. It's hard to believe now, but it was all farmed. Corn and soybean rotation is what it was. Across the road here was the same way, three years ago it was all farmland.

Narrator:
Here's a look at Aden's crop a few years ago.

Dale Aden:
You can see the crop up here is just fine, but down here it's all drowned out.

Narrator:
Here's that same spot today—a wetland with a thriving wildlife population. These days the sound of tractors on the Aden family farm has been replaced by a different sound.

Dale Aden:
I call it music—I guess—wildlife music and it's just wonderful to hear.

Narrator:
And Aden is happy to sit back and listen.

Dale Aden:
I couldn't be happier for the way it's turned out.

Unit 7: The Black Diamonds of Provence

Narrator:
In a small village in Provence, France, residents have gathered to give thanks. While they sing and pray to Saint Anthony, these church members are praying for something different—a good truffle harvest. At the annual truffle mass, the collection plate is filling up, and not just with cash. In Richerenches, truffles are sometimes called "black diamonds." At a price of up to $1000 U.S. per pound, they're one of the world's most expensive foods. The name Richerenches means "rich earth," appropriate for this village. Half of France's black truffles are transported through the town's market, up to $180,000 U.S. worth a day. They're all looking for truffles, and not just any one will do, either.

Pierre-Andre Valayer, Truffle Broker:
It's the most important market of truffles in France. So if you want to buy some truffle, you have to be in Richerenches to buy something. So for the sellers, it's the same thing. If you want to sell well, they have to come to Richerenches.

Narrator:
Provence generally brings to mind summer holidays, lazy afternoons, and ancient customs. In winter, though, the small town's pace speeds up considerably. Many of the region's farmers also work as truffle hunters. Most of the business is done discretely from

the backs of the brokers' cars. One small bag of truffles is worth hundreds of U.S. dollars, so the trade is certainly lucrative.

Philippe Oger, Truffle Eater:
I do think they buy apartments and so on . . . on the Riviera with this money. I know that.

Narrator:
The buying and selling of truffles is mainly a cash business; it's usually under the table. This means that the brokers often don't pay any taxes on the money they earn and neither do the hunters. Most people presume that truffles are only an expensive luxury for the rich; however, regular people who cook at home often spend money on them, too. France's gourmet food companies also buy truffles from the brokers and export them to restaurants in the U.S., Japan, and elsewhere. The demand is high, but unfortunately, the supply is decreasing.

Herve Poron, Truffle Exporter:
Today, if you find 100 tons, it's a very good production. In fact, it's most of the time it's more like 20, 30, or 50 tons . . . compared to 1000, 100 years ago.

Narrator:
The best truffles are deep black, with white veins, but there are fewer and fewer of them available these days. One major reason for the decrease could be the recent changes in Provence's truffle-growing environment.

Herve Poron:
Because to grow truffles you need woods, and the woods have disappeared. And what is left is not often very well taken care of . . . so we're desperate for woods. That explains the lower production today.

Narrator:
Truffles grow underground, around tree roots. If there aren't as many trees left, there are fewer places for truffles to grow. Provence is a farm region where farmers grow lavender, and grapes for the famous wines. Now only a few places remain that allow truffle growth. Truffle hunter Joel Barthelemy is looking for those places with the help of his yellow lab, Jade. Jade is a trained sniffer dog. All dogs have sensitive noses, but sniffer dogs' are exceptional. However, there are other factors involved.

Joel Barthelemy, Truffle Hunter:
The dog has to pay attention, and he has to love his master. You can do all the training you want, but the dog has to want to please his master.

Narrator:
Jade seems to have the capacity for both of these requirements. She's found something and gets a treat for her effort. As the two hunters continue their search for truffles, it seems that for today at least, there's no truffle shortage here. Perhaps Saint Anthony has listened to the truffle hunters' prayers after all.

Unit 8: Paraguay Shaman

Narrator:
Somewhere in this forest, maybe in this plant or that herb, there might be a cure for diabetes, or malaria, or even common fevers and colds. But as the plants disappear, so too do the potential cures.

The rainforests of Paraguay have long been a source of medicinal cures.

Traditional folk healers often lead the way to the plants that provide the medicines.

Paraguay's renowned healers, called "shamans" have a deep knowledge of local medicinal plants—the equivalent of the knowledge contained in an entire medical library.

But Paraguay has one of the highest deforestation rates in the world. That's why researchers believe it's a priority to record the shaman's extensive knowledge—before the forest disappears.

The journey begins in Paraguay's isolated Mbaracayú Forest Nature Reserve and the nearby native community of Tekoha Ryapu, where shaman Gervasio lives.

To reach Gervasio, a group of researchers set out on a long journey through the reserve.

Meanwhile, at the village, Gervasio is using chants and prayers, perhaps to establish a spiritual connection, or bond, with the forest.

When he feels ready, Gervasio and his wife lead the group on the search.

They are looking for a root called Suruvi, also known as *Jatropha isabelli*, which is used for various ailments.

Scientists are very interested in this family of plants for cancer research.

Gervasio brings the root back to the village, where his wife inserts it into a pot of water to prepare tea.

Scientists have published a book to help record and transmit Gervasio's forest knowledge. The book helps people easily identify and study local plants.

Recording and analyzing Paraguayan plants for possible medical cures is urgent business; some may

even call it an emergency. Medicinal plants that were once healthy and multiplying are now disappearing—and so too is the possibility of finding new medical cures.

Unit 9: Animal Minds

Narrator:
When you look at some animals, it seems as if they are alert, thinking beings. But just how smart are they? And how can you tell the difference between intelligence and evolutionary instincts?

Scientists used to think that while an animal might sometimes appear smart, every move was really the result of training or instinct. A rat in a familiar maze, they said, was moving as unconsciously as a train goes down the tracks. Until the early 1900s, when one rat outsmarted the maze—it climbed onto the mesh roof and headed straight for the food. Scientists deduced the rat must have formed a mental map of the maze—and remembered where the food was.

Pretty smart.

Are dolphins intelligent? One researcher has put dolphins to the test to find the answer to this question. Behavioral biologist Karen Pryor has come to Marine World Africa USA to help out with a medical exam.

Karen Pryor, Behavioral Biologist:
That's a form of targeting, right there!

Narrator:
This dolphin has been trained to breathe on cue so doctors can give her a checkup.

Karen Pryor:
Let's do one more. Good girl. Now, the other side.

Narrator:
It's one of the techniques Pryor established.

Karen Pryor:
Thank you!

Karen Pryor:
We don't use any coercion. We don't have leashes or bridles or whips or spurs. We, we let the animal sort of do what it's doing, and we tell it when we like that. With a whistle followed by a bucket of fish.

Narrator:
It could be that Pryor's gentle touch rewarded her with a look at the dolphin mind.

Karen Pryor:

I think one of the reasons we see so much of their, what we call intelligence, is that we train them without coercion. It's the, it's this beautiful method of shaping behavior.

Thank you! I'm not supposed to laugh, either, 'cause they know but that means the trainers really aren't aware.

Narrator:

In the late 1960s, Pryor discovered that dolphins could play more sophisticated games than anyone had dreamed. She found that dolphins share a skill we think of as uniquely human—creativity.

In her experiment, she picked a new behavior each day and rewarded the dolphin for it throughout the session. Every day, the dolphin would start off with the behavior rewarded the day before, but Pryor was waiting for something new.

Karen Pryor:

It took us about two weeks to run through the normal behaviors . . . there was nothing new there . . . that was our criterion . . . so we couldn't reinforce her. She became despondent almost . . . we were very upset, too. Second session, third session kept going like this. We wondered if maybe that was going to be the end of the experiment. And then we go to session 16. And the animal came rushing out, offered us a flip we'd never seen . . . we reinforced that. Instead of doing that again, she offered us a tail swipe we'd never seen. We reinforced that. She began offering us all kinds of behavior that we hadn't seen in such a mad flurry that finally we could hardly choose what to throw fish at. The trainer gave her the whole bucket.

Narrator:

Pryor had discovered that dolphins have a kind of imagination. It was a revelation for researchers.

Karen Pryor:

Science has always leaned over backwards about all animals to say that, you know, there's nothing going on in there that you can't see on the outside . . . they're just responding to conditioned stimuli. It might be that our creative dolphin experiment was one of the first to make it irrevocably clear that the animals are doing something on their own also. Something of a cognitive nature.

Narrator:

And dolphins aren't alone . . . elephants do indeed have a good memory, primates use a variety of tools from sticks to stones . . .

Woman:

Good boy!

Narrator:

And some parrots have a pretty wide vocabulary and have been trained to understand the words they are using.

Woman:

How many?

Parrot:

Two.

Woman:

Right!

Narrator:

Understanding that humans aren't alone when it comes to intelligence shows just how far we've come. Turns out we're not so unique after all.

Unit 10: Slow Food

Narrator:

The fertile hills between Florence and Siena are home to some of the world's best known vineyards.

This is Chianti, one of Italy's famous wine regions. Greve, population 4000, is the center for the wine trade and other local products like mushrooms and cheese.

This is a place that appreciates tradition. Greve is a place where time is never rushed.

Paolo Saturnini, Mayor of Greve:

Our challenge and our duty is to try to maintain the soul, the essence, the specialness of Greve, in Chianti, and all the other slow cities.

Narrator:

Greve's mayor, and mayors from three other Italian cities, created the Slow Cities League. Their mission—to keep their hometowns from moving into the fast lane.

Out of that, came the Slow Food movement.

It's simple—preserve the pleasures of good living, good food, family, and friends. Now the movement has gone international, with more than 100,000 members worldwide.

Sandro Checcuci, Greve Resident:

It's very nice to live here because we have a nice atmosphere, we have a nice landscapes. And so, when you have nice things to see, a nice place to live in, it's very easy.

Narrator:

Salvatore Tescano left the fast life behind. He ran an American-style restaurant in Florence, where he spent his days serving up burgers.

Five years ago, he dumped his fryer and moved to Greve, where he's opened a new restaurant.

Salvatore Tescano, Slow Food Chef:
It means taking the time, finding the rhythm that lets you live more calmly. In a lot of ways, starting, of course, with what you eat.

Narrator:
In the mountains of Pistoia, in northern Tuscany, generations of farmers have produced a pecorino cheese that they say is one of a kind. Made from the raw milk of black sheep, the cheese is hand molded twice a day.

But this tradition had been dying out, until slow food stepped in. With a campaign to organize the farmers and promote the cheese, both are making a comeback.

Luana Pagliai, Cheese Maker:
It's brought us a kind of fame. Not everyone knew about our product. The project is getting us noticed.

Luciano Bertini, Slow Food Farmer:
From Singapore to Macao, in New York, in Rome, you always find the same pizza, the same hamburgers. Slow food doesn't want this. Slow food wants the specialness of every product to be respected.

Narrator:
Greve is not trying to escape the modern world; it's a city that is simply enjoying itself and doing its best to take it slow.